W9-ANV-854

# I Dwell in Possibility

*The Cross-Cultural Memoir Series*
*Available from The Feminist Press*

*Lion Woman's Legacy: An Armenian-American Memoir,*
by Arlene Voski Avakian
*The Seasons: Death and Transfiguration,* by Jo Sinclair
*Fault Lines,* by Meena Alexander

# I Dwell in Possibility

## A Memoir by Toni McNaron

*The Cross-Cultural Memoir Series*

THE FEMINIST PRESS
at The City University of New York
New York

Published 1992 by The Feminist Press at The City University of New York,
311 East 94th Street, New York, NY 10128
Distributed by The Talman Company, 150 Fifth Avenue, New York, NY
10011

96 95 94 93 92 5 4 3 2 1

*Library of Congress Cataloging-in-Publication Data*
McNaron, Toni A. H.
    I dwell in possibility: a memoir / by Toni McNaron.
        p. cm.
    ISBN 1-55861-049-9 (cloth) : $35.00. — ISBN 1-55861-050-2 (pap.) : $12.95
    1. McNaron, Toni A. H. 2. English teachers—United States—Biography.
3. Alcoholics—United States—Biography. 4. Feminists—United States—
Biography. 5. Lesbians—United States—Biography. 6. Alabama—Social
conditions. 7. Racism—Alabama. I. Title.
PE64.M38A3    1992
976.1'781063'092—dc20
[B]                                                                    91-3105
                                                                          CIP

This publication is made possible, in part, by public funds from the
New York State Council on the Arts and the National Endowment for
the Arts. The Feminist Press would also like to thank Janet E. Brown
for her generosity.

Cover photographs courtesy of Toni McNaron
*Cover design:* Lucinda Geist
*Text design:* Paula Martinac

Printed on acid-free paper by McNaughton & Gunn, Inc.

*To Theresa Louise Hurley and Erskine Lamar McNaron*

I dwell in Possibility —
A fairer House than Prose —
More numerous of Windows —
Superior — for Doors —

Of Chambers as the Cedars —
Impregnable of Eye —
And for an Everlasting Roof
The Gambrels of the Sky —

Of Visitors — the fairest —
For Occupation — This —
The spreading wide my narrow Hands —
To gather Paradise —

*Emily Dickinson*

# Contents

# Acknowledgments

*B*ecause this work has been fostered by so many, I feel compelled to acknowledge some of the most important of them: the Graduate School of the University of Minnesota for a summer research grant that allowed me to make much more rapid progress than normally possible; my brother-in-law, Leon, who helped me purchase a home computer without which the numerous revisions, full of "block moves," would have proved daunting; Anita Kunin for providing me with photocopies of the early manuscript, thereby facilitating my finding my publisher; my women's writing group for reading and responding to early portions of the first two sections; Chris Gordon, Judy Remington, and Ellie Siegel for reading manuscript drafts and giving me essential editorial suggestions; Kathy Casto, my editor at The Feminist Press, for her clarity and good humor.

Florence Howe's expert editorial skills, together with her extraordinary generosity, have challenged and touched me all along the way. I am indebted to my dear friends and colleagues, Shirley Garner and Mimi Sprengnether, not only for their quick and trenchant responses to specific sections but more importantly for their unflinching belief in me and in the value of this project. My sister, Betty, has given me a singular gift: she has been willing to suspend her inherent distrust for the genre of autobiographical writing to lend me her steady support and periodic commiseration when I was under the particular stress of meeting deadlines.

Finally, I acknowledge my family: Blue and Slate, our dog and cat, who have kept me company many a late night or early morning as I sat before the typewriter or computer unable to articulate what my memory was offering me; and Susan Cygnet, my partner, who has helped me learn that intimacy is worth the effort and risk involved and who has spurred me to voice my ideas and feelings even, or most especially, when I feel reluctant to do so.

# Preface

*In* 1940, when I was about three, my mother planted a small magnolia tree in our backyard. It had come from a friend whose family lived in the heart of agricultural Alabama. This friend believed having the sapling would remind my mother of her childhood days in Selma.

In all my young years of driving around the South, I never saw a magnolia tree growing in a black family's yard or a black section of town. I concluded that even the trees, like the picture show, water fountains, restrooms, and library, were for "Whites Only." In 1987, after I had been living in the North for over twenty years, I attended a National Women's Studies Association conference held at Spelman College in Atlanta, Georgia. Founded in 1880, this black women's college boasts stately buildings, open grounds, and a solid row of magnolias along its outer fence. As I walked onto campus the first evening, I remembered my earlier impressions of where they could grow.

I caught my breath at their majesty: the trees rising conically, reaching for the sky, their waxy leaves so green as to appear almost black, their branches clotted all the way up with great white blooms. As a child, I believed some giant had placed the blooms among the leaves as a whimsical gesture.

On the ground beneath one tree, I found several brilliant red seed cores from fallen flower heads, full of prickly whiskers that had once held graceful petals in place. In my hand, they were pulpy, and the whiskers sprang back softly when I pushed them against the center.

Also on the ground were several petals from fallen blooms. Picking up one, now a deep ochre, I felt its succulent thickness and realized for the first time what helps keep the blooms intact for so long.

These artful petals are actually useful, sucking in each afternoon's rain, holding moisture against the next day's relentless heat.

The South and its signs are more complicated than I could know growing up in their midst. My growing up itself was more complicated than I sometimes constructed it. Perhaps, I thought, by studying myself as carefully as I had these magnolias, I could unearth my own mysteries.

It all began when Sara Evans, a feminist colleague in history at the University of Minnesota, taped my memories of the civil rights movement in Birmingham. She enjoined me to write my story since I had been present at events of great historical moment. The project quickly broadened to include early memories of playing with black children, only later to be taught to feel superior to them. Once I had opened that door to my childhood, other powerful scenes crowded into my consciousness. Eventually I shifted from the original focus on race to a more open-ended exploration into the formation of the self I now consider "me."

As I explored my earliest memories of family and my gradual sense that we were different from the black families who lived so near us geographically, I soon found myself enmeshed in other central questions of my growing up: Why did my father call me "Son"? Why did my mother "protect" me from other children? Why did I never tell her the most important things about myself? I saw that the self that I was shaping differed significantly from the one my parents had imagined. I remembered a woman who felt confused and isolated, who was an alcoholic. Yet I also began to connect my developing creativity with a sense of myself as a sexual person, my emergence as a lesbian, and my passion for literature and teaching.

This memoir has been more than six years in the making—an incredibly long time for someone who prefers breaking through plaster walls to sweeping up the debris, washing or hanging out clothes to folding and putting them away, hatching a grand idea to tracing down footnotes or laboring on a third or fourth revision. Now my part of the process is over, a fact that fills me with excitement and satisfaction. My lingering discomfort with the work's being read by strangers, however, comes from my sure knowledge that others in this account would tell different stories from the ones that I record. My fantasies are wild: "Someone will sue me," even though everyone in my family except my sister Betty is long dead; "Betty will never speak to me again, deny me my mother's antiques, turn me from her door when I visit," though she has adjusted to my telling her that I am a lesbian, an alcoholic, an autobiographer, and someone who found growing up in our family painful as well as wonderful.

None of these things will happen. Instead, I will live with my periodic concern that I have been unfair, lopsided, cruel, vindictive. The act of putting my life onto paper has allowed me to see it more distinctly, both in its worst and best lights. I accept that it is populated by individuals who were who they had to be rather than who I might have wanted them to be. By facing their ghosts, I stand strangely less encumbered by their ideas of me. I think of Virginia Woolf and Maxine Hong Kingston, and keep coming out of the shadows.

*Toni McNaron*

# I Dwell in Possibility

# *Part I*

*Top:* birthday party, 1941; *bottom:* the author's mother at Christmas, 1963.
Courtesy of Toni McNaron.

# Out of the Nest

*I* grew up in a one-story white frame house, with living room, dining room, and kitchen on one side of a long hall, three bedrooms and a bath on the other. The house was in Fairfield, Alabama, home of Tennessee Coal and Iron (TCI), a subsidiary of United States Steel. Called the Pittsburgh of the South, TCI boasted a model steel workers' town, with low-cost housing and schools located near the plant. Nothing was said about the grit that appeared on window sills and furniture within hours of dusting. Because the worst of the manual labor in the hellish blast furnaces was done by blacks, they outnumbered whites. Everyone in Birmingham, the city to which Fairfield was attached, worked directly for "the company" or for one of its necessary feeder industries and services. It was the late thirties, and the South had only just begun to pull out of the Great Depression.

My father progressed from working in the wire mill as junior bookkeeper to being chief accountant for TCI, and we lived where we did for his convenience. He liked to come home for lunch, and the mill was only about ten minutes from our house. Though an unpretentious house in a working-class neighborhood, my home was full of antiques. A few of them, including a delicate drop-leaf, three-drawer sewing table, came down the Mississippi on a flatboat with my maternal great-grandmother. With her French Huguenot family, she had fled one of many persecutions and landed in Canada. Some of the other fine pieces were gifts to my mother, primarily from my sister but occasionally from my father. I remember a fishing trip from which he returned with a four-branch gas chandelier and no fish. He had spied it in the barn of a farm where he had stopped to get fresh eggs. Painted red, it was being used by the local chickens, attested to by wisps of straw still falling from the lamp bases. My father bought it for a couple of dollars, and we all watched as it became a gorgeous brass light that hung from then on in our living room.

Most of the antique furniture was acquired by my mother in her many jaunts to shops filled with old chests and tables, china, silver, and other bric-a-brac. In the forties, Alabama shopkeepers were not always aware of the value of their holdings, but my mother knew wood grains, silver markings, porcelain symbols. Often I accompanied her to serve as decoy. We would arrive at a shop and browse until the proprietor asked if he could help us. Somehow, Mamie (the name my sister had used as a baby that became what most people called my mother) turned the conversation to me, and I launched into one of my distracting recitals. Since I knew names of rivers, oceans, continents, and other phyla, I could charm adults fairly easily. While I spouted off something years ahead of my comprehension, my mother slipped into remoter rooms of unfinished furniture. Using the pearl-handled penknife always in her purse, she quickly chipped through some colored paint on a washstand or end table. When she found cherry or mahoghany, or, on rare occasions, rosewood, she returned to me smiling. At the next lull in whatever conversation the owner and I were having, she would say in all innocence, "Oh, I happened to notice the little painted piece in back—how much is that if I just take it with me now and not bother you with refinishing it?" If the price was right, a bargain was struck, and the piece piled into the back of our old black Plymouth. Once home, and the newest treasure in the basement, she and I stripped off the bad color, restoring the wood to its original beauty.

Perhaps had my mother lived in another age or been able to tell herself a different story, she might have opened an elegant little shop. Then she could have bought up old painted pieces, restored them, and sold them to people wanting the pleasure of owning them. Instead, we accumulated pieces of antique furniture as my schoolmates' parents might collect matchboxes or miniature china horses. Inside my house, I often felt overwhelmed by objects I had been told were priceless and feared I might accidently knock to the floor at any moment.

My mother seldom did anything on a small scale. Though she was only four feet eleven inches tall, her imagination and energy formed a force field that lent her at least an additional foot. This commanding presence left me often feeling eclipsed, effaced, though Mamie clearly adored me. I still remember going into our house on Holly Court some five months after she had died and being met instantly by the smell of her perfume. It was as if she had just stepped out and would return at any moment.

When I first knew her, she was already forty, so I have very little sense of her as a girl or young woman. Old photos show her in typical twenties styles—tight-fitting black dresses with lace, low-slung wide belts, large ornamental pins on her equally large bodice, funny hats with feathers. One story from her youth that I heard repeatedly was about a dance in Montgomery to which she went, along with Zelda Sayre of whom my mother was an acknowledged look alike. She and Zelda reputedly decided to play a joke on Scott Fitzgerald, in town on furlough from the army. My mother was to "play" Zelda for a time to see if Scott could tell the difference. I listened as Mamie spun her tale about dancing with the dashing soldier who would become one of America's great writers. The joke seems to have worked, at least in her reminiscence.

But the person I knew in childhood had changed in some major ways from that storybook character. No longer svelte, my mother was always either on a diet or about to go on one. Given her frame, at 160 or so, she was twenty to thirty pounds overweight. Rising in the morning full of resolution, she ate her two squares of zwieback and drank a cup of tea while pointing out her virtue to us egg and toast munchers. By lunch, resolve had weakened to allow a taste of whatever dessert she had made for the rest of us; by dinner, caution had flown into the southern air. Mamie was a fine and proud cook, preferring French dishes with rich sauces and elaborate sweets of all sorts. Her cream puffs were legendary, shared with many townspeople when she had to make her contracted monies for the church coffers. Birthdays brought out all her creative talents, not only in the cake of one's choice but in the side dishes: sweet potatoes mashed and put into scooped-out orange halves complete with handles; fried chicken wings or pork chops dressed in paper "shoes" to keep fingers greaseless; tiny Parker House rolls shaped like miniature English pasties.

Her weight in no way obscured her elegance. Most weekdays, Mamie wore a house dress and a smock during the morning as she cleaned or cooked. In mid-afternoon, she took a leisurely bath and "dressed"—nice clothes over massive foundation garments, careful make-up to give her a certain old world beauty. Her hair was brownish with auburn tints, often worn wrapped around a thick rat that lent a halo effect not unlike Greer Garson. The wreath, which softened her face, also cast her backward in time.

Throughout my childhood, my mother wore tiny pince-nez glasses. Whenever she took them off, two bright red ellipses appeared on either side of her patrician nose. I called these "holes" and worried because they took so long to fade. When she finally succumbed to tortoise-shell glasses with regulation ear pieces, she lost some of her exoticism.

Early in the twentieth century, when she was nearing twenty, Mamie had won a scholarship to study piano outside the South. But before she could leave Selma, Alabama, she met, fell in love with, and married Mac, as she called my father. They carried on a brief courtship when he was on shore leave from Newport News, Virginia, and were married over Thanksgiving of 1917, because Daddy could get away at holiday time. Most of the photographs in their early years are of them in bathing suits or other casual wear at some beach with lots of relatives. A little later they appear with my sister, Betty, born about a year after they were wed.

My father was handsome in a craggy sort of way. About five feet six or seven, he had steel blue eyes that stare out of photographs much as they did in real life. He seems almost always to have worn his hair in a close crew cut. It was totally gray when I was born, the story being that it turned overnight after his father died. When I knew him, he too was overweight, though he never seemed to be doing anything to change that. My mother tried to get him to wear belts, but he insisted they cut him and so he preferred suspenders. They allowed him to buy trousers that were loose, that let him breathe. As a child I often watched in excited horror on those occasions when his trousers inched down over his stomach, lower and lower, until, suddenly recalling them, he hitched them back to his waist. He was the perfect antidote to Mamie, in her half-body girdles and massive brassieres.

But his laxity in the matter of fitted clothes was delusive. I was constantly surprised by the particular forms of his fastidiousness. One that seemed especially romantic to me as a child involved his donning a smoking jacket some weekday evenings after supper and on weekends for most of the afternoon. I thought him dashing and relaxed, especially in the silk one I gave him when I was twelve. The other manifestation felt much more oppressive. It involved forcing me to be letter and number perfect in school subjects. Nights often found me sitting on the cedar chest across from his favorite easy chair. We were there to go over my history or geography lesson, and Daddy defined that activity as follows: he would announce a topic heading; I would recite, word for word, the material underneath. If I missed even a preposition or conjunction, I had to do it over. Similarly, when I brought home tests graded 97 or 98, his only response was, "Well, why didn't you get 100?"

Of course I adored him, as my first memory of him shows: It is early Christmas morning, and I am nine months old. Warm in my flannel sack, I come out of sleep to see my father leaning over my baby bed. His face smiles, his eyes twinkle; his prematurely gray hair is cut unusually crew for the holiday. He calls to me: "Wake up, Jay Bird Blue, it's Christmas."

Daddy had another special name for me—Son—that he used in private for the first six years of my life. In the South, a saying went, "If you can kiss your elbow, you'll turn into a boy." One summer when I wanted desperately to be Daddy's son and was old enough to realize that I was only a daughter, I would sit in my back yard, alone, in my seersucker playsuit, contorting my arms, trying to get a lip over to an elbow. Once I even asked a girl friend to bend my arm further than I could. That night I lay awake in my canopied bed aching from my trial.

Failing the elbow trick, I tried other devices to pass. I asked for and got boys' toys: a jungle gym, chemistry sets, Lincoln logs, tinker toys, baseballs and gloves and bats, and all manner of guns during World War II. I wore cowboy shirts with my school skirts; I learned to run fast, to play hard ball, to shoot marbles, and to throw a pocketknife so that it landed blade in ground.

When Daddy stopped calling me Son, my attempts to be one merely became more subtle. To avoid being a "dizzy blond," I learned all I could as fast as I could. Because Daddy once showed me pictures of the Axis army's territories and chuckled when I tried to say the French or German names, I studied history with a passion. Because I heard him humming the tune to "Ghost Riders in the Sky," I read cowboy books until I could spout the lingo like a native. Because my father once said he admired Alan Ladd in *Whispering Smith*, I wore two six-shooters and leather chaps even in the hottest summer weather. When I saw neighbor boys working in the yard or on the family car so their dads could read the Sunday funnies, I pretended to like mowing the grass and washing our old Plymouth. When I began menstruating, I denied my pain so I wouldn't be like "those silly girls" who stayed home from school the first day, lying under heating pads or hot water bottles. I carried books for boys I had crushes on in junior and senior high school, not even aware of how confused I was about my gender identity. Embarrassed in adolescence not to be able to shave my face, I took a razor to my underarms every morning, causing rashes that stung most of the day.

As I was growing up, I longed to hear my father call me Jay Bird Blue or some other term of endearment. But he stopped calling me pet names or any names as he and I got older. Something about me was causing my idol to fade from sight. Rare moments, to which I have attached tremendous importance, stand out. When I was four or so, he occasionally let me crawl up into his lap after supper and listen while he read me the daily funnies: "Major Hoople's Boarding House," "Gasoline Alley," "Hazel," "Dagwood and Blondie"—domestic strips in which well-meaning men were henpecked by imposing women.

In about 1943, I decided that my father bore some physical resemblance to Adolf Hitler—he too wore a small mustache in the center of his upper lip and had dark eyebrows. I would beg him to let me wet comb his crew cut over to the right. With his hair plastered down, the image was remarkably like the Führer's. When he indulged me in this fantasy, I imagined him powerful and assertive, full of words and passion.

Wanting desperately to spend time with him away from home, I asked to go fishing from the time I was about seven. Though he often promised—"The very next trip, you can go, but not just now"—I never got to go on one of these magical adventures. He preferred the company of his friend Mr. Kelton, a huge beefy man over six feet tall, whom my mother disliked intensely. On lucky Saturday afternoons, Daddy offered to take me for a treat, when he was not off fishing. What we actually did was go over to Mr. Kelton's house, and he and Daddy talked, while I played relatively unsupervised in a back yard, fenced in for Mr. Kelton's hound dog.

Once when I was ten, Daddy took me to a professional baseball game at night under huge flood lights that attracted thousands of southern summer bugs. Birmingham had two baseball teams—the Barons and the Black Barons. The Barons were a farm team for the Boston Red Sox, while the Black Barons trained the earliest blacks who broke into major league baseball. Spectators for each team were absolutely segregated. Sitting in the bleachers with my father, I felt excited to be there. I ate a hot dog and drank Coca-Cola in a paper cup with Walt Dropo's picture on it. Walt was my hero since he, like I, was a left-handed first baseman. Near the end of play, Daddy bought me an ice cream sandwich. But he was annoyed by my questions: "Why do they fall onto the ground near home plate?" "Can we move down into those seats where nobody's sitting and we could see more?" "Why is that man with the red face yelling at the umpire?" "Wasn't that a strike, not a ball?" "Why can't I have a Popsicle?" He never took me to another ball game.

With his sudden death in 1954 when I was almost seventeen, my father became even more a mystery to me than his shadowy presence had caused him to seem. From that time until I entered therapy twenty-five years later, I made up stories about him and what he would think about his daughter/"Son" as I matured.

. Early memories of my mother are much more troubled. I see her face, moon-round, smiling but often slightly strained, coming closer than was comfortable for me. "Don't cross the street, honey, you'll get hurt." Hearing her say this, I feel instantly defiant and angry. Within half an hour, I've gone outside, toddled over to the curbing, looked across the road at nothing of interest, and crossed that street. No hurt comes to me, so I feel tricked.

Mamie seemed full of "don'ts," sentences telling me what not to do in order to avoid danger: "Don't go barefoot outside, you'll get impetigo." "Don't go swimming in public, you'll get polio." "Don't run and play, you'll get overexertion exhaustion." "Don't get your nice starched white pinafore wrinkled." "Don't go out of your yard, the stray dogs will get you." "Don't lie in the dirt, you'll get eaten by ants." "Don't play pitch, you'll hurt your fingers for piano practice." "Don't perspire, it's not nice." "Don't spit out your watermelon seeds, it's common." "Don't ever eat ice cream and watermelon on the same day or you'll die like Mrs. Munson did last Fourth of July." I explored all these warnings and found only one true—when I played pitch frantically with a hard ball, I did sprain fingers, making piano playing virtually impossible.

My mother was acting out of her best sense of what was necessary for me to become only a slightly modernized version of the southern belle she had been. Two images of me clearly illustrate her hopes: All through childhood, I wore my golden blond hair waist long. Wanting me to look like someone in *Gone with the Wind*, my mother rolled hunks of my thick hair on worn-out boys' socks that she scavenged from neighbors with growing sons. Trying to sleep on eight or ten wads of hair was an ordeal, and I felt only relief when my locks were finally shorn as I entered junior high. All through childhood, I also wore a starched white pinafore each morning over my dotted swiss or polka dot piqué dresses. Mamie would get me ready for a morning presumably of play, put her hands lovingly on my shoulders, look me hard in the eyes, and say: "Now, go outside and have a good time, honey, but remember not to get your little pinafore wrinkled or dirty, in case we have company this afternoon."

My way of coping with so many don'ts was to lie, not merely to avoid trouble but as a way of life. Most of the time I wasn't found out, but fear haunted me. When I was caught, it was shameful and full of pain for us both. One summer between college terms, I insisted, when Mamie asked if I was bored with spending so much time with her, that I liked playing two-handed solitaire every afternoon and sitting in front of the TV trying to think of something other than the programs or her occasional contented snoring. I wrote my true feelings to my roommate and buried her answering letter in my underwear drawer. My mother periodically inspected my drawers, insuring that my clothes were neatly stacked. The day she met me at the front door, tears in her eyes and Jean's letter in her hands, I lied extra hard to calm her and to cover my rage. "There's only a month left till we can go back to Tuscaloosa and freedom" meant that Jean was unhappy with her home life, not that I had said anything about mine. "Your mom is like mine—they want their little girls close, just in case" was really saying how much we appreciated the loving watchfulness from our mothers as we got older. "Just put on a smiling face and count the days": I couldn't construct any other meaning for that one.

If I managed to get away with most of my lies, my disobedient acts were more flagrant and perceptible. Mamie's mode of dealing with me was effective. As an active child, I ran and played as many hours as possible. Feeling trapped inside my house, I stayed outside except for lunch and occasional bathroom breaks, though I even preferred to squat in our back yard behind a hydrangea bush so as not to interrupt my play. Knowing all this, Mamie devised "Punishment." Never spanked, I was forced to sit perfectly still in a rocking chair in my parents' bedroom every time I disobeyed. There was a direct correlation between degree of defiance and number of minutes in that chair. The range was from five to thirty: five minutes can be a long time for puppies and little girls; thirty an eternity. I couldn't take anything of mine into the room—no crayons, paper, books, games. They would distract me from contemplating what a "bad girl" I had just been. My mother never understood that I was trying to be a bad girl, since that was the closest I could get to being a boy.

What I did, shut in that room without a clock to let me see how my confinement was progressing, was fantasize. Within a few months, I was able to become sufficiently involved so that sometimes, out of sheer spite, I refused to leave. Mamie would come to the still-closed door when the last minutes were passing and say, "Time's up, honey, you can go out and play now." Mostly I just sat out my fantasy, prolonging the last scenes while she waited for my appearance. Rarely, I said, "Just a minute, I'm busy." She'd stand it as long as she could and then burst into her own room and urge me out into family space. Once or twice she cried from sheer frustration, saying over and over, "I just don't know why you hurt me this way."

After one of my refusals to leave the room on her schedule, Mamie smarted around the house for the rest of that day overlooking smaller disobediences. I comprehended that I had won something; I felt smug and mean and lonely.

Most of my schoolmates lived in situations where at least the bathroom was private. I did not. The excuse went something like: "Oh, honey, excuse me, but we only have one bathroom and I just have to. . . ." There was a turn bolt on that door and my sister used it. When I tried, I was sharply reprimanded for inconveniencing Mamie who, after all, was responsible for dinner or lunch or whatever was currently important. More than I resented those intrusions, I disliked being called in while she bathed and dressed for the day. We talked there, or I was asked to help her into one of her several armoring garments—brassiere, massive girdle, tight-fitting slip. The intimacy and role reversals that surrounded these meetings several times a week for years seem even at this great distance to be troublesome.

I always sat on a little wicker clothes hamper, my eight-year-old feet barely touching the cool tile floor. I stayed very still, hoping my mother would forget I was there. Mouse quiet, I gazed at her, drying from her morning bath. She stood before me, huge and strong and all soft, rounded folds—layers of folds—face, breasts, stomach, thighs, ass, or as she insisted on calling it, "derrière."

Once dry, she would start all over, this time with a powder puff bigger than my whole hand. The powder made me want to sneeze, but I would hold fingers like a clothespin on my nose so she would go on, forgetting me. With short quick motions, she dusted under her melon bosoms, slowly so they poised between rise and flop. Then she moved down to her satin stomach with its big open space she called a navel— to me a cave. Then her puff-hidden hand moved down, but I have blocked that scene. At this point I would jump off the hamper and ask "why" about some silly thing. I wanted to make her dress; I could not watch her any more.

My question broke into her lazy ritual, and she started to pile on ladies' armor that crushed her lovely folds. First, a vest, soft but hiding. Then a brassiere one size too small so that her floppy breasts looked like iron ones. Was she really a lady knight in disguise? Then came the girdle I helped her close; I snapped the snaps—one . . . two . . . three . . . four— from waist to . . . Then came hooks and eyes over what I eventually learned was pubic hair. Then soft panties over that and a clingy slip over everything. At the very last, she smeared on Mum, a white cream for marble-shaved underarms, rouged her cheeks, and lined her full lips with a hard red stick.

Then she would loom over me—a statue in a mask—ready to fight her own dragons, I thought. I could not see any skin and had no hope for a soft hug; I would hurt myself on some new-made edge.

The other person living in our house was my sister, Betty. Sixteen and a half when I was born, she had been an only child until then. My first knowledge of her stems from a story Mamie told: when Betty found out that I was on the way, she is supposed to have replied, "If I can't name the brat, I won't speak to it." My mother recounted this to relatives, neighbors, friends. She found it humorous, but I did not like being called "brat" or "it." Betty was allowed to name me, and she chose Toni. Had I been a boy, I would have been called Tony. Many people do not understand the fine point of this gender-based spelling, so that all my life I have gotten mail addressed to Mr. McNaron. Once when I was going to church camp, I was mistakenly put into the boys' cabin, only to be moved immediately upon arrival.

My sister is essentially verbal. From the beginning, she taught me words that I at first had no idea about, which I remembered by sound or later by spelling: "postprandial divertissement" was one of my earliest phrases, along with "marsupials are indigenous to Australia" and "the prolixity of *lapins* is horrific." I see her sitting beside me rattling off these words, being amused and proud when I could repeat them to her latest swain.

In order to get finer instruction in Greek and French, Betty went to New Orleans to Sophie Newcomb College, then the women's arm of Tulane University, but returned after one semester with a case of severe homesickness. The family doctor advised bringing her back home in

November, but Daddy insisted she stay in New Orleans the whole semester; otherwise, he could not get a partial tuition refund. The story I always heard was that for the rest of that fall, Betty would call Mamie and cry into the long distance telephone.

Born a year after my parents were married, Betty was reared largely by her maternal grandparents. The Hurleys lived in Selma, Alabama, the seat of southern culture and agriculture. Adoring Betty, they lavished upon her clothes ordered from Bergdorf Goodman in New York, toys from Switzerland, and unconditional love. Since my mother's father worked for a railroad, Mamie had unlimited passes to travel the eighty miles south from Birmingham. Mamie spent the last month or so of her pregnancy back home, and my father commuted on weekends. Once Betty was born, Mamie remained with her mother for several more months.

Grandparental showering at such an early age convinced Betty that her family was without fault or flaw and that she would always be taken care of. When I was growing up under strict rules about keeping my room pristine at all times, my closet neat, and all my clothes properly hung or drawered, I chafed under tales of Betty's youth. It seems that she often let her nightgown slip from her body onto the floor, only to have the faithful old family servant, Annie Belle Royal, come along to pick it up and put it away. I could not make sense out of two antithetical codes for children with the same mother.

Though the South of Betty's youth and courting age was different from my mother's, both women fulfilled the requirements of "belle." My sister was what the forties termed glamorous. I remember one photo in particular; lightly tinted, it shows Betty in a soft hat with a huge brim that dips over her face just like Garbo's or Rita Hayworth's always did. Her smile is subtle, even alluring, and her soft hazel eyes glance upward from slightly shaded lids.

My sister had her own food story, as did everyone in our family. Determined to be thin at any cost but adoring sweets, she established a bizarre regimen. Breakfast was usually one piece of cheese toast and a mammoth cup of hot tea; lunch, a Hershey bar and Coca-Cola; dinner, tiny servings of food topped by a large dessert. If her morning ritual on the scale found the indicator pointing beyond her top weight (110 pounds), she ate virtually nothing that day except the Hershey bar and Coca-Cola. Next day, when things were back to acceptable, the earlier plan resumed. To this day, Betty has retained what can only be called a girlish figure, feeding others sumptuous meals while nibbling at

Lilliputian helpings herself. Recently her doctor warned her that her blood sugar level was dangerously high, that sweets were off her diet. Realizing the genuine crisis this constituted, I quickly searched my co-op shelves for substitute snacks. But sesame sticks and trail mix hardly replace Lundt's latest delight, a giant Hershey, or bulk chocolate triangles by the pound.

Her looks and charm made her quite popular with boys, who somehow did not hold it against her that she was also extremely smart. Since I was a flop at "boys" because they resented my success at my studies, I held my sister in some degree of awe. Betty was unwilling to sit home and pine, however, so she hid her all-A report cards, telling chums that she "did all right" at the end of each grading period. When I was preschool age, she had endless beaux wishing to marry her, all of whom she carefully kept at bay. Several of them paid court to Mamie, sensing that the way to Betty's heart was through her mother. Others chose to focus on me in their struggle for supremacy: I was carried off to bed many nights on the shoulders of a sweet hulk of a man named "Box" Willingham, who threw me into the air to my delight and let me blow his army sergeant's whistle. These World War II veterans played with me the way other children's dads did, and I loved them fiercely.

Every now and then, Betty would prefer me out of the living room so she and her current visitor could be "alone." In addition to the proverbial nickel for an ice cream cone, I was bought off in clever ways. The most original was the time Betty finagled me into turning the crank of her old blue Victrola while she and Tookie Teague waltzed. I was intrigued by the magical machine that made sounds if you cranked and by the graceful swirls my sister made. She negotiated the furniture and ornaments so much better than I.

During the war when men were off fighting Germans, Betty worked as a public school teacher. I picture her, frantic in our living room, watching a high school senior doing calisthenics that she herself would have to lead her class in the next day; or helping Mamie cut out endless patterns of leaves for borders in her third-grade room; or standing in tears in the middle of the floor having vainly tried to locate middle C on a pitch pipe, readying herself to teach music class. Finally, she got to be the librarian for a year until the regular guardian returned from her stint in the navy.

Books suited my sister better than basketballs or chalk pointers, so after being replaced in the schools, she found her way to the Birmingham Public Library. Beginning in the circulation department, checking out books, she quickly rose to be head of the popular literature wing. In those days, libraries tried to maintain quiet. Betty loved jewelry, especially gold charm bracelets. I can still hear her clinking delicately around shelves, urging three more novels on one patron, four more books on camping on another. Circulation doubled during her first year in the job, since her customers, especially the men, simply could not refuse her recommendations. Who knows whether they read every word, but they certainly exposed themselves to much more culture and information than they had intended. Though she complained about the hours, my sister probably liked her job—not exactly a salon, her section of the library was definitely her domain.

Betty left the library in the early sixties, returning to teaching, this time in a private school across town from where we lived. But in 1963, in December, our mother died suddenly, and Betty was permanently changed. One sign was her decision never to return to work. She asked a friend to bring any personal belongings from her desk when he came to pay his respects. Her last check was mailed to her at home.

We had what is now thought of as a closed nuclear family. When I was born in 1937, three of my grandparents were dead and the fourth died when I was three. My parents were old enough to be my grandparents, and my sister could have been a youngish mother. Though one of my mother's brothers and one of my father's sisters lived in Birmingham, I spent very little time in their homes or getting to know them. They visited us at Christmas, and occasionally we went to their houses for some special event. They called on my parents when they needed help, or when one of their sons (they all had only boys) got into some kind of trouble. I resented their arriving on our doorstep with their newest crisis, expecting Mamie or Daddy to solve it. I resented even more Mamie's and Daddy's persistent willingness to do just that, even when it meant hardship or strain for them.

My family's insularity meant I was shut out of my history as well as on-going holiday clan gatherings. Neither parent liked to talk about the past: my mother said it was too painful; my father simply never mentioned his. I have been told that the annual July 4th celebrations in Selma took place on my mother's parents' lawn and that Mamie's father worked for the railroad. Mostly, he dressed himself in starched white shirts and immaculate suits, summer or winter. Daddy was born and reared on Sand Mountain, at the tail of the Appalachians. His family was supposedly dirt poor and uncultured. My father's father walked out on him, his mother, and two sisters when Daddy was in his teens, forcing him to end his youth and go to work to help support the family.

I know these shadowy ancestors from faded pictures, shown me under duress and at my insistence. I held back questions and responses so as not to upset whoever was showing them. Daddy's father looks like a slightly ill kempt, overgrown kid, usually with some old hound dog at his feet, holding a bottle or glass in one hand, a string of dead fish in the other. His eyes are not quite focused, and he looks as if he could run at any moment. The first time I saw a snapshot of him after I had gone through treatment for years of alcoholic drinking, I felt I was meeting a kinsman. My father's refusal to touch liquor at home suddenly made more sense.

Daddy's mother came to live with him and my mother and sister when Betty was a child. Mamie told a story about sterilizing dishes and glasses in order to protect her child, only to have Mrs. McNaron, who suffered from tuberculosis, go into fits of hurt or affronted self-pity over the special treatment. Whenever my mother and father were in deep wrangles, Mamie would drag out her recital of these scenes, guaranteeing a yelled out, "I don't want to hear that story one more time, Old Lady" (my father's affectionate name for his wife). In the single snapshot of her that I have seen, my paternal grandmother stares out of eyes filled with betrayal, holds herself like a ramrod, seems afraid to smile. She is as thin and sparse and held in as her husband is fat, messy, and without boundaries. I would describe her as handsome rather than beautiful, him as childish and irresponsible.

I have many more photographs of Mamie's side of the family, especially of her father. He is dressed to the hilt: rounded high collars centered by tasteful ties always adorned with a stick pin, never lacking a suit coat, framed in oval, arty tintypes taken by a professional photographer in downtown Selma. "Doc," as Mamie's father was called, smiles from his neat borders and reminds me of the Mona Lisa— reputedly enigmatic if not downright profound but vapid to me. In the full-standing photos, this saintly creature always has a pocket watch, visible from the gold chain and jeweled fob that show just below the center of his buttoned vest. Betty remembers him as "the sweetest man that ever lived." All I remember about him is a walk down Holly Court hill when I was a baby of about two and a half. I needed to hold his hand to steady myself. Because it would have been less than gentlemanly to walk any way other than upright, I had to strain my short arm because he was too tall to walk upright and still reach down to my level.

Mamie's mother looks like a matriarch from the United Daughters of the Confederacy, though we never belonged to that group: buxom and tightly corseted; tall and big boned; eyes looking straight ahead, unflinching and steely; hair pulled back from her face severely, only to roll into a soft circle around her head. When Betty showed me this picture a few years ago, my unvoiced but immediate response was, "I wouldn't want to have her mad at me 'cause she could hold on to it forever."

My mother's mother died quite suddenly one summer in Foley, Alabama, in a movie house. Every year, my family vacationed there, staying in the cabin owned by Mamie's parents. Foley boasted a picture show among its more modern attractions and Mamie's mother took Betty and a boy cousin to afternoon matinees as often as the feature changed. There, in the darkened theater, my grandmother had a heart attack, and while my sister held her head her cousin ran for a doctor. My grandmother died, and my mother fell into a depression that lasted three years before my father intervened. At his insistence, they visited Dr. John, the family doctor. When my father asked what they might do to "cure Old Lady," Dr. John recommended having another child. Though my parents were almost forty, I was conceived. Whenever Mamie told the story of Dr. John's suggesting that she and Mac have a baby to "cheer Theresa up," I felt like running. I grew up in the shadow of that expectation, always trying to please, so often sensing that what I did was not quite enough.

I felt too important to the adults in my house. They kept close watch over me, encouraging me to be what they were not or could not be, reluctant to let me be myself. As a result, my childhood was full of instances in which I very much wanted their attention, but when it came in quantities, I would feel compelled to pull away. For instance, my junior high school teachers seemed intent on having us create "projects," assignments that caused me considerable consternation. Visual effects were to accompany our written reports, and we all knew that decorations determined whether our work received a B for competence or an A for "creativity." Part of me welcomed the help readily forthcoming from Mamie, with Betty as her assistant, since I was not particularly artistic. They would cheerfully volunteer to make my covers, correct my spelling, encourage me to do yet more reading and writing to insure the coveted A. Somewhere in the middle of this process, my gratitude would turn sour, and I would feel taken over, unable to own my work but equally unable to snatch it from them.

My family taught me to see myself as superior to virtually everyone and to isolate myself in the name of precocity or independence or some other large, empty word. One result was that I developed an extraordinarily active imagination, another was few companions my own age. Angry and confused, I took my feelings outside where I ran and played, day after day, to the point of exhaustion.

# First Lessons

*O*ne house, a hedge, and an un-paved alley from where I grew up was the "colored section" of town, popularly known as the "quarters" or "nigger town." The former term recalled the plantation days of slavery, while the latter reflected more contemporary race hatred. The world across that alley fascinated me. When I was three and four, I would sit by my bedroom window and look over at unpainted wooden houses where people lived who were supposed to be different from me. Occasionally, cruising policemen yelled at them, "Get your ass inside, nigger"; after a judicious time lapse, the figures returned to their porches and resumed their activities.

There were three houses up the slant alley. The one nearest the top had once been whitewashed, and traces of peeling green trim persisted. All were built of weathered boards with spaces between, offering no protection against heat, rain, cold, or dust. The family in the first house had a beat-up jalopy that mostly did not run. When they wanted to use it, they would push it into the alley, then try to start it. If the engine failed to turn over, they quickly pushed the car back into their packed dirt yard before the garbage truck filled with white people's trash came or before some white teenaged boy decided to gun his motor all the way up that alley, raising so much dust that it drifted across the vacant lot to my window sills.

Behind "my" three houses (I thought of them as somehow special to me) lay miles of equally poor dwellings in which many hundred blacks eked out whatever existence they could. The neighborhood stretched up a gradual hill so that from my watch-window I could just barely make out houses and an occasional church tower way off in the distance. Within its boundaries, that part of town contained several classes of blacks. The absolute poorest lived nearest us—an odd phenomenon—while middle-class people had better houses further within the tangle of short streets that made up the center of the section. These houses had brick foundations with clapboard siding from about half way up. Window boxes graced virtually every house, as did old rusty gliders painted fresh every other spring. In every yard grew brilliant flowers—waist-high zinnias in reds, oranges, and yellows; fertile roses that looked like they should be wearing blue ribbons; the tallest black-eyed susans I had ever seen. I learned about these distinctions as I rode with my father to take Hettie, our housekeeper, and her successor, Josephine, home when they worked past dark.

When I was ready for junior high school, I had to get to the other side of Fairfield. To walk there the proper way, through white neighborhoods and shopping areas, took about half an hour. But there was a shorter route: once on the street below our house, I could cut ten minutes by going down a little side street that took me over the imaginary line from between white and black Fairfield. I would walk right through the black section, past a tiny store where I could stop for a few jawbreakers or Tootsie Roll Pops on the way home. I was usually the only white child in the place, and the man behind the counter always grinned as he asked, "How you today, Miss?" Along the counter behind which he stood were big jars filled with all kinds of hard candies, "penny" candies that cost two or three cents in white stores. Once I asked my parents why the A & P lied about its candy and the black man's store told the truth. I got no answer but was scolded yet again for refusing to take the "long" (read white) route to school. One of the things I liked about this route was the absence of other white schoolchildren, since in their presence I felt awkward and isolated. In the black neighborhood, I felt more at ease partly because black women on their porches often spoke to me as I went along, ignorant of the pressure I created for them and their children.

The entire South of my childhood was unreconstructed. Blacks were not allowed into white neighborhoods except to get to the houses where they might work. Though Fairfield had a larger population of Negroes (as we called blacks then if we were being polite) than whites, this numerical majority did not matter at all, since every remotely powerful office was held by white men. There were no hotels in Birmingham where blacks could stay except for Gaston Motor Court, owned by one of the few black attorneys in Birmingham but still located miles out of town. Though blacks were allowed to spend money in downtown stores, I never saw them except in department stores my mother said were "common," visited by us only when we needed some specific item unavailable anywhere else. The only exception was Loveman, Joseph, and Loeb, a major department store where blacks did shop regularly.

Once when I was small, my mother and I were in Loveman's looking for some cotton mesh gloves. I never liked these trips downtown, and, on this occasion, I manufactured a major thirst that meant I needed to leave my mother at the counter to find a drinking fountain. I found two fountains, one lower than the other. Since I still could barely reach the regular ones, I used the one nearer my level. As I drank, I felt myself yanked away with a force that almost cost me my footing. Mamie dragged me to one side, whispering loudly, "Can't you read that this one is for coloreds?" I had not seen the clearly painted black letters on the cream wall above the porcelain basin, COLORED. Beside it, above the fountain that was too high for me, I saw an equally clear sign reading WHITE.

"Is the water different in the fountains?" I innocently asked. "Of course not," my mother whispered in a tone that made me think I might be demented. "Then why can't I use the one that's easier for me to get water from?" We had never talked about race relations in our home and so whatever was going on eluded my childishly literal mind. "Just do as I ask, please, honey. Now come on back and try on these nice beige gloves I've found for you."

In the next weeks, I noticed other things: when Daddy took Hettie home, she rode in the back seat, leaving him alone in the front. If children from across the alley ran carelessly into the paved street, their mothers called in voices that sounded like Mamie's when she was afraid I had fallen and hurt myself badly. We kept the dishes and glasses used by Hettie and the yard man, Charlie, in different places from our own. I felt hurt and angry about the car and dishes, since I adored Hettie and Charlie and couldn't comprehend why they were being treated differently. Occasionally at Loveman's I sneaked a quick drink from the forbidden fountains, but my motive was to disobey my mother.

Even though we lived close to Fairfield's black section, no one ever talked about "them," and I was told by my family not to pay any attention to the things I might see or hear from "across the alley." But I needed time away from all the beautiful objects waiting to be knocked to the floor, and I needed very early to disobey. So I began to travel the short physical distance past the last white house, slip through the hedge, and arrive at alien ground—the alley. Though I spent play time in that unpaved area between what I knew were entirely different worlds, I seldom went into the yard of a black person's house. Once or twice I ventured into a field near the three ramshackle houses to play softball with a group of blacks and a few whites who did not live on my block.

I played in the alley often. Two or three other white children not yet in school who lived on my block also played there, along with nine or ten black boys and girls. A black boy, older than the rest, taught me to play marbles, and I was good. We dug out little cup holes in the clay and drew boundaries with a stick; then everyone put the same number of marbles inside the circle as ante. Then one by one we used our special shooter to try and knock marbles into holes. Every marble we got to go into a hole was a keeper. If we lost all our players and only had a shooter, it was legal to put it inside the circle, matched by five to ten regular marbles of anyone who wanted to risk that big a loss. I always risked, winning some stunning shooters called rollerpackers. The risk answered some deep impulse that was being systematically repressed in the rest of my life.

To be a proper southern girl, I needed to learn prudence at all costs, since one false move might reveal some unacceptable tendency. At my first birthday party, for instance, we played the games popular among white children of the time: drop the clothespin in the milk bottle, pin the tail on the donkey, drop the handkerchief, blindman's buff, and how-many-little-words-can-you-make-from-this-big-word. Mamie had bought wonderful prizes to be given the winners— brightly colored tops, packages of metal jacks, wooden paddles with tiny red rubber balls attached by long rubber strings, bags of cat's eye marbles complete with a shooter. I won all the games, but my mother made me give the prizes to my guests, saying, "You wouldn't want your little friends to think you're selfish or greedy, would you?" What I wanted was fairness, but I saw that being polite might well exclude that possibility.

By the fifth grade of my all-white school, I comprehended that life among my so-called white peers was far more hazardous and cruel than it had been in the alley. None of us who played there minded whether we lost or won on a given day; it was exciting just to make holes, draw circles, and risk. Consequently, when I saw white boys playing marbles using pretty much the same strategy I had learned, I asked to play with them. They let me but giggled behind their hands at some private joke. When I won, consistently and heavily, their giggles turned into ugly snarls. They talked about me in ways that caused girls to avoid me, especially in the restroom. The back of my neck stung and turned red in spite of my willpower, but I went ahead and used the toilet when what I wanted most was to run out of the bathroom, out of the school, out of my world. But I refused to play marbles less well than I knew how, so the process of exclusion and derision continued.

As it did, I gradually formed distinctly negative attitudes toward white boys. I did not like how mean and nasty they could be to the black children across the alley from me. They routinely dropped terrified cats and kittens off high back porches, laughing uproariously when they landed with thuds I could hear from two houses away. And I very much hated them when they rubbed my nose in pink buttercup flowers until I sneezed and coughed my way into my house. Without knowing it, I was coming to associate white boys with bullies who went after white girls and all blacks.

Given these strained relations with my white classmates, I still puzzle over why that black boy taught me to play marbles so well and over why he and other black boys did not seem to mind when I won their marbles. Surely it is facile to say they won mine too and so it evened out. Did they already feel like such total losers in the world around them that a few marbles more or less couldn't matter? Did the black boy have a fantasy that I would do just what I did and so teach me well in order to cause me pain? Did he do it to get back at the white boys who routinely shot BB guns into his front yard, scaring him and his sisters back into their house? Did he, like I, sense without words some connection between us deeper than color and gender? Or were we just having fun, was it just a game?

I refer to my alley associates as "that black boy" or "a black girl" because we never told names, white or black, though we played together for several years. In fact we hardly used words at all, which was another blessing about the alley. Inside my house, language was everything, and everyone knew lots more of it than I did, no matter how hard I tried to catch up. I now believe that we maintained that amazing anonymity and silence as protection. My mother often asked me who I was with "out there in all that red clay dust." Because I knew nobody's name, I could answer truthfully, "I don't know, they're just some kids—we have fun and I like them." Perhaps their mothers asked similar questions. But somebody could have gotten into lots of trouble if the grownups had traced our gang. Our silence had its painful edge, since it acknowledged the impossibility of any of our becoming friends.

When I was about to enter the first grade, my mother took me aside and tried to tell me something about race relations in the South. Her success was only slightly greater than when she tried years later to tell me about menstruation by saying, to calm my fears at blood coming out of me, "Oh, honey, be glad, now you can have babies." All I heard that afternoon when I was seven was that I was forbidden to play in the alley. That was on a Sunday, the usual day for long talkings-to by my mother. On Monday, I started school and hated it instantly.

On the first day of first grade, everyone's mother brought her reluctant child inside a hot, stuffy old brick building, into a strange room full of small desks and large blackboards. Presiding over it all was a woman I would come to see as kindly enough, but my initial encounter with Miss Leslie left me angry and confused. It seems that part of our "lessons" was to be the acquisition of manners—of which I already had more than enough as far as I was concerned. But Miss Leslie felt it her social duty to show her little girls and boys how to set a table properly and how to sit by a *papier maché* fireplace and engage in chat, that essential southern practice.

In an attempt to involve us in setting up these ersatz spaces, she asked the class to bring various items from home: cushions for the little straight chairs we were to chat in; paper place mats for the little table where we were to have tea; vases for flowers or other decorations. Then she looked at the fireplace area, turned to us with a deep smile, and said: "Now the last thing we need may be hard to find, since not everyone will have one in their home. But we lack a little hearth broom." I was confused about what she wanted, since she pronounced hearth "herth." Guessing what she meant, since we did have a red straw broom by our fireplace that I used regularly to sweep up ashes or stray coal pieces, I raised my hand eagerly. "I can bring a hearth broom from home—we have one." I pronounced the word as it should be.

"Well, thank you, my dear, I'm sure you can, but first you must learn to pronounce it correctly—"herth," not "harth"—come along now, I'm sure you can say that."

Proper pronunciation was sacred in our household. I knew that h-e-a-r-t-h did not rhyme with e-a-r-t-h, even though they might look alike if you took away the "h." My confidence in the correctness of my way of saying it urged me on to what was probably stupid bravery. I looked Miss Leslie in the eye and said, "Oh, no ma'am, it's "harth," not "herth."

My mother whispered in my unbelieving ear, "Honey, just say what the teacher asks you to here and keep saying it right at home. And say you're sorry, like a good girl. Go on, now." This from the same person who drilled correctness into me, even refusing to let me use street slang in order to blend in with the other children on my block. My anger flared as I turned on my mother and spat out, "You tell her *you're* sorry if you are—I'm not sorry—I'm right and I don't understand why you want me to lie."

Deciding not to push the issue further just then, Miss Leslie went ahead with her plans for next day, saying only, "Why don't you bring along your little broom and we'll put it by this nice fireplace and you can show us all how you sweep the ashes." When the long half-day finally ended, my mother went up to the teacher's desk and spoke in hushed tones. I have no idea what she said, but I was disappointed in her for seeming to collude with someone who could not even pronounce a simple word correctly.

We got out at noon, and by two o'clock I was back in my play clothes, sitting in the alley with my black playmates. After a few days, I noticed that the handful of other white children who occasionally played there were gone. Other parents may have conducted similar awkward, muddled conversations about no longer playing in the clay strip between worlds. No matter how muddled the message, the others obeyed. I was slow to grasp that my entry into that dull and hypocritical space where first grade happened was my formal exposure to southern racial and sexual politics. In that school room, no such Never Never land as my alley could exist. There, everything was black or white, and I was definitely white.

As a child, I came into contact with two black women, both of whom worked for my family as domestic servants: Hettie Holmes and Josephine Zeak. Mamie took an interest in Hettie's welfare, giving her old clothes and food to take home to Mr. Holmes. As a child who loved to choose for myself, I wondered if Hettie might not prefer money to go downtown and buy something new.

On several occasions, Mamie sent Daddy to the local jail on

Sunday mornings to bail Hettie out. Hettie, my mother told me, drank whiskey on the weekend and fought with her husband, who drank whiskey all week. Their weapons were knives, and Hettie came to work more than once with new cut marks on her neck and upper arms, though never on her powerful and beautiful face. I imagined Mr. Holmes agreed with me about her face. Once, when I raged against him for hurting her, she said laughingly: "Oh, sugar, you should see him, he looks a whole lot worse." They stayed married all the time I knew her.

Hettie was short, dark skinned, and pudgy, wore faded house-dresses, and cleaned our house in bare feet. But to me at three and five, she seemed mysterious, warm, and free spirited. She dipped Red Devil snuff from little flat aluminum cans. Wanting to do everything she did, one morning I asked her to let me have some snuff. "No, child, this'll make you some sick." I insisted, putting Hettie into an ancient black–white tug in which a child of five can order a grown woman to do her bidding. I won, of course, and took a small pinch of the rich brown smelly stuff. Sticking it carefully between my gum and lower lip, I tried hard to copy my model. In about three minutes, I felt lightheaded, then nauseated for the rest of the morning. After that I was content to watch my hero fill her own lower lip until it stuck out bravely.

Hettie Holmes cooked things my mother did not know how to fix. Her corn bread—crisp and delicate all at once—tasted so good I ate it without butter or jelly. Her version of pork chops and onions had a succulence and pungency that spoiled me for all future offerings of that popular southern dish. Hettie could serve peas and beans that still tasted of peas and beans, unlike my mother's, which had no particular taste because they were disguised in a thick French sauce.

My mother prepared *haute cuisine* when I wanted greasy vegetables from a frying pan. The frying pan urge obsessed me for months. Hettie made our lunch and served it in the dining room where we always ate. Then she had her own food at a table in the kitchen, carefully placed so Mamie could see and talk with her. Mamie enjoyed Hettie's company but could not conceive in 1943 of their eating in the same physical space. Hettie took the cast-iron pan from which our food had just been served, set it on a dish towel on her table, and ate directly from it. When she had eaten all she could with a fork, she took a piece of bread and sopped up remaining traces of gravy or "pot licker." I was punished severely for using my bread that way.

Whenever Mamie went to town to shop or attend her many clubs (garden, book, church auxiliary, forensic, library), I lunched out of that frying pan, sitting proudly at the kitchen table. Hettie, on the other hand, watched and listened nervously for Mamie's possible untimely return. At least once, we were almost caught. I was in the middle of pork chops and onions, peas, and corn bread, when Mamie rang the door bell at the front screen door. While Hettie kept my mother at bay with some story about her hands being in dishwater, I dumped my food onto a china plate and ran for the dining room. When I first saw Lillian Smith's title, *Strange Fruit*, I recalled those stolen childhood lunches at which I could relax about whether I was using the correct implement or putting my glass back at the right angle in relation to my knife and plate.

In Alabama, torrential downpours can drop inches of rain in a very short time. We lived on the plateau of a high hillside that had been terraced for housing. Houses across the street had many cement steps going from the street up to their front porches, while our front entrance was on the street level. When it rained hard, the water surged down those stone steps into our yard before it ran down the hill toward our back alley. I was scared of those sheets of water. If a storm began on an afternoon when Hettie was keeping me, she stopped whatever she was doing to stand beside me at the living room window. I was fixed in amazement at the deluge of clay-colored water washing down, making creases in all the lawns, noisy even through our closed windows, bringing small objects with it. Standing behind me, her hand resting reassuringly on my back, Hettie would talk in her low, husky voice: "God's making soup out of rain for his people and what you see washing down the steps is his pots boiling over, like mine do in the kitchen if I go off and forget them." She told me the trees were not going to blow over but were yawning to wake up and feel the wind blow through them. She told me lightning was a message from the Lord telling us to work harder and look especially to our house-keeping. She told me thunder was Jesus in his private bowling alley, knocking over ten golden pins, having fun for a change.

Hettie Holmes stopped working for us when I was about nine, and I never heard of her again. When I asked why she was not coming to work, I received no answer. I was angry and hurt to have so central a person removed from my daily life without a word of explanation. Maybe she became more alcoholic and could not work a steady job; maybe Daddy stopped being willing to bail her out of jail; maybe she cooked up one mess too many of greasy magic peas and corn bread for Mamie's ego. Maybe she got tired of being grateful to Mamie for handouts. Or maybe she secretly resented being bailed out of jail by my father. I made up lots of maybes. But none of them took away my ache or filled the void I felt when Hettie vanished. She is surely long dead but I think of her sometimes when it storms or when I eat black-eyed peas that never quite taste right.

Shortly after Hettie Holmes stopped working for us, we heard about a young black woman reputed to be good at cleaning and ironing. She arrived one day in 1947 and stayed until we sold the house in 1964 after Mamie died. Josephine Zeak was her name, and I liked her right away. I had never known a person whose name began with "z." Josephine was tall and thin with cocoa brown skin and shiny straightened black hair. Her nose was Western, her cheek bones were statuesque African. She wore stockings and spoke softly. Her dresses had belts. She used a napkin when she ate her lunch and read magazines while her food digested. It was a major source of irritation to my mother and sister that Josephine would not hop up from lunch to scrub the kitchen floor or at least wash the lunch dishes. She insisted on half an hour between her last mouthful and any resumption of work, so that her food could digest properly. I remember Mamie getting up from her lunch, returning to her knees to finish polishing a part of the floor between the living and dining rooms that got waxed once a week and was hazardous to walk on. While she did that, Josephine waited for her hamburger patty to settle, reading to my mother from *Life* magazine about some movie actor they both liked. She refused to wash curtains, wax floors, or iron with starch, leaving those odious tasks for my mother.

When Josephine arrived, I thought myself old enough to take some responsibility in training her. Dusting and vacuuming were my specialities, so I "taught" her to do those things. She was canny enough to mask her feelings, never letting on that she already knew how to do such chores all too well. In her early thirties when I met her, she had been cleaning houses since she was a teenager. Whereas Hettie Holmes had come every day unless she was too hung over or in jail, Josephine stipulated which three days a week she could come and what her hours would be. Because Mamie had never dealt with a black person who was not completely deferential, she was speechless. All she could do was complain to Betty about Josephine's "insolence" and how that was probably tied to her being light skinned. Neither of them considered firing or confronting her.

Sometimes Josephine and I cleaned the bedrooms together so she would have time to iron in the afternoons. Those were good times for me because I went into the basement where the ironing board stayed and talked to Josephine. I learned about her two daughters and soon met Joann, who was only three or four months older than I. Our talks about school subjects and dating seemed stiff to me. Joann was dating and I was not, so I felt inferior when that topic came up. But when we talked about anything else, she hung back, trying to show what her mother undoubtedly would have taught her was appropriate deference. We graduated from high school the same year, and that next fall she married a soldier named Sport and moved to Georgia, while I went to the white state university. One rainy afternoon in the basement Josephine shared a dream with me: she was determined to help her girls advance themselves, so they would not have to clean houses.

Sometimes I read to Josephine while she ironed, and then we discussed what I had read. As I grew older, I realized how unfair it was for anyone so intelligent to have to clean white ladies' houses in order to make money. Many years after she came to work for us, I asked her about all this, and she said, "I once thought of being something, but then I married and had the babies and it did not seem very practical to try. It was easy to get work cleaning houses. White ladies liked me to do that but didn't particularly want me to do other things."

Since my exodus from the South in 1961, my contact with Josephine has been mostly through our monthly letters. Hers are full of the weather, her health, her children, grandchildren, great-grandchildren, the white ladies she has worked for, her hopes that I am well and happy. When I went to Wisconsin to graduate school and her older daughter went to Alaska with her army husband, Josephine said she felt lonely and less useful. But on one occasion, she was more helpful to me than either of us understood at the time. I was in the process of writing my Ph.D. dissertation. My mother and sister had just spent the summer with me in Madison, Wisconsin, and I could see that Mamie was not well and that Betty was discontented. That fall, just months before my mother died of a heart attack, Josephine called me long distance (a huge cost to her) to say she was worried about "Miss Mamie." Under strenuous questioning, she revealed that Betty was pushing harder than usual to leave Holly Court. My sister had wanted to move across town to a better neighborhood for years. My mother flatly refused—perhaps that was the only time she refused my sister.

She owned her house; it was her only security; she liked having Betty and her husband live with her. To reverse that arrangement would mean a loss of power. As Josephine talked with me, she cried, saying, "Oh, Toni, I'm scared for Miss Mamie." I sat right down and wrote my mother immediately, supporting her wish to stay where she felt more secure. Josephine had taken a great risk to speak so directly to me.

Though I have never told Josephine in so many words that I am a lesbian, she has known about several women with whom I have lived. She has accepted this part of me as easily as she did my telling her at ten how to vacuum. She sends greetings to my present lover, remembers her name, is happy that I am not living alone. Each time I have moved, she has written to say, "Wish I could come help clean so your space will be fit to live in." Statements like this one are followed by, "Smile," written in parentheses. Her sense of humor continues to touch me as does her determination to grow old gracefully. A few years ago she moved away from her husband, Mr. Zeak (she never called him anything else in front of me). She wrote me that things had not been so good between them, and she had decided to live more peacefully in her old age. Now she rents an apartment in the same building as her sister. Her income gets smaller every year since housecleaning has become too strenuous. Though she worked hard for over fifty years, she has no pension and virtually no Social Security. Her daughters help her out financially, and my sister and I send her money occasionally, which she calls a "token." When I see the word, I feel that no amount we ever send can make up for the years of cheap labor she gave us. Her meaning for the word is that my sister or I have sent her another sign of how much we value and care for her.

On a trip south in 1974, I looked forward most of all to seeing Josephine. She invited me to her house for lunch, and I accepted gladly. The psychosomatic laryngitis I had developed shortly after my uncle had greeted me with, "God made them niggers black, you know," magically vanished as I crossed Josephine's threshold. Her space was safe space, a place where I could speak without fear of offending. The decorations in her house were a strange blend of simple furniture and linoleum on the floors and exquisite ornaments from our house on Holly Court, given to her first by Mamie and then by Betty after Mamie's death.

We were to have lunch in the kitchen so I stood and talked with her while she fixed things. She had remembered my favorite lunch: Campbell's tomato soup and a hamburger made of ground round steak on bread with mayonnaise and catsup. I cried while Josephine stirred my soup; no one else that trip seemed to focus on me at all, preferring to make me into who or what they expected. Maybe that was part of why I always loved the women who worked for us so fiercely and was so devastated when they vanished: they gave me sympathy, kindness, and affectionate acceptance without being able to demand anything in return.

When I noticed that Josephine was cooking only one hamburger patty, I asked why. "Oh, I ate my lunch before you came, so I could listen better to all you have to say." Then I noticed only one place setting at the table. "Oh, I'll just stand here by the stove, in case you want something more; then when you finish, we can go into the living room and have a nice talk." I felt wounded for both of us and insisted that she sit with me while I ate.

I decided to ask her about being black in Fairfield, Alabama, and she decided to tell me. She spoke with tears in her eyes about Dr. King and his vision. She spoke with fear in her eyes about young blacks, especially men, out of jobs, restless, eager to act violently toward anyone in their way. She admitted that it had made her angry to be treated badly by white ladies and hurt her not to be able to give her children more of what she wished for them. I told her I was in favor of total integration. She replied, "Oh, child, I'm too old and grew up a long time ago; if we go that far, it's just more hurt and blood for us here." Her worst terror was that, as some blacks rebelled, all would be punished. So she preferred moderation, a slower pace. From my position of white safety, I told her the pace was killingly slow now and that I wanted change within my lifetime.

After a couple of hours, Josephine began noticeably to fidget. When I asked, she admitted, "I'm a little worried about how long you've been here. My neighbors are sure to have seen the car when it drove up; they'll know it held a white lady." I had stayed longer than any errand could have possibly taken and so must not be an employer. Recently a "nice colored lady" from her church had been slapped around by young black boys because she had been seen being too friendly with some white person at a grocery store on Fairfield's main street. Josephine was frightened and yet sad to have to wish me gone. I asked her to come outside and let me take a picture of her, which she did. I could get her to do this, against her better judgment, because the basic power imbalance between us was still present. Having hugged in her kitchen, I was careful not to appear too close or to touch her. It felt entirely too familiar to me, holding in spontaneous affection for a woman I love.

For many years, Josephine sent me a homemade pound cake at Christmas. That meant laying in eggs, sugar, flour, butter, vanilla, ingredients alone at a cost of about eight dollars. Josephine made five dollars a day, cleaning houses. To make my cake, she took a day off, losing her much-needed money, in order to sift, mash, and beat by hand. Then she went to elaborate lengths to wrap my cake so it would hold its freshness through the U.S. mail. It came in a cardboard box, mailed first class, marked fragile, handle with care—expensive. Inside the big box was a bakery box secured into the heavier one by layers of grocery store brown bags. These would have cost her as well, since stores gave free extra bags only to whites. Inside the boxes lay the cake, made in a doughnut hole pan, even more delicate than if it were solid. The cake was wrapped first in waxed paper, then aluminum foil, then paper toweling. Each material was folded with utmost attention to closing out any air that could dry the texture. Wads of paper towels were gently stuffed into the center, so the form arrived intact. Tissue paper wrapped the bakery box, holding it firmly yet softly in its container. Every year when it came, I cried: all that time and love and sacrifice for me. I was possessive about my cake, unwilling to share it even with lovers. Several years ago, I gave up sugar but could not bring myself to tell Josephine for a long time afterward. I liked feeling that taken care of. I still miss my package.

Hettie and Josephine filled that peculiarly southern role of black mothers to a white child, mothers marked by the cruel inequities of a racist culture. I took advantage of them even while I adored them and would fight to defend them if neighbor children called them "nigger." My mother had severely punished me the day I came in from playing with friends on the block and asked if our yard man was a "shiftless old nigger." "Never let me hear you call any of the colored people who work here by that common, white-trash word, do you hear me?" I heard her and never did it again, since my mother had gone on to say, once her fury had abated, that it would hurt their feelings badly to hear me say that word. Though I often took spiteful pleasure in disobeying my mother, about this subject I lived up to her demand. I did that because I loved Hettie and Josephine more than almost anybody in my life and because they loved me back through the dense barriers of race. But their love had to filter through an ingrained and justified fear and hatred of my whiteness. They surely made distinctions between me and the faceless white boys who shot up their front yards with BB guns. For all I know, they defended me against names used within their own world for the racist bigots who lounged on the street corners of town. But the trap of racism held us, so I have to live with knowing that my love for them was mixed with my liking having power over someone in my world, and their love for me was interlaced with ambiguity and maintained at perhaps too high a price to their own sense of selfhood.

A black man named Charlie Teague mowed our lawn once a week and helped my mother in her large garden. He was very big and dark and full of an infectious laugh that hid his worries from whites. While he cut the grass or weeded, he sang or talked to himself. His monologues were hard to follow, since the whole left side of his face was full of Brown Mule chewing tobacco. After my disaster with snuff, I stood in awe of him: how did Charlie stay upright with all that raw tobacco lodged in his mouth? Every five minutes of so, he shot out a long, straight stream of juice that arced perfectly through the hot air to land with a mighty splat on the sidewalk or in the gutter or the dust.

I felt proud when Charlie deigned to talk to me instead of himself. He would stop work, wipe sweat off his face, and listen to my latest story. During the 1940s, like most children, I had a helmet and machine gun. I also carried an old World War I medal my father had given me, and a lot of hostility that emerged when I played soldier. Charlie indulged my fantasies by calling me Sergeant, or, when he felt especially playful, Sarge. He would pretend to take orders from me about mowing or weeding, answering me with a mock salute and a "Yessir, Sarge, whatever you say."

One July day, Charlie was working in our side yard, overgrown with high weeds because my mother had recently been in the hospital to see if a lump in her breast was malignant. He was using a big sickle that had once been fire engine red and was almost as tall as I. Deciding that I wanted to swing that sickle, I asked Charlie for it. When he demurred, pleading that it was too heavy for me, I commanded him as a white army sergeant to let me use that tool. He obeyed as a black hired man.

Feeling cocky, I swung the big blade out to the right. That part went fine, but then the sickle fell back toward me, grazing my right big toe. A large slice of me went with it, stuck to the grassy blade, and my toe began to bleed. Afraid it would not stop, I held my toe under the yard hose, since cold water had often stopped my nicks and cuts from bleeding. This had no effect except to make little pools of reddish water in the dust. Charlie was scared speechless and did not even bother to say "I told you so." What difference would that make to my hysterical mother when she found out that he let me swing the blade?

After a long time, my blood slowed enough for me to walk a few steps in my sandals before having to mop my toe. I sneaked into the house and ran for my room to put on socks to hide the wound. Lunch was ready, and Mamie expected me to take Charlie's tray out to him as I usually did. He ate what we did, even if he had special dishes that stayed in the basement. His tea was served in an old Blue Plate mayonnaise quart jar full of ice cubes and a lemon slice. Once I asked why Charlie's dishes were kept in our basement when Hettie Holmes's special plates were just stacked on a separate shelf in the kitchen. Whatever Mamie said, the message was that since Charlie was a man, he did dirtier things than Hettie when he was at home or on the streets.

Eager not to arouse any suspicion by my delay, I hurriedly pulled on the darkest blue and red socks I owned, strapped on my sandals and walked to the kitchen to get the tray. By now my toe was throbbing, but I refused to limp or show any signs of pain. When I took the tray out to Charlie, he was still wearing a look of terror, but I smiled innocently and told him just to call if he wanted more corn or iced tea. Back inside, my socks soaked up the blood, and I got through lunch. When I took them off, later, blood had clotted so thickly that the right one had to be gently peeled away. I never told on Charlie, and Charlie never told on me. Occasionally one of us would make a veiled reference to "the blade" or "that big toe" and fall into gales of laughter.

Every fall I saved enough of my allowance to let me buy Charlie a Christmas present: several plugs of Brown Mule and a quart of Mogen David red wine, his favorite thing to drink. Mamie gave him old shirts and pants of my father's plus some food she made. Charlie always showed delight over his presents, laughing more than usual, breaking off an extra big chew of tobacco since he felt flush with his supply from me, talking loudly about "what wonderful white folks ya'll are."

Like other black people in my life, at some point Charlie simply vanished. By that time, I had stopped asking where they went or why they no longer came to our house, but I never learned to stop missing them.

In 1950, while American soldiers were killing Asians in Korea, I entered a high school full of white boys who rode through the black section of town at night and on weekends, shooting it up or throwing glass bottles into streets, onto lawns, against sides of houses. All that seemed very far away to me as I struggled vainly to keep my starched Peter Pan collars straight, my bobby socks rolled to just the right length, and my lipstick on past second period math. I had trouble making friends my own age and often felt lonely. I have almost no clear memories of those years.

But I do remember sitting on my bed for hours, looking out my burglar-barred windows at the alley, the three houses down its slope, and further off, the expanse of dwellings that made up the black neighborhood. In my yearning for something I could not have named, I romanticized the people who lived there even as I continued to benefit from my automatically privileged position. We were all caught in the web of southern racism and sexism. Those blacks who lived in solid brick houses on paved streets in the center of their community near churches and food markets were imprisoned by their color. Once out of their neat yards filled with tall red–orange callas and prize-quality roses, they were as vulnerable as their poorest fellows living in wooden shanties along dirt roads full of potholes. Similarly, though hardly with the same possibilities of permanence, when I ventured away from my house and yard into the larger world of white teenage activities, I felt like an exposed failure, no matter how many A's or honors I accumulated.

One night during this time stands vividly in my memory. I awoke to an eerie glow, sat up in bed, and raised my shade. Columns of flame deep inside the black section frightened me enough to cause me to wake my parents. We heard faint sounds of one or two fire engines though the flames ranged over blocks, burning out of control. (Blacks depended on the city of Fairfield for public services, so I suspect one or two engines was all they ever got.) I sat on the edge of my bed crying until almost daylight, long after Mamie and Daddy had gone back to bed and encouraged me to do the same. The flames finally subsided, replaced by ominous clouds of black and then ugly grey smoke. To me, it seemed as though that smoke came from the people, not the fire. Years later when I saw pictures of columns of smoke from the ovens of the Holocaust, I would flash back to that night in Alabama.

Though I searched the white newspaper for several days, I found no word about the big fire. There was lots of news about the local domino club's victory over a neighboring team, majorettes from Fairfield High who attended a conference of other majorettes, the latest discount on chicken at the Piggly Wiggly—nothing about what must have been the worst fire in my town's history. I wanted to go see where it had been, but my parents refused to take me near the place. When Josephine came to work the next day, I asked her about it, but she brushed me off, saying, "Some folks say white boys from the high school lit a Coke bottle filled with gasoline-coated rags and threw it into some lady's yard, but I'm sure it was just old newspapers stacked in a building." I remembered the stories about boys at school who routinely invaded the black world, looking for idle amusement, and I knew who started the fire. Breaking my silence about that fire now, forty years later, I feel a ferocity coupled with that sense of helplessness that was to wash over me more often the older I got.

# Child's Play

"Toni's so talented—she can amuse herself for hours." My mother said this often to our family and friends as proof of my creativity and resourcefulness. Hearing it, I always see myself sitting alone in a room, coloring or reading or building some new fantasy world.

The story began in my baby bed with its several rows of colored wooden beads strung on thin metal rods like an abacus. From the time I could stand, I moved the beads in endless mutations to produce colors and spaces. At three, I was given a little slate with a real abacus for its top. When my mother handed me my slate and piece of chalk, she said: "Here, honey, now draw a cat or print your ABC's." As long as she watched, I demonstrated what I gather were my precocious motor and mental skills. But as soon as she went into some other room, I put down the chalk and began to count and arrange the beads. I loved the click of one against another and the gliding sound as I moved a whole row from left to right, fast. Their bright reds, blues, greens, and yellows cheered me up, reminding me of my baby bed and of how much I liked standing up in it, staring at the big colored spheres.

At about four, I began to catch my feces in my hands before they fell into the toilet bowl, take them into my bedroom and hide them in an old shoebox my sister gave me. That box stayed under my bed, near the windows. When the grownups were busy elsewhere, I would steal into my room, crawl down between my bed and the wall, haul out my box and make wonderful creations. At its height my collection included ten figures and four or five cars. One day as I was busily executing my new idea for a giraffe, my mother discovered me. Deeply shocked, she gave me a severe lecture about "niceness," then punished me by having me sit quietly in a chair for some five minutes. A

37

few days later, she presented me with a box of colored modelling clay, but I refused to use it, saying, "Clay is for babies."

I learned during this earliest phase of my artistic development that what I made could not last long, and that lesson was reinforced throughout my childhood. As payroll master for his company, my father brought home bags of bills and change every Thursday, only to take them away on Fridays to hand out in small brown envelopes to the workers. But while they were in our house, I could dump out and play with their contents. Each unbleached muslin bag from the First National Bank of Fairfield could hold several hundred copper pennies. I loved to hear them tumble onto my bedroom floor, then watch them scatter under my bed, into corners, out into the hall. Because Daddy worried that a coin or two might get lost under some piece of furniture, he urged me to play on the living room rug. The public nature of this space frustrated me, since people tracked back and forth on their way out the door. In the middle of an elaborate design, a large foot could invade my work area, disrupting my pennies, causing me to cry quietly as I tried to restore them.

The pennies served as borders for buildings, people, objects. But almost as soon as I had finished a town or barnyard or sentence, Mamie came and scooped them up because she needed the room for something, or Daddy rebagged them so he could get to bed in time to feel rested at 4:00 A.M., his wake-up hour.

The effect of these interruptions on my creativity was marked. Unlike some I know, I never kept a diary or journal, and I have no signs of childhood art, though I engaged almost daily in the act of making. I remember feeling quiet and steadied by such activities, safer than when talking. From a very early age, I was able to lose myself in such creative play, going far from 5130 Holly Court, Fairfield, Alabama. But writing any of it down seemed dangerous to me; someone could easily take my stories or plans away if they existed on paper. So I lived out my mother's proud boast—I did indeed amuse myself for hours, leaving no record for anyone to find, not even me.

I was a skinny child with a head full of long blond hair that I wore in curls like Scarlett O'Hara. This hair was mostly a bother as I ran wildly outside. Summers, Mamie plaited it into two stubbly braids held with rubber bands that pulled and were covered with grosgrain ribbons of various colors. Try as she did, my mother seemed incapable of making tight, neat braids like I saw on girls at school, but at least my neck was partly cleared so sweat could roll down easier. Every late afternoon, my hair had to be brushed, since my rambunctious playing tangled it horribly. Tender headed, I cried through most of this ritual. But all adults seemed convinced that my hair was my "crowning glory," so there was no getting away from the torture. To this day, I have to force myself to brush the recommended fifty strokes and prefer simply to wash my hair and run my hands through it as it dries.

The reason I was skinny is my food story. At a rather early age I learned that if I did not eat my lunch or dinner, my mother would stay at the table coaxing me. Wanting her undivided attention sometimes fiercely, I began what must have been a tedious ritual. I picked and poked at my food until my father and sister were long gone from the table. Then Mamie and I were left to battle out the carrots or spinach or even mashed potatoes and gravy. "Eat, honey," was the refrain to which I turned deaf ears, knowing I could outsit her and keep her talking.

The hard part of my regimen was that food got cold and inedible, so that finally no one would have wanted to have it. To handle this unforeseen development, I figured out how to toss bits of congealed vegetables or cold meat down the big furnace duct that came up to the dining room floor and was covered with a metal grating that I polished monthly to keep its brass coating shiny. While Mamie was in the kitchen getting another glass of iced tea, I would deftly get rid of some of the odious food. When she returned, I would brag about my cooperative behavior, "See all I've eaten while you were gone; aren't I a good and brave girl now?" My poor mother praised me for what she took to be eating but what in reality was lying and having sure wrist action that later helped me throw a baseball to first base with amazing accuracy.

One day when I was about eleven and had been tossing unwanted food down the grate for years, I was shocked to learn that we were going to have the furnace cleaned out. On the appointed day, I made myself scarce the moment the burly white workman arrived at about nine in the morning. Ironically, we were all having lunch when he knocked on the basement door, came into our dining room, and unwrapped a small bundle. "I can't tell how this stuff ever got into your furnace, ma'am, but I took it out. Do you want me to throw it away or what?" To my horror, the bundle contained parched chicken bones, unrecognizably shrunken things that must once have been carrots or beans or squash, dust-coated blobs of years-old potatoes.

My mother graciously scooped it all up, saying over her shoulder as she fled into the kitchen, "Oh, never mind, I can just put it here in the trash, probably a cat or mouse did it." Lame by any measure, and we both knew it.

When Mamie returned from the back porch, she sat down resignedly and looked right at me. "Toni, honey, how could you have told me such stories all these years. I thought you were trying to eat, and you were doing something no nice person could imagine. Wherever did you get such an idea in the first place?" I answered not at all but glumly chewed the vegetable before me. I never really answered Mamie, and she never required it. From then on, I had to invent new schemes to cover my not eating. Stashing small amounts in a pocket or trying to attract the cat's attention without also alerting my mother were far less effective than the furnace trick had been.

Though I resisted real food, for years I played something called "store" and a variation I named "drugstore." Mamie saved Rice Krispies and Grapenuts Flakes containers, Quaker Oats tins, RC Cola bottles, Oxydol boxes. Being resourceful, I also badgered our next door neighbor lady for such rareties as Black Jack shoe polish cans, Sauer's almond extract bottles, and Blue Bonnet margarine holders. On makeshift shelves or tall cardboard crates, I set up my wares, each marked with a tiny price tag, and sat patiently waiting for other children to come "buy" something. We never actually paid money for such empties but gave each other rocks or shards of pretty colored glass that had been given designated values.

"Drugstore" was beautiful. I saved old medicine bottles, of which we seemed to have a great abundance, what with the vague illnesses that kept me home from school and my mother's various potions. Into each clear bottle went first tap water, then a few drops of food dye. The result was a rainbow of bottles, each having a label on which I wrote the virtues of the exotic contents. "Sure cure for toenails hanging part way off." "Take one spoonful daily and never again have circles under your eyes." "Drink regularly for itchy heads or rashes between your toes." Each evening, I stored all the pretty liquids in the basement, only to set up the entire show next day even though almost no one ever came to see or buy my magic elixirs. The colors fascinated me, just as the beads on my baby bed had years before and just as organic chemistry and stained-glass windows would years later.

My artistic flair was inhibited by all the rules of public school.

Teachers wanted me to sit still for hours, coloring within the lines, making trees green and cows brown and people light pink. Once in second grade I argued for the trueness of a picture. I had drawn a brown person and a pink cow because I had seen brown people out in country fields with scrawny pinkish-red cows. My teacher, driven by racism as much as a narrow view of art, threw my piece of construction paper into the waste basket, saying, "If you insist that there are brown people and pink cows, I'll report you to the principal who will talk to your mother about your disrespectful attitude." I got a C in conduct that semester.

As a very little girl, I loved to make musical sounds—song snatches, whistles, simple noises that felt good. My mother sang and encouraged me to hum along with her at home and church. In grammar school, I learned there was someone called "the music teacher" who would come to our classes one hour a week. I was elated, since it meant I would learn real tunes and words. I even fancied being able to teach Mamie a song. The teacher was a tall, thin woman with fading auburn hair and big feet and hands. She would stride into our classroom, go straight to the old spinet that was wildly out of tune, and begin playing some song whose lyrics were much too advanced for us. I learned "On the Road to Mandalay" without having any idea where or what Mandalay was. But I was quite drawn to "flying fishes"; they reminded me of brown people and pink cows, and I wished I lived "in China across the bay" since maybe there they would let me color as I saw things and not worry about the lines.

The music teacher did not like my voice because it was too low. She forced me to sing soprano notes. I squeaked and cracked and sounded awful. Everyone laughed at me for singing off key, and my record began to say I was "unmusical." To help me retain self-respect and some interest in singing, my mother assured me, "Just keep singing out as loudly as you want at church, honey, and if it isn't quite right, no one will mind." She also told me that singing an octave lower than other girls was perfectly all right, that if I ever joined a choir, I would be placed with people called altos because their voices were "mellow." That word became a lifeline to counter "unmusical" as I fought to hang on to my love of making sounds. No wonder I came to prefer cellos and French horns, contraltos and basses, the left hand on the piano, fog horns at sea.

Too many of the people who taught me spent most of their time trying to help marginally literate students. Consequently the few teachers who did excite me remain in my mind like crystal. Much of my free time was spent in their rooms, where I helped them arrange borders above the blackboard or clean their space. I often lost potential friends because I chose to answer the questions teachers asked in class. Although it was painful not to be accepted, I did not regret my choices even when I was making them. Those women were generous to me, in class and out. They told me extra things about geography or math or sentence diagramming; they let me take heavy books or satchels full of our homework to their cars; occasionally they even asked me to read spelling quizzes or other students' test papers when the answers just involved numbers or letters.

The first time this happened was in second grade. My teacher was Miss Virginia Lindsay, a slight honey-blond woman in her late thirties. She was known for her long hikes even in damp Alabama winters and for her summer travels to exotic places not in America. After about three months as her pupil, I was allowed to help grade spelling papers on Wednesdays after lunch. I would bolt my food and race back to Miss Lindsay's room where we sat together at her big desk. She gave me a red pencil like hers to put check marks beside misspelled words. Being left-handed, I made check marks that looked backwards, so I learned to reverse them. I would not give away our secret. Miss Lindsay always patted me on the arm when we were done and said, "You'll make a fine teacher someday."

In fifth-grade, a tall, fleshy, not-so-smart woman named Bernice Brown taught us things I already knew, but she was warm and affectionate and liked me. One afternoon she took me aside, and put her arm around me: "Now, Toni, you know, don't you, that you're a special little girl who will keep going to school for a long time? And when you've gotten big degrees and I'm old, I'll feel so proud that you were in my fifth-grade room. And if you aren't popular, just wait till you're older." The elliptical nature of her last remark haunted me even as the rest of her speech made me feel special and proud.

And I remember Miss Gray, a wiry woman probably only two or three years from retirement, who taught sixth-grade math with an iron fist. On rainy days after she had drilled us in fractions or simple equations or long word problems, she showed us a softer side. She would recite long poems, my favorite being one that began, "Now, William, come here sir." Miss Gray never prepared us for her shift from math to poetry but suddenly would turn her small head capped by thinning frizzly hair and bellow out this or some other first line. I always jumped at first but then settled in for the treat that her recitation was. The lasting thing Miss Gray taught me was that math and poetry do not need to be disconnected. She primed me for my later fascination with Jacob Bronowski and Buckminster Fuller, who urged adults to stop talking about the gulf between science and the humanities.

But most of the time I was just bored by what went on in that stuffy brick building where too many students did not know how to read or write. I began being absent often, having one form or another of a cold-flu-sore-throat ailment just bad enough to keep me home but not so bad as to keep me from reading or playing games by myself. My report cards tell it all: for the first eight years of school, I consistently ran up higher numbers in the "times absent" column than in the "times present" one, though I collected zeroes in the "times tardy" slot. One school year they went: first semester—absent 64 days, present 26; second semester—absent 57 days, present 33. In the space for accompanying remarks appears: "Toni seems quite bright, but could you encourage her to come to school more often?"

When I did not attend school, I had to stay in bed quietly during the mornings, since I was "sick." However, if by lunch time I had no fever, I could play quietly in the side yard during the afternoon. I quickly found ways to insure a reading of 98.5 degrees. As soon as Mamie placed the cool tube under my tongue, I maneuvered it on top. The only drawback to this practice was that sometimes the result was so low as to raise suspicion. But when it worked, I could get up as long as I promised not to run around.

Most days I played the same solitary game. Outside our bathroom window stood a massive oak tree. Forgetting mosquitos, gnats, and other southern bugs that attack anyone who stays outside for more than a few minutes, I spent hours hunkered down on the ground.

First I would scoop out dirt from around roots, then mold wet clay tunnels that leaned against them, and finally turn twigs and carefully sculpted leaves into road signs that meant "Right Turn Only" or "Do Not Enter" or "Danger High Voltage." They only meant that to me, but then if I were not there, things merely looked scuffed up, as if a squirrel had scratched around for stray acorns. Once my highway was complete, I carefully smuggled tiny metal cars and trucks outside. Though for some reason unknown to me my parents bought me such toys never intended for little girls, they were to stay in the house so as not to get dirty or broken. For hours I intently moved cars and trucks along my dirt roads, twisting and turning through the system of tunnels and overpasses. Sometimes several cars stopped at once so the riders could get out to share inside information about road conditions or talk about where to go next. Occasionally a truck turned over going too fast around a sharp curve. Upset, I rushed vehicles to the scene to rescue the unlucky driver and his family who were with him on an outing. If asked the name of my game, I would have said without blinking an eye, "Running Away." I imagined going first into town, then to places nearby whose names I knew—Bessemer, Tarrant City, Dolomite, Powderly, Ensley. If I needed to go farther away, I picked Mobile or Florida or Mandalay.

Though I could play alone for an unusually long time without becoming distracted, this ability became a way to handle my increasing sense of difference from other children my age and the resulting isolation. Occasionally an exception emerged, some child in our neighborhood or at school with whom I formed a tight bond at least for a brief period. I have photographs of two of these friends. One is a tiny snapshot of Sue Brooks and me at my third birthday party. Binky (Sue's nickname) and I are perched on a little stepstool placed on the sidewalk as part of some game. We are each holding a balloon chosen from the great cache Mamie had suspended from the dining room chandelier. We are looking innocently and intently into one another's faces, seemingly with no heed of the camera, the photographer, or the other children. The outside world had vanished for that frozen moment.

The other photo dates from high school days. I am at Sarah Jones's house after school, palling around with her and Sue Hood, another schoolmate. The three of us were fast friends for a year until Sarah and Sue began having predictable dates with boys, and I sunk further into my inability to secure any such prize. On this afternoon, we are posing suggestively: Sarah lounges on her front step while I stand near her in a pose I'd seen Hedy Lamarr strike in movies. We look content and connected, something I was not to feel often outside the confines of my home.

When I was eight, I made my first and only penny peep show and experienced a devastating blow to my efforts to share my creative self outside my family. My mother carefully taught me how to construct such a spectacle. First you must find a sloping hillside (we had a huge one in our vacant lot filled with flower beds). Then you take a trowel—

or better yet your hands—and burrow into the slope. When the space is the right size, you line it with cardboard to keep out falling dirt and curious bugs. With the frame complete, the real work begins. A penny peep show is made up of tiny bits of paper or material, formed into recognizable objects, all placed in that hollowed-out space and covered with a piece of window glass. The glass in turn is covered with a cloth or strip of cardboard, thus hiding your "show" from view. People are then invited to take a peep at the cost of a penny. These projects were popular in my childhood, and I paid lots of pennies to see other children's shows.

When I came to make my own, I decided to be more elaborate in my choice of objects to put in the boxed-in space. I made tables and chairs of match sticks, painstakingly gluing each slim stick to its fellows. I constructed people from wads of cotton, dressing them in scraps of cloth from my mother's hooked rug work basket. Finally, I wrapped live flowers in tiny waxed-paper containers that would hold water longer than newspaper. After almost a week of preparations, I invited neighbor children and even a few select adults to "peep" by writing crude invitations that I dropped into mailboxes. On the appointed day, I stationed myself beside my wonder half an hour before showtime, just in case someone tried to get a free sneak preview. As viewers began to arrive and give me their pennies, my heart pounded with what I would only later understand to be artist's nerves before an unveiling.

After about ten people had come, I took advantage of a lull to run inside to the bathroom. Less than five minutes later, I returned to find the glass smashed in, the flowers crushed, and the little matchstick furniture in shambles. I burst into angry tears and screams that lasted over an hour. I was inconsolable, filled with fury for whoever had destroyed some inner part of me that I had lovingly presented to be "peeped" at. My mother never convinced me to build another show, though she often would sit on the ground with me and begin putting things together from the dirt around us. I would watch her for a few moments and then break into sobs until she had to take me inside and comfort me with candy or some other sweet.

The next Easter Mamie gave me a gorgeous spun sugar egg: a peep show with an isinglass window that opened onto a resplendent garden filled with every imaginable flower and a bunny for good measure. The next year, she began giving me special decorated eggs made of thin milk glass. Each bore my name, the date, and some lovely design: tiny blue forget-me-nots; a bouquet of purple violets; a wreath of yellow jonquils. I have moved this collection around with me over the past thirty-five years.

I do not remember making anything for a long time after my peep show was wrecked. Determined to protect myself, I retreated into my head, where images and creations seemed safer than when set out for public display. I crammed in story after story of little girls who saved friends from disaster and then gradually focused on horses or cats or more exotic animals once I had read Kipling. In the animal stories, I was always the undying champion who rescued them from capture and caging in zoos, or from natural predators.

One of my favorites, which I told myself from the ages of eight to eleven, with minor variations, focused on the same subject as my game with trucks among the oak roots—running away:

> A little girl packs a wicker picnic basket with all the leftover fried chicken and biscuits from her mother's refrigerator, leaving room for her floppy-eared harlequin rabbit and a story book. Then she tiptoes out of her house while her mother fixes lunch. She runs as fast as she can, as long as she can, and winds up on the edge of town where the road begins to open onto lush meadows filled with butterflies and brown-skinned hopping rabbits.
>
> She runs into the very center of this grass sea, plops down with her cache of chicken and biscuits, and begins unwrapping little packets of food. She can never eat just the one she's made for that afternoon but keeps at it until all the food is gone. Her stomach full, she lies down in the field, reads a little, quickly falls into a sleep filled with magical dreams. Usually she is awakened by a beautiful yellow and blue butterfly lighting on her nose or by a furry rabbit sniffing loudly around her hair and face. These interruptions never frighten her, because she never wakes to find it dark.
>
> Once the little girl sits up, she realizes that she is hungry. It is dusk and the sun is going down. She begins to feel cold and lonely, hugs her rabbit to her chest, and sings herself back to sleep. She is protected during the night by fairies or brownies and rises to a glorious sunrise and a little dish of Cream of Wheat.

After eating, she sets out for far places that she always reaches safely. These journeys lead the little girl to cities and countries whose names her big sister has taught her, places like Borneo and Atlanta and Walla Walla, Washington, her favorite place in the world to say out loud.

My stories never had endings. I just stopped telling them or let them trail off into shadowy scenes while I went into the kitchen to help my mother do the dishes. As I retrace their outline, I realize that what is missing is another human being. Though I was able to surround my heroine with benign and affectionate nature, I could not conceive a companion of her own kind.

The closest I ever came to such a person was my make-believe baby sister. Between the ages of seven and ten, disliking dolls, I fabricated Sarah Sue, much my junior. I bossed her around unmercifully but defended her from the ornaments that were likely to slip off their marble-top tables at any moment and from the adults who could interrupt her at their whim. She was an admiring audience for my roly poly bug collections, my June bug captures, my skating up and down the sidewalk that marked our property boundaries. She consoled me about having to eat at least one or two of the carrots on my plate or about having to sit quietly after lunch in the summer. When my mother took me downtown while she shopped at all her favorite department stores, Sarah Sue listened to my endless complaining and shared my dislike of such activities. I do not remember why I stopped creating her, but I suspect it had something to do with her getting too big to handle and having a will of her own. In any event, I eventually gave her up rather than continuing to drag her around as a flimsy sign of my imaginary power.

Just about the time I lost Sarah Sue, I entered into one of the most purely creative if bizarre stages of my young life. I felt increasing pressure to become more lady-like, as Mamie talked about brassieres and lipstick and ruffled dresses. I decided to withdraw from the irksome business of growing up, since I knew that I did not want to become a southern lady, learning how to faint without hurting myself or letting my skirt rise above my knees, or how to lower my eyes, hold them down, and then raise them slowly and alluringly. While my mother indoctrinated me into the culture she believed I was destined for, something inside me resisted fiercely. Sensing that Toni, the defiant ten year old, would lose, I cleverly chose to become a horse. I had already read many cowboy stories as well as technical studies of horses that described breeds, named body parts, and defined various gaits and habits.

Borrowing from one of my favorite radio programs, "Tennessee Jed and His Great Horse Smokey," I became Smokey. Weekday afternoons an hour before the "Lone Ranger," the show was a southern version of the classic masked Samaritan. Having no gender, Smokey was a means for me to escape the confining behaviors appropriate for adolescent girls. I whinnied at the table when I wanted something, and my parents acknowledged but did not disrupt my fantasy. Years later, when I took psychology courses and learned that children are hospitalized for far less severe antisocial or withdrawal symptoms, I felt grateful to my family. Instead of mincing like a preadolescent girl, for two years I cantered, galloped, trotted, and occasionally even pranced.

During this period, my sister visited Boston. Her gift to me upon her return was a treasured black leather bridle, complete with steel bit. With that bit between my teeth, and her (or my mother) holding the reins, I ran around our front yard, neighing.

In the middle of my dilemma over how to express my creative energy without its being ridiculed, interrupted, or destroyed, my mother asked if I would like to take piano lessons. At first, I recoiled from the suggestion, since it would mean sitting inside for long periods and I preferred to run. But Mamie felt strongly that one of her daughters should play the piano, given her own talent and love for music.

After weeks of discussion, I agreed. My first teacher, Mrs. Bowen, lived near us and taught in her home. After about a year with her, I transferred to the Birmingham Conservatory of Music and half-hour lessons from Miss Edith Plosser. I was excited to have a music teacher with such an unusual name, though she seemed cold and stern. Her repeated complaint was that I did not practice seriously or long enough. Since we did not own a piano, practice meant calling our across-the-street neighbor, Nell Hill, to find out when it was convenient for me to come over to her house where there was an out-of-tune upright. At the same time that she complained about my sketchy practicing, Miss Plosser thought me potentially talented, so she set me to such masters as Bach, Scarlatti, and Clementi. They had no tunes and were terribly demanding technically. I began to cut practice times shorter than usual.

Once I was safely ensconced at the conservatory, Mamie convinced my father that I had to have a piano. Somehow, one was procured—a Betsy Ross spinet, made in America of partly seasoned wood because of the Second World War. Since our house was already liberally furnished, my piano was placed in the hallway outside my bedroom door. My sister's bedroom was at the end of that hall, so when I practiced, she was trapped in or barred from her room. Any time she interrupted, I welcomed the break, though the situation must have irritated Betty.

My third teacher, Mr. Parker, was over six feet tall with jet black hair and deep-set, searching eyes. His hands were enormous, reaching an octave plus two with ease. His span and temperament inclined him toward Franz Liszt, so I studied most of Liszt's corpus. My hands are also fairly large and by sheer determination, I can play an octave plus two. I gave that measure of determination because I was amazed at the raw emotion within the music. A part of me otherwise unknown and unencouraged was awakened, and putting my passion into the ivory keyboard had less risk than my previously chosen media. My interpretations pleased Mr. Parker, so he set me to such equally romantic giants as Rachmaninoff, Katchaturian, and the mature Chopin. I suddenly turned from a phlegmatic pupil into someone who went eagerly to her turquoise velvet piano stool and stayed there, hoping my sister would not need to get into or out of her bedroom, pounding away at the forte passages, rendering soft parts with maximum tragic sadness.

At first I exulted in the forte passages, hitting the keys with such ferocity that I sometimes made the crystal vase that sat atop the piano vibrate. After seeing Rubenstein at our local auditorium, I began to raise myself off the piano stool as I banged some percussive chord of a Chopin étude or Rachmaninoff concerto. Gradually, as I came to trust both the piano and myself more, I let myself pour years of accumulated melancholy and aloneness into the pianissimo phrases, knowing without language that the keyboard was a safer repository for such emotions than writing or speech. After all, the moment I struck the key, the act was over. Musical tears could always be explained away as deriving from Chopin's romanticism or Brahms's sweetness. Not having to "own" the emotions that sounded from my fingers emboldened me to express myself more deeply and fully than in any other circumstance or medium.

Playing the piano gave me even more satisfaction than playing pitch with a hard ball. Like my hero, Walt Dropo, I was left-handed and preferred to play first base, since it was one of the few instances in which being left-handed counted for rather than against me. I had a beautiful leather hardball glove with Walt's signature on the claw, and the clean "splop" of a ball landing solidly in the pocket of that mitt brought me small but distinct rushes through my mid-twenties when I finally abandoned playing pitch.

My two outlets became counterproductive, since the ferocity with which I played pitch endangered my hands for executing delicate piano runs. Mamie, of course, wanted me to give up pitch, but I refused. Once I went so far as to limit baseball to two hours a day during the month immediately preceding a major recital. I remember occasionally going to lessons (in the musty house where Mr. Parker and his ailing mother lived) with a sprained finger. My thumb took the worst beating: if I reached to catch a side ball incorrectly, my thumb bent back on itself from the force of the throw. When that happened, swelling set in, lasting at least three days. Often I could not play a note intended for the right thumb because mine was too big for the space between keys.

The worst scene in this battle of wits with my mother and between the selves warring within me occurred the month before my senior recital. After several solo pieces, I was to end by playing a Katchaturian duo with my teacher. By this point in my career, I knew I was good, at least at broadly romantic music. Maybe I panicked at the prospect of a career as a pianist. In any event, I entered into my pitch activity with renewed concentration, extending my allotment by however many minutes it took Mamie to realize my time was up.

A week before the big event at the concert grand, as I was catching a particularly hard throw by my playmate, Kenny, I felt searing pain. As my thumb folded back, I knew I had sprained it badly. I began immediately soaking my swollen finger religiously. After two days, my thumb barely fit into the key area. Lying about my pain, I practiced with a strange enthusiasm, leaving off my baseball fetish entirely. The night of my performance, pains shot from my thumb up into my right arm. No one knew I had taken six aspirin just before leaving home. I executed my solo pieces with clarity and passion, and in the final duo, Mr. Parker and I played superbly. The audience applauded enthusiastically, but I took that recital as further proof of something I was coming increasingly to believe and practice: people seemed satisfied, even pleased, with performances at which not quite all of me was present or in which not quite all of me was engaged.

# *My Mother, My Muse*

*P*art of my coming to conscious-
ness as a feminist has been a growing understanding that my mother
was indeed an artist, whose media included church work, flower
gardening, and decorating her home. In the South of her youth, girls
seldom resisted the cultural pressures to marry and become mothers.
My mother seems genuinely to have enjoyed her home and family. But
the person talented enough to win a music scholarship surely must
also have needed creative outlets. The intensity with which she carried
out her Altar Guild duties, planted new bulbs, arranged flowers
throughout the house, or created beauty in our living room impressed
me even as a young child. As I struggled not to fear or suppress my
own creativity, I believe I watched Mamie more closely, looking for
clues to becoming a woman with deep longings for aesthetic and
spiritual fulfillment.

I frankly have no idea what would have been done about my
spiritual training without my mother's influence. Whatever Daddy
may have believed about Christianity or any other religious system,
he felt no need to attend church or to discuss religion with me as I was
growing up. Once he did tell me that the part of the Bible he liked best
was Psalm 1, so I read it repeatedly, trying to discover some clue about
him or me or God. The psalm speaks angrily about the ways of the
wicked being like "chaff which the wind driveth away," and of the
wicked themselves perishing. One's only hope seems to be not to walk
"in the counsel of the wicked" or sit "in the seat of the scorners," which
to my father may have meant doing tax forms free for people whom
the world deemed unworthy. To my young mind, however, these
images called up harshness and punishment; they advocated strict-
ness to the letter of the law if a person wanted to escape terrible con-

sequences. I did not find the God behind this psalm appealing and was not surprised that my father preferred to stay home on Sundays and read the paper.

But Christ was important to my mother, and she talked to me about him often. Her stories centered around a nice man who helped everyone, judged people not by their actions but rather by their inner wishes, and worked breathtaking miracles without a wand or vial or any of the aids that characters in my fairy tales needed. My mother also made sure I attended services with her regularly and that I found a serious personal belief system.

My experience with Christianity was aesthetic more than it was either theological or doctrinal. I loved the smells, sights, sounds, and, after confirmation, tastes that surrounded my hour in church. Being an Episcopalian was largely a sensory matter. Kneeling and rising at moments of joy and thanksgiving excited me. As I grew more ardent in my practice, I stayed on my knees throughout the Communion service. Some people knelt until it was their pew's turn to go up to the altar; the few who became my models resumed this distinctly less comfortable posture after they returned to their seats, witnessing more directly to the rigorous nature of the event.

Almost every Saturday afternoon, my mother went to church to perform some volunteer service. She waxed the floors twice a year, polished the pews every two months, washed and ironed altar linens once a month, and served altar duty at least that often. I asked to go with her because I liked being in church when no one was there. Cool even in summer, the atmosphere made me feel eerie—not scared exactly but more like someone in a fairy tale, stepping back in time. While Mamie did her chores, I walked or crawled around under pews, smelling the stale candle wax and lingering scent from the past Sunday's flowers. As I got older, I sometimes sat praying hard at the innermost rail reserved for the rector or bishop when he visited yearly for confirmation. My prayers were selfish, full of requests for more friends and less work around the house, for longer vacations and fewer days in school. I felt holy and important, very much an actor. I still remember standing outside myself, watching me on my knees, thinking, "God will surely hear me this time and show me a sign." My Bible story pictures showed blind men suddenly seeing, lame old women throwing down crutches, and lots of people eating from the same few fish and loaves of bread. Our Sunday school teacher told us these scenes were miracles proving Christ's power as God and confirming the faith of some believers. I thought I was a believer and wanted something dramatic to happen. Since questioning came to me quite young, I needed a sign to show that I could keep believing. If Mamie came upon me kneeling so devoutly, she smiled and gently encouraged me to move back to a regular pew, saying, "Now, honey, I'm glad you're praying but not here where Bishop Carpenter does. You come back here to our family pew and pray all you want."

My mother insisted that going to church in the wrong frame of mind lessened the experience. Rather than forcing me to say prayers or make lists of my wrongs, she suggested we leave time to read together from the Bible before going to service. Once we had eaten a light breakfast and dressed, including putting on our hats but not our gloves, we sat on my bed to prepare. Until I was about ten she read to me—always psalms—but from then on, I was expected to take my turn. We read our favorite psalm: the twenty-fourth for me; the ninety-first for her. Mine spoke of "clean hands and a pure heart," of not lifting up one's "soul unto vanity" or swearing deceitfully; I felt exhilarated just thinking about the "everlasting doors" through which the "King of Glory" would enter (heaven I assumed), and hopeful that I might "ascend the hill of the Lord" someday. Mamie's was all about protection in the face of one's direst enemies—"the pestilence that walkest in darkness," and "the destruction that wasteth at noonday." The "thou" of this psalm survives while ten thousand fall at his right hand and a thousand at his side. I caught my breath to think of the angels who could keep "thee" from dashing a foot against a stone or from falling at all. And I simply thrilled to hear, "Thou shalt tread on the lion and the adder, the young lion and the serpent shalt thou trample under foot."

Fired and comforted by our readings, we donned our gloves and set off for Christ Episcopal Church, some ten or twelve blocks from home. At the Communion rail I left my troubles (Why did my school-mates shun me? Would I ever have a teacher who interested me? Why couldn't I have an Erector Set when lots of boys I knew were getting them?), nagging guilt (I should have taken the garbage out before Mamie had to ask me three times; I ought to have memorized every word of my history lesson so Daddy would be really proud of me for getting a perfect score; I must start keeping my fingernails cleaner so Mamie won't have to worry so about my unladylikeness), even surface shame (Why had I lied to my teacher when she asked if I had helped Billy Mayo with his math? Would I really be punished for wishing my mother would stop badgering me to pick up my clothes before I left my room to go take a bath? Was I mean not to care that my playmate from across the street had gotten a rope burn when I lassoed him?). I was certain as I melted the awkward wafer and swallowed watered-down wine that I ingested calm and a powerful shield of protection. At no time did I seriously believe that these were even symbolic of Jesus's body and blood; they were a way to unify my ragged parts, to heal my raw places.

By the time I was ten, I was helping Mamie set up the altar for early Communion. I handled the objects that made church possible: beaten silver pitchers; a smooth silver plate that held little flat wafers that I eventually learned had no taste and often stuck to the roof of my mouth; linen napkins each with a beautifully embroidered cross and meticulously stitched border; the wine cup with its silver outside and gold inside, decorated with cross and dove; the choir cross on its polished wooden pole. As I carried that cross from its locked closet, where it was stored during the week, into the dimly lit nave and buckled it into its leather halter at the head of the choir stalls, I imagined myself a monk attending his Lord on some solemn occasion. All the objects seemed mysterious and came to inhabit my fantasies about escape and rescue, this time of a kind man named Jesus whom all the officials wanted dead. I imagined myself running to warn Jesus about the mean Pharisees who were coming for him, or beating up Sadducees who tried to trick him, or (most exciting fantasy of all) scaling the cross in time to cut Christ down before he died so the world could benefit longer from his good ideas.

When I was twelve, I learned names for all these holy toys—cruet, paten, chalice—and became fascinated by the changing seasons of the church year. Every time we went from one to the next, all the altar fittings changed color—from lime green to royal purple, white on holy days, black for Good Friday, scarlet for saints' days. Green and purple lasted the longest, causing me to conclude that there was a relationship between peace and growth, majesty and sacrifice. The symbolism for each color was woven into my daily thinking by the time I was in high school. Watching Mamie handling altar cloths or ironing little chalice napkins with more attention than she gave to Daddy's shirts impressed upon me that the house of God deserved my utmost care, that its ornaments were even more precious than the ones at home.

All through high school and college, as my Protestant friends drifted away or actively revolted against their religions, I increased my piety. My love for language and poetry kept me religiously active even when I knew that the theology no longer moved me. *The Book of Common Prayer* is after all a work of major literary merit, written in the sixteenth century by Thomas Cranmer, slightly before the King James Bible group completed its monumental task. At eighteen, I had invested Cranmer with mammoth physical and spiritual dimensions and felt personally attached to a man who could write such powerful prose. My favorite parts were the Collects—short readings intended for specific occasions such as sickness, travel, times of the day, the seasons. Some were also for people in certain circumstances or professions: prisoners, teachers, men at sea, the poor and dying. The imagery, the simplicity of diction, the uncanny understanding of the human condition and the human heart touched me. Phrases still float to the surface when I am extremely happy, sad, or tired: "O Lord, support us all the day long, until the shadows lengthen and the evening comes, and the busy world is hushed, and the fever of life is over," "Bless all who teach and all who learn," "Deliver us, we beseech thee, in our several callings, from the service of mammon," "Relieve the distressed, protect the innocent, awaken the guilty."

By attending chapel several times a week as a college student, I discovered a service—evening prayer—I had never attended at home, full of such sheer poetry as, "Let the floods clap their hands, and let the hills be joyful," or "He hath showed strength with his arm; he hath scattered the proud in the imagination of their hearts." Only Shakespeare and Keats evoked comparable shivers or yielded comparable rewards to my mind and spirit. During my senior year in college, partly to render service to the Episcopal Student Center and partly to satisfy my curiosity, I formally analyzed the Communion service only to discover that its structure was not unlike any well-made drama. Beginning slowly and quietly, the service builds gradually through recitations, prayers, and confessions spoken by the entire congregation. At the climax, when host and wine were elevated, my excitement rose with them. As I eagerly awaited my turn to walk the length of the aisle, I felt as if I were on my way to see a close friend. The fact that he was permanently out of town was softened by the mystical connection I could achieve by "receiving the sacrament."

The Episcopal church seldom mentions heaven and never deals in hell; the confessions indicate that through our daily actions, we make our own here on earth. The best mode of living is to recognize how we "have erred and strayed from Thy ways like lost sheep." Our best plan for salvation is to stop doing "those things we ought not to have done," and initiate "those things which we ought to have done." To succeed in this essentially ethical rather than theological program promises "health in us." In the midst of one of my several emotional crises during college, I looked up "salvation" in the dictionary and found that its root had to do with health of the spirit. As adulthood crept nearer and seemed more frightening, I needed such health badly. I spent increasing time in meditation and religious study, reading about Joan of Arc and the desert fathers, wondering how they escaped having to date and marry.

This vast store of magic and comfort might not have been mine without Mamie's need to exert herself in devotion to her church and her equally clear need to have me accompany her. I can only conjecture to what extent her seemingly domestic labors in church were in fact powerfully aesthetic for her. But I know that the church buoyed my mother. After a childhood and youth lived in the heart of a privileged South, she chose to make her life with a man who moved her to a dusty, industrial, working-class area. Her tastes were elegant and expensive, yet my father never made more than an adequate salary. Finally, Mamie's health was problematic for the last fifteen years of her life. On the one hand, her stamina was amazing to watch and hard to match, as I learned when we spent a month on vacation together. She outwalked me and was undaunted by attending nine plays in seven days in New York City. But her neuritis and arthritis clouded many of her days and pained her nights, and her shortness of breath scared her. Evenings when her body must have seemed strangely at odds with her spirit, Mamie would ask me to sit on the side of her bed and read that familiar Ninety-first Psalm to her slowly, sometimes twice for good measure. After my father's death, she told me repeatedly that without the church and her faith she could not have gone on. Yet that faith manifested itself in dailiness, never becoming theoretical or doctrinal.

She showed me how crucial a woman's view of Christian theology can be, and when I read Barbara Meyerhoff's moving account of a community of elderly Jews (*Number Our Days*), I understood perfectly what one of the women meant by "domestic religion"—a string of daily rituals over which the women in a family preside, that "makes the adrenaline flow" and "changes your entire view on things." Underscoring the femaleness of this phenomenon, a speaker insists,

"These things were injected into you in childhood and chained together with that beautiful grandmother, so ever since infancy you can't know life without it. . . . [I]n this domestic religion, you could never get rid of it. You could not just put it aside when you don't agree anymore. When it goes in this way, I describe, Jewish comes up in you from the roots and it stays with you all your life."

I no longer attend church services or adhere to the formal belief system of my past, but when I enter cool, dimly lit churches, tears come unbidden but familiar. I remember my mother, specifically and tenderly, going about her housewifely duties at church, infusing her and my very breath with something deeply spiritual and unforgettable, something that rises above creeds and denominational hypocrisies, something I cannot "put aside because [I] don't agree anymore."

My mother's yard and garden were legendary in our community. The actual gardening, which went on almost all year, began six months before I was born. Moving from their former house because the new arrival necessitated their having more room, my parents had also bought the vacant lot next door. During her last months of pregnancy, Mamie planted hundreds of iris and jonquil bulbs, sitting on a pillow and sliding down the inclining slope of our yard. That space became a magnificent display of flowers and shrubs.

At its very center stood a terra cotta birdbath. From that core fanned out a series of ever-widening circles bordered by rocks that were always kept in place and free from choking weeds. Within the first circle, surrounding the birdbath, old-fashioned pinks covered the entire ground area. The next somewhat wider circle contained special varieties of jonquils with multicolored centers; Mamie spaced these further apart to allow the best growing conditions for the bulbs and the best viewing for us. Concentric to this middle bed, the largest circle completed the central bedding expanse and housed gorgeous rose bushes in varying shades of red, yellow, and orange.

A second bordering system, made up of long, rectangular beds in which annuals were grown from seed, ran parallel to the lot line. Mamie had a major objection to the idea of using bedding plants. Perhaps it was an attempt to save money somewhere in her life, but I suspect that her motives stemmed from a desire first to watch seeds sending up shoots and then to separate the seedlings with her own hands.

These long edges of the garden area were especially showy at the height of summer: tough zinnias with their scratchy stems; brilliant marigolds, cosmos, dahlias, daisies of many varieties; sweet william and alyssum, baby's breath, ageratum, dwarf marigolds, tiny zinnias, blue phlox, fever few.

At the end of a bed that edged the property line grew the strangest and most wonderful of all Mamie's flowers—spider lilies. Their blossoms, at the tops of very tall single stalks, were deep fuchsia with slender tendrils. At their centers were tiny stamen with fuzzy black ends. They had no leaves and were airy and royal. When I moved to the midwest, I searched unsuccessfully for such a lily.

In our backyard there was a magnolia tree that had been planted in 1940 when I was only three. As I waited impatiently for it to grow, Mamie told me gothic stories of mammoth magnolias in Selma, where she had grown up in the first decades of the twentieth century. Our tiny tree had been given to us by a family friend whose father was a judge in the small town of Camden, in the heart of agricultural Alabama. Our friend fancied that having the sapling in her yard would help my mother survive in industrial Fairfield, reminding her of a gracious era vanished with her childhood.

By the time I was in high school, that magnolia was still only about three or four feet tall and was not giving my mother what she wanted most—sumptuous white blossoms, shade from the flaring heat of the sun, and that unmistakably sweet aroma. Then, one day, we were out driving in the country just outside Fairfield when we spied a magnolia tree in full growth and bloom. Nearby stood an old farmhouse to which my father walked to ask the woman of the house if he might buy a bloom or two for his wife. She agreed, and from that day onward, when Mamie was having a special celebration during late spring or summer, Daddy drove out to "our" magnolia, as we thought of it, and brought back a precious blossom or two. My mother lovingly washed off ants or other small bugs that had taken up residence in the spacious hollows and floated the massive flowers in a sterling silver bowl in the center of our dining room table.

Though the magnolia stayed small, we boasted a gigantic oak nearby. Around the base of this great tree, Mamie planted snowdrop bulbs. She said they hardly ever did well for her, but a few survived the damp winters and numerous squirrels who loved the taste of their leaves. They bloomed in February as the true harbinger of spring. All through January, from the time I was eight or nine until well into my teens, I watched them closely, going out back and turning over a few

of the leaves my mother so scrupulously placed over them to hide
them from the squirrels and to keep them warm. Finally a day would
come when the first yellow-green showed above the mulch and dank
earth. On that day, Mamie would let me remove the leaves and pour
the first water lovingly from a kitchen pitcher. When the snow drops
bloomed, I would sit beside them, drawn to the perfectly marked spot
of green in the center of each scallop of each bloom. They were special
because they were the only flower we grew that was green and
because when I looked at the blossoms hanging their heads, I felt less
alone in my shyness.

As soon as I knew about saving money, I began to reserve portions
of my allowance each year for a special present. Two months before
Mamie's September birthday, I looked through fancy iris catalogues,
chose one specimen variety and proudly sent off my seven or eight
dollars. She had never grown specimen iris. The hundreds that
bloomed down our hillside were plain white, deep purple, sky blue,
or lemon yellow fringed in brown. My mother loved those gifts from
me because they allowed her to have one of a kind. Greeted with total
enthusiasm, each year's iris was planted immediately in a bed made
specially for the collection I had promised in a card accompanying the
first bulb, which was called Black Orpheus.

Though my mother's talents for interior decoration were always
in evidence, at Christmas time she outdid herself. A small touch that
nonetheless delighted every child who came into our house was her
wishbone tree. Mamie would buy the tiniest tree she could find at the
YMCA lot, place it on a tier-top table in the living room, and hang on
its delicate branches scores of gilded wishbones, saved from Sunday
chickens and from the big hens she boiled up periodically for salad. All
around this display were little boxes wrapped and bowed, each
containing some bright trinket from the ten-cent store. Each child was
allowed to select a wishbone from the tree and pull it with Mamie. The
child who got the lucky piece took away a prize in one of the boxes.
Those who got the unlucky piece received a handful of hard candies.
Since Mamie seemed to enjoy the event as much as the children,
everyone won.

Aside from this small ornament to cheer up children, everything
about our decorations was a major production. Our front door project
involved hours of hard scratchy work. I was allowed to help, so I know
what it entailed. Around the facing, Mamie hung a swag of long-

needled pine cuttings, intertwined with lights. She made her own swags because none she saw was thick enough for her taste. During my high school and college years, she and I would sit on the kitchen floor for hours, securing small clumps of pine to fat rope by wrapping picture wire around the sprig and then tying that to the rope. These clumps were overlapped like roofing shingles, the end result being a thick mass of pine with no hint of a rope beneath. Once we had tacked the swag to the wooden frame of the door, it remained to lace strings of multicolored lights through that mat of greens. I soon grasped that the swags sold at tree lots or florists were sparser in order to make it easier to attach lights. But my mother knew that expediency did not always coincide with beauty, and she chose beauty every time.

Once the swag was finished, Mamie began on our holiday wreath. She bought a basic green wreath with the tightest weave she could find. Then for days she gilded fresh fruit, sprinkling each piece while still wet with gold and silver sparkles purchased at a costume shop. These had to be nursed while they dried, since if they fell over they might lose sparkles. Once the fruit was dry, Mamie stuffed each piece into a length of old stocking saved from the rag bag, thereby making it possible to secure fruit to wreath. She loved della Robbia art, having seen pictures of the brothers' work, so her meticulous labor was an imitation of their ceramic designs.

The masterpiece of Christmas decorations was the living room mirror above the fireplace mantel. A huge pier mirror, it reached from the edge of the mantel to the ceiling. Mamie decided that something hanging from the top would be pretty reflected in the glass. She found a branch fallen from one of our trees, which became the base of her creation. After painting it white, she spent hours atop our rickety step ladder, with one knee on the top step, figuring how to get that branch to stay in the space between the top of the mirror and the ceiling. Finally she managed to get a tack or two into the ceiling and a curtain hook screwed into the mirror top. Achieving this sweet victory only spurred her on. She spent the next few days shopping for exactly the right balls and wire on which to string them. She wanted invisible wire that would create an illusion of floating magic in the mirror. Satisfied, she began attaching thin wire onto eight silver balls varying in size from huge to miniature.

Climbing back up on the ladder, she worked with this infinitesimal wire, trying to get the balls tied to the delicate, now-brittle branch twigs without breaking the branch or dropping the balls. Once a small twig did snap off, and one very large ball smashed to bits on the tile hearth. My mother glued the twig back onto its stem and marked it so she would never try to hang a ball from it in the future. Having replaced the big ball, she went back to work nimbly attaching wires to twigs. The result was a happy Mamie and a stunning mobile that not only was reflected in the mirror but moved gently whenever we had a fire. The motion and the shimmering images mesmerized me.

Few people commented on my mother's artwork. If she minded, it did not keep her from reassembling her mobile every year. The hardest part of the operation was storing the branch, since she was convinced she would never find a better one. We wrapped it in Kleenex, then in paper toweling, then newspapers, and finally stored it on a shelf in the basement far away from everything else. Ten years later, it was still intact and only needed a yearly coat of white enamel to resume its original splendor.

The photograph of Mamie that means the most to me shows her standing in front of the fireplace with her mobile above her head. It was taken two days after my father had died suddenly of a heart attack. She is as carefully dressed as ever and her hair and make-up are in place. But her face reveals a woman in deep grief. I remember thinking when it was taken that we probably would not have the tree branch up on the ceiling again. I was wrong, and that is why the photograph stands out in my memory. The next Christmas, my mother climbed back up the rickety ladder and turned her living room once again into a palace of art.

Many things changed when her husband died. But two things stayed the same—her garden and her decorating. She obviously had discovered that some creative acts are worth the pain they involve because life without them would be too bleak and empty to bear.

# Part II

*Top left:* the author and her mother, 1957; *right:* the author, 1948; *bottom:* the author in Mississippi, 1959. Courtesy of Toni McNaron.

# Men Come and Go

When I was thirteen, our family circle changed. It was 1950, and my sister married a man named Leon. I think I fell in love with him the way girls that age often do with older men. The first time I met him, he rode home with us from the Birmingham Public Library where he had been visiting Betty during her evening shift. Recently mustered out of the navy and beginning college on the GI bill, he was wearing a pea coat and dark blue high shoes of some sort. I thought him very dashing, and when he drove up to our house a few weeks later in a red and black Model A Ford, complete with rumble seat, I was his. It never dented my vision of him that the car seldom started once it arrived, and many's the time I was thrilled to pump the gas peddle vigorously while Leon turned the hand crank that stuck out of the radiator. I even liked it when the jalopy stalled on the streets of Fairfield, and we had to hop out and push it to an incline so the battery could reengage on the way down. That Model A had a horn with a rasp that irritated adults and pleased me. When Leon and Betty drove out into the country for Sunday afternoon courting, I was often asked to come along and ride in the rumble seat. The seat had no padding and my bottom was sore by the time we got home, but nothing would have kept me away. Little did I realize that I was serving as chaperone for my sister and perhaps for Leon too.

Openly jealous of Betty, I complained loudly to Leon who told me that he was coming to see Betty as an excuse to play with me. When I heard that they were to be married, I went to him in tears of rage and hurt, only to hear the same line—by marrying Betty, he would see more of me, and we could play more often and more easily.

When he asked my sister where she wanted to live, she replied with surprise, "I want to live at home, of course." Leon moved into Betty's bedroom. He did not seem to mind, since he inherited the use of a big basement in which he played at welding, photographic developing, and building fancy wooden things on his lathe. He let me watch and even showed me how to use power tools and big machines. I especially loved to pull down the handle of his free-standing power drill and watch it quickly eat through the thickest piece of wood I could find. And I was hypnotized by the vats of photographic fluids into which he slid blank sheets of paper and out of which he drew images of people or places. The moment the image began to emerge was magical and persistent. Leon taught me how to mix and lay cement, how to turn a staircase banister or a lamp base on a lathe, how not to be afraid of electricity. I learned to use nail sets and screw sinkers, so that all my finished surfaces came out smooth, nails and screws invisible.

For the years Leon lived in our house while Daddy was alive, they had arguments. My father did not particularly like his new son-in-law—maybe because Leon played with me in ways Daddy did not; maybe because he was very handy around the house and began winning Mamie's praise by fixing electric outlets, small appliances, sash cords, or by painting the outside of the house and making her helpful objects like a cast-iron rack to hold fireplace wood. Saturdays and Sundays were the most intense, with all five of us home much of each day, getting into each other's way no matter how separate we tried to be. The conflict over my father's chair and parceling out the Sunday fried chicken are cases in point. Though we owned numerous chairs from various historic periods, Daddy's was the lone stuffed armchair, placed near a good reading lamp. I learned never to sit in it when he was home, but Leon somehow missed this message. He occasionally just wandered into the living room and sat down in the Chair to read the paper for a while before dinner. Should Daddy come out of his bedroom and find Leon there, he'd frown and return, not to appear until Mamie announced dinner. At dinner we were sure to have a scene—never over the chair, since my father was too silent or lazy to confront the issue. The set-to would come over some topic of conversation on which Leon ventured an opinion. Daddy would fume and curse for a minute or two, then retreat into his usual silence.

For many years, when the four of us had eaten chicken, all had been well, since everyone got the pieces asked for, even down to giblets. I liked the heart best, Betty the gizzard, Daddy the liver, and

Mamie the neck. After my father's death, it came out that my mother had lied about her preferences. She had always sworn that her favorite pieces were the back and wings, pieces with virtually no meat. Once Daddy was dead, she began eating breasts, pulley bones,* even a leg or thigh occasionally.

When Leon began eating Sunday dinner with us, our delicate balance was tipped irreparably. He liked only white meat; my father liked only white meat. Betty took small pieces of white meat and a thigh while I liked only dark meat. We were all thrown. Either because Leon and Daddy were men or to keep the peace (unless these reasons are synonymous), we let them have their preferences. Neither Betty nor I was satisfied, forced into silent competition over a chicken thigh.

When I graduated from high school, Leon convinced me to declare myself a physics major at the University of Alabama. Russia had just launched Sputnik, and he was fiercely anti-Red. He berated fields of study like literature and jobs like teaching (things I thought fit me), saying "any girl" could do them. My math talents became his constant focus, while he played down the fact that I had caused a minor explosion in the chemistry lab twice in one semester. Wanting him to continue to think I was special, I listened. Still adoring him, I agreed. When at the end of my sophomore year, I had accumulated ten credits of C's and D's in physics and was miserable doing problems and never talking theory, I phoned my family to tell them I was becoming an English major. Mamie was a little disappointed; Betty supported my doing something verbal; Leon barely spoke to me for the next year. Even though I kept my math minor, I had failed him, preferring to do what any girl could to becoming the famous scientist he fantasized I might be.

Since sexuality never was discussed in our household I grew up ignorant and wary. When junior high boys began making references to the lengths and shapes of their penises, I was one of the last girls to understand. For a long time, I thought the cry in assembly of "six inches" as some boy touched his lower body meant that the boys were having some bizarre bathroom contest involving the measuring of turds. When I overheard girls in the lunch line say, "Nobody could have one eight inches long, 'cause it'd stick out of his pants in front,"

---

* A wishbone.

I realized my mistake and instantly felt profoundly out of step.

The summer I was fourteen, I got an older boy from across the street to let me lie on his squeaky glider while he lay on me, moved his hips from side to side, and breathed heavily. I had heard the glider from my own porch where I played with roly-poly bugs, watching them roll into tight balls whenever I poked them with finger or stick. I had also heard girls giggle ecstatically and felt compelled to see what caused both sounds. The experience was singularly boring. All I really felt was out of breath from the weight of Bobby's big body as it stayed flattened against mine. I pretended to like it, though, because somewhere I understood that was expected by him and by a code to which I was trying blindly to conform. But there was no fun in it. I preferred to crawl on my own belly in our basement across the red clay that smelled moist and rank all summer and was cool and smooth against my bare skin.

When I heard about "making out," I decided sex was uniformly unappealing, noisy, and dull. Part of my response came from early conditioning. From the time I was about three, I had slept in a canopied bed. On top of each of the four posters little pine cones were fitted down into the post, holding a lightweight frame in place. Over that skeletal form was draped a canopy, always white, always frilly like gauze or mosquito netting. When I was eleven and twelve, I fantasized often about becoming an orchestra conductor. Having been given my first record player—a square black box for playing 45 RPM records— and my first red plastic RCA records, I sat in my bed at night with my door partially closed, listening to Tchaikovsky or Rachmaninoff or Brahms. As the scores became more exciting, I began to conduct, swaying to the music, picturing myself complete with tuxedo and baton, doing what Eugene Ormandy and Toscanini did. Invariably, just at the climax of the score, the pine cones jarred loose and the frame slipped, bringing the canopy down dangerously close to my face. Of course, I could not finish my conducting, since I had to rescue the frilly netting from my passionate engagement with the music.

My mother would hear the frame slip and rush in to remind me that if I were that active, my bed would never last me into my own home. When I imagined my schoolmates thrashing around in a back seat of a car or on their family's temporarily abandoned sofa, I felt depressed. Any such vigorous movements in the name of sexual pleasure would surely bring down the canopy. So I internalized my culture's wish for me not to be too active in my own sexual enjoyment—to leave that to the males or, if one really wanted to be nice, to leave it out altogether. Sedate sex became the only kind I could fancy occurring in that bed that was to accompany me into my married life.

Since in high school dating seemed the only socially acceptable behavior, I tried, albeit unsuccessfully, to attract boys. I remember having a major crush on Harold Smith. Complete with thick, moist Victor Mature lips, Harold seemed mostly not to see me. To change his mind, I embarked on a vigorous campaign, carrying his books from class to locker, biking past his house each afternoon after school hoping he would be outside mowing or raking leaves or playing with his baby brother whose hair was even redder than his. My crush lasted well over a year without the slightest encouragement from my idol.

As time passed, my frenzy grew. Once I had a driver's license, I began driving past his house. If I was doing errands and spotted his car (I had of course memorized the license plate number), I would follow him to the grocery store or magazine stand or movie house. Though I constructed many fantasies about what would happen if I went into any of these places and just happened to run into Harold, I never had the courage to do it.

Because I was so fixated on my own crush, I missed a rather significant detail about Harold Smith: he did not date other girls either. He spent time at school horsing around with the boys; otherwise he was at home. The story was that his father did not live with them and that he took care of his mother.

On the few miraculous occasions when I had a date, it was usually with some skinny young man who avoided all unnecessary physical contact. Each time I managed to bring one of these strays home, the same event took place in our living room, which we called the sitting room. My mother would have on her usual afternoon attire: a muted linen dress if it were spring or fall; a dark blue or brown dress in winter; white linen with eyelet-embroidered neckline or cotton splashed with flower patterns in summer. For jewelry, she wore a bracelet, earrings, several rings, and an antique pin. Shod in heels and hose, carefully made-up and coiffed, my mother presented herself as lovely, gracious, and more formal than not.

Once the boy and I were inside, he was ushered onto the settee, while I sat in the gentleman's chair. Mamie sat utterly erect in the lady's chair and began her interview:

"Where do you live?" was her standard opening.

Whatever address came back was not right. Too far away, too close to downtown, a lower-class neighborhood, too near the mill, a section of town with apartment houses. No one ever came from the south side, which was the area Mamie wanted me to marry into.

"What does your father do?" she asked needlessly, since she had already decided against the boy from his first reply.

I usually felt like running out of the room as each boy told of his father's unacceptable job. The only person who saw through her was Joe Wheatley, whom I met my first year in college and who became my best friend for the next ten years. Joe was canny and read Mamie's rejection from her slight sneer and her change of position in the chair. His family was Irish, and Joe felt fierce pride in his heritage. When asked what his father did, he smiled thinly, even meanly, saying: "He runs the only Irish restaurant in Alabama." My mother was speechless for several seconds.

Once these excruciating interviews were over and the boy had gone permanently, Mamie would try to impress upon me yet again the importance of family and address.

One of the things my mother regretted was her inability to "bring out" her daughters into society. In Birmingham, Alabama, as in all major southern cities during my youth, spring meant more than jonquils and azaleas. Spring was debutante season. Between early April and mid-May the local newspaper was filled with long descriptions of afternoon teas held on spacious lawns under green and white striped canvas tents, of weekend brunches in solaria decked with orchids grown in adjacent greenhouses, of early evening buffets at which short white suit coats were acceptable if shirts met tuxedo standards—frilled fronts and cuffs with thin black edging that stood out when militantly starched. Concessions were made to the wealthiest families; their daughters were displayed at seated dinners of no less than five courses, followed by midnight-to-dawn dancing parties at the most expensive and exclusive of the city's country clubs. I knew what the deb wore, what her mother and father wore, what flowers and music provided the backdrop, which others from the season's crop of debs were invited, what refreshments were served, and the society editor's personal sense of the ambience. It became clear that some debutante parties and balls were more successful than others, and that this ranking was conveyed by the most subtle details and nuances of reporting. I recall one unfortunate girl who had served only sparkling burgundy at her cocktail tea for three hundred rather than the requisite champagne.

Whenever Mamie bewailed her failure to give me such a "coming out," I honestly reassured her that I would have wanted no part of such a thing. Just to read a newspaper account gave me a severe stomach-ache:

Miss Camilla Carstairs was presented last evening under a starry canopy in the arbor of the BCC (Birmingham Country Club). Her mother, Agatha, and her father, Reginald, crowned her in a jeweled tiara interlaced with white orchids. Champagne flowed freely all evening and canapes supplied by Ross's Catering Service adorned several banquet-length tables covered in lime green linen with centerpieces of ice blue daisies requested by the deb as a sign of simplicity and wholeness. Miss Carstairs, or Cam as her close friends call her, was radiant with a glow that combined health and delight. Her party of complementary debs was composed of ten other lovelies, all coming out this season. Each of the girls presented Camilla with a bouquet of roses in varying shades of yellow or orange. Dance music was provided by a live band from Mobile, the Musical Mobilians. The festivities lasted until the wee hours, topped off by a bird breakfast lavishly donated by the proud father. Mrs. Carstairs was seen discreetly dabbing her eyes at several moments during the evening.

Putting myself in such a situation, I knew that I would have been all thumbs and feet, that my repartee would have been too serious and direct, my choice of flowers and music old-fashioned, and that my guest list would have included absolutely no one that anyone else knew as part of the current circle. In a word, I understood that I was not a debutante by any stretch of my mother's imagination and felt relief that our circumstances cut off all possibility of a debut.

Only one young man ever met my mother's standards—Don Reed, whom I also got to know during my first year in college. In response to her query about his address, he simply responded "Hartselle," which was a tiny town near Huntsville on the northern border of Alabama. Because it was a small, quiet hamlet about which she knew nothing, Mamie could romanticize the geography. When asked what his father did, Don could say, "He's dead," cutting off any further remarks, since any mention of death of a parent catapulted my mother into her own grief for hers. Because he was mannered, deferential, and an English major with verbal facility, he kept his head above water in our living room. In fact, he did that well enough to be asked into the dining room on several occasions to share one of Mamie's elegant meals.

My mother would have liked me to marry Don, and his family seemed equally interested in the match. What everyone probably knew, but no one acknowledged, of course, was that he was not the least interested in marrying me or any female. But we spent lots of time together out of genuine affection for one another and let our families think whatever was convenient. Their fantasies about our engagement meant fewer lectures about going out with someone.

My mother treated girls much as she did boys, saying about virtually any who spent time with me, "She's so frivolous; how can you stand to waste your time with anybody so silly? Why don't you try to find someone your equal?"

Yet, what my mother feared most was my leaving her. I remember getting an invitation during my fifteenth summer to attend a church camp weekend at a lake near Birmingham. Rarely was I included in such affairs, since I never could provide a date and consequently would be a loose wheel in paired activities. I was terribly excited and wanted to go with the intensity of the passed over. When I told Mamie, I assumed she would be happy, since she pushed me into social activities, saying I needed to spend time with people my own age because she and Daddy were so much older. But when I announced my invitation, her face fell. It seems she had planned an all-day excursion to Elmwood Cemetery, complete with a fried chicken picnic.

These outings were fairly common. We would pack the car with lawn mower, clippers, trowels, spades, rakes, Vigaro or bone meal or cow manure depending on what we were going to plant, and the plants, bushes, or flowers to be set into the ground. Sitting in the back seat of our Plymouth, I often felt like part of the garden supplies. But I still liked going. As on vacation at Fort Walton, time spent at the cemetery was easy and pleasant. Nobody had behaviors for me to adhere to, and working in the ground always brought my mother peace, even at the place where her parents were buried. Though our lot was big enough for eight graves, only my mother's mother and father were there. The remaining six plots were for her and Daddy, Betty and her husband, me and mine. On our work excursions we took lunches and plenty of iced or hot tea, which we ate and drank on an ornamental granite slab bench. These macabre visits to my grand-parents' dwelling left me feeling oddly deprived when classmates talked about their wonderful visits to a grandmother or grandfather, complete with laden tables, country air, and cuddly love.

As soon as Mamie told me about the projected trip, I felt guilty. I was proposing going off to have fun with live teenagers, leaving her without her best worker. "How can you be so selfish? But I needn't ask—all of you are the same. If it's more important to you to go and have your fun than to . . . ." I broke in, tearfully, saying, "I'll cancel; I didn't know you had plans for us. I'm sorry to upset you; you know how much I love you. I'd rather dig holes with you than lie around in the sun with some silly kids." She refused to hear of such a thing, announcing stonily that I had to go now that I had accepted. I begged her to let me call and say I was sick with one of my several chest and throat ailments, since by that time I could not imagine having fun. But on the appointed morning, I was sent off with a melancholy wish to enjoy myself.

I lay on the pier, alone, most of Saturday and again Sunday morning, getting scorched from sun bouncing off water. By the time the group dropped me at home, I was already blistering. Unable to sleep lying down, over the next week I peeled off every inch of exposed skin and reeked of Noxema. Mamie cared for me beautifully, having first lectured about my terrible habit of going off with strangers and forgetting everything I knew about being responsible. "Part of my not wanting you to go to this camp was my fear that you'd do something like this and hurt yourself just to be one of the group." "You'll do anything to be liked, you know, and I worry about that impressionable part of you." "Why can't you set the standards rather than lowering yourself to other people's?" I was asked twice more during high school to go on some kind of overnight group outing. Both times I refused.

My junior year I had crushes on two people—Ann, president of the senior class, and Victor, president of the student council. Ann was a Roman Catholic, one of the few in my school, which meant that some mornings she came to school smelling of incense, which fascinated me, and on Ash Wednesday her forehead bore the mark of her priest's thumb—a sure sign to me that she was closer to God and the angels than the rest of us. I began talking to Ann at football games: she was there representing the senior class on the arm of a handsome college freshman active in the Catholic Youth League; I was there selling pop and candy to help my gym teacher. As football season became basketball season, Ann stopped coming with the college freshman and on a few occasions even helped sell pop and candy. When I asked her for a school snapshot, she smiled beatifically and gave me one.

I carried that picture in my purse for years, long after she graduated from high school and long after she killed herself during her second autumn in college for reasons seemingly unknown to anyone. "But she was such a devout girl," or "She was such a good girl," or "I can't understand why such a pretty girl would do such a dark thing" were the things our parents said. My fantasy was that maybe Ann became increasingly lonely for my company. I remember our last conversation: it was late summer and she was going back to college, much to my sorrow. She talked about sin and guilt and punishment. When I tried to say that she did not have to worry about such dour subjects, she flashed her pale blue eyes at me and said, "You can't possibly know what terrible things I've done and can't stop doing— I sometimes think life is just too unfair to be lived!" I never saw or spoke with Ann again. But for several weeks that junior year, I felt I had arrived: the great Ann was my campaign manager (I was running for the student council for the next year, and she thought me the best candidate). She made one amusing if blatantly racist poster for me that showed a Chinese man saying, "You pullee no bonee, You votee for Toni." I rode onto the council on Ann's skirttails.

Victor was not tall or dark or handsome—he was thick without being muscular, had never gone out for any athletics, and had jet black curly hair that was outside the acceptable norms for boy's hair in Fairfield, Alabama in 1953. But he could talk about current events, school politics, and even movies and records. In my high school full of children of United States Steel workers, these abilities set Victor apart. Even his name did that—most boys were called Bob or Bill or Jim, with an occasional Harry or Steve.

At first Victor, like all the other boys, ignored me, but little by little I slid into his consciousness. Flattery and pure adoration provided the oil, and finally he began stiff exchanges in the halls or at student council meetings, which I attended on the pretext of needing to watch how things were done so I could be a better member the next year when he was gone. He even asked me to dance at the junior–senior prom, which I attended with the boy across the street who was a foot shorter and two years younger than I.

Victor did something no one from Fairfield High School had done in recent memory: he went to Harvard. If I had fancied him before, when I learned that he had won a scholarship there, his rating surpassed any scale of measure I knew. He agreed to write me about the Great University and did, though his letters were short and businesslike. But when I won a Kiwanis Club trip to Washington and New York, Victor wrote out of what seemed the blue saying he would come down to the City while I was there and we could go to dinner.

I suffered through the Washington segment of the trip and the bus tour of New York City ending in a visit to the United Nations and a posed picture with Henry Cabot Lodge, who had graciously agreed to speak to us about the work of the U.N. Finally it was six o'clock, and Victor appeared at the Waldorf Astoria Hotel where the Kiwanis Club was putting us up. We went to what I am sure was an elegant dinner at what I am sure was an elegant restaurant. All I remember about the evening was a moment at my hotel room door about one in the morning. I had never before been out so late with a boy; I had never ended any of my scattered dates away from Holly Court, Fairfield, Alabama. Now I was in New York, and a Harvard man and I had walked all over Manhattan after dinner. At each curb, Victor had taken my arm ever so gently to show that he was attentive. Once back at the Waldorf, he did not leave me in the lobby, but insisted on taking me up to my room, "It's so late for a young lady to be in the halls alone."

After I had taken out my key and unlocked the door, Victor took my right hand in his and said shyly, "I've really had a good time, Toni. Thank you for the evening." Then he leaned over and kissed me on the mouth—a thoroughly 1950s American kiss. I never told anyone back home about that kiss, and only my family knew of the date. He wrote two or three short, impersonal notes about classes and springtime in Cambridge, then all correspondence stopped, and he went out of my life. Too ashamed to ask for any explanation, I reached two negative decisions: I simply did not know how to maneuver relations between the sexes; it did not pay to get too close to anyone, since they could so quickly and easily vanish.

The other important men in my life during this period were my high school principal and my music teacher, both considerably older than I. Early in my sophomore year, we got a new principal—Henderson Walker, or Hank to his friends. A little taller than my father or Leon, he had sandy hair slightly waved on each side of a deep part down the middle. His eyes were clear blue with just the beginning of laugh lines at their edges, and a smile often lit up his face. I think it was this essential happiness of person that first attracted me, since the men I had known worried a lot and the boys were mostly angry.

One morning during his first week at school, I got a pass to the library and went instead to the main office to "see Mr. Walker." I never expected to do that, but shortly after I sat down to wait, he came out himself and asked me into his office and shut the door. Such privacy and respect quite went to my head and I could only say such balmy things as, "Welcome to our school, Mr. Walker," and "If there's anything I can do to help you get acquainted, just ask." After days of hearing about almost nothing but the principal from me, my mother agreed to ask him and his wife to dinner. I wrote out the invitation, and they accepted.

From that evening on, Hank and Dot (they insisted I call them that, though of course not "Hank" at school) became fast friends of mine and my family's. He took particular interest in my brain, encouraging me as no one had except Mamie. Any time we passed in the halls, Hank made a point of asking me about my classes or family. Occasionally, he drove me home in his canary yellow convertible, which was the envy of all the boys in school, until things soured for my hero. Because I was so enamored of him, I must have been oblivious to the growing stir in both the faculty and student body. As it turned out, a lot of people did not like Henderson Walker—he put on airs, was too familiar with students, did not automatically believe the faculty about school events, talked of bringing in teachers with dangerously new ideas.

Suddenly the gym teacher, a close friend of my sister and a frequent visitor at our house, announced one evening that Mr. Walker had been asked by the board of education to resign without delay. He had been accused by one of the boys in the senior class of improper behavior toward him. Not entirely sure what that meant, I sensed it had to do with something sexual. Later, Dot's tone of voice and the discomfort in the air of our living room seemed to confirm this. She had come personally because she, like everyone else at the high school, knew how fond of him I had become; she did not want me to be unduly hurt by hearing students talking about him in the halls or lunch room.

The next day, I went promptly to Hank's office to find him looking drawn and anxious. "I've heard all about the charge, and I don't for a moment believe it, you have my total support and trust, and I'll defend you to anyone who says untrue things about you." My words tumbled out from love and an inarticulate identification with whatever it was people thought about this lovely man who had paid me such kind attention. Hank cried his thanks, saying, "It means so much to have your faith, Toni, you are so special a person in this world. I suspect you may be able to understand all this." I could not and was puzzled by his thinking I could, but I certainly did understand that the first man who had accepted me for who I was without needing me to be more or other was being maligned and driven out of his job by people for whom I had little or no respect.

I kept up with Henderson Walker, learning that he worked first at the biggest department store in Birmingham selling men's clothing, then as part of an interior decorating firm. But he cared passionately about the education of the young and finally found a job in a little town far enough away to have escaped the poisonous grapevine that prevented his working in any school in the metropolitan area. He drove over an hour each way in order to continue his work with young people.

When Mr. Parker, my music teacher, was introducing me to Rachmaninoff, Chopin, and Liszt, he already had a Ph.D. from Indiana University's School of Music—that meant he was extremely good both at theory and performance. I suspect he yearned to be a concert performer but could not figure out how to do that under his circumstances. His father had died, leaving him the sole care and support for his ailing mother with whom he lived and in the front of whose house he gave music lessons so as not to leave her unattended for long.

I remember the smell of that room—faintly medicinal and distinctly stuffy. I studied on an upright, black piano with a marbled surface where the varnish had cracked from too much dry furnace heat forced by the prolonged dampness of southern winters. If there were any windows in that room, I do not remember them—certainly they were never opened to the outside air or light. Since the room was just inside the front door, I assume it had once been a foyer when Mr. Parker's house had been a place of human traffic. Now it admitted pupils for the prescribed forty-five minute lessons.

At the end of our first year together as pupil and teacher, he began asking me to go to movies with him on Saturdays and to Sunday League at the big Baptist church of which he was a solid member. Adoring the picture show, I liked the former, but League bored me with its incessant singing and dreary homilies followed by "fellowship" in the basement. This latter activity consisted of cookies, punch, and stiff conversation.

As months passed into years, Mr. Parker on rare occasions held my hand in the movies or put his arm ever so tentatively around my shoulders as we sat having root beer floats at a drive-in afterwards. Then it happened—he proposed marriage. It was a Saturday in early July after my graduation from high school. We had been to some movie and had drunk the ritual float and were parked in front of my house. Eager to get inside because nothing was happening, I opened the door only to be stopped by Mr. Parker's intense request, "Wait, Toni, not just yet."

"I care for you deeply and for your beautiful playing. I want you to marry me."

Stunned but not speechless, I replied, "I can't do that, Mr. Parker, I'm going to college."

"Oh, I know, and I don't want to change that. I'll just wait until you are finished. We'd be engaged, of course."

"I can't do that, Mr. Parker, I'm going to college." I am convinced that I repeated myself because, in my state of shock, I had no more words available.

"You just have a one-track mind, Toni."

"Well, you just have a marriage-track mind."

With this heaven-sent quip, I left the car and raced into my house to find my mother who would surely comfort me in my hour of total need. Mamie was bathing, so I barged in and sat on the wicker clothes hamper where I had perched as a child. I blurted out, "Oh, Mamie, something terrible has happened—Mr. Parker has asked me to marry him, but don't worry, I refused and told him I had to go to college and that he had a marriage-track mind to expect me to do anything else."

To my further shock and amazement, Mamie began fussing at me. She was not angry at this man, my teacher, for behaving in such an uncalled for way. She was mad at me for being "rude" to "someone as lovely as Billie" (she had long since dropped the "Mr." that I insisted on retaining). She actually wanted me to say I was sorry and that I would reconsider his generous offer. Not since the first day of first grade, when she had urged me to apologize for pronouncing "hearth" correctly when my teacher did not, had I been so deeply upset with my mother's reading of a scene involving me.

I did not apologize to Mr. Parker any more than I had to Miss Leslie all those years before. Mamie talked with him, though I never learned what she said. He and I stopped seeing each other, which caused me to feel only relief. But at the same time, I lost an approved escort. The rest of that summer I simply stayed home or went out with my family as usual.

My senior year in high school, 1954, was momentous for me and for the South. My father died on New Year's Day, and in the spring, the Supreme Court ruled on Brown vs. Board of Education. I scarcely comprehended either, and only over time could I feel what they had meant to me. In one way, the two events crossed without my bidding. I had planned to go to the University of North Carolina at Chapel Hill or to Duke because they were good southern colleges where I might learn something after eleven years of boredom in Fairfield's public schools. Daddy's sudden death ended that dream, forcing me to attend the state university in Tuscaloosa.

The weather that New Year's Day was warmish, even for Alabama winters. We had not had rain for about a week, so my bones felt less chilled than usual. After a holiday breakfast of waffles and bacon, I had gone outside to play pitch with myself. Daddy came out the front door about eleven, threw the hardball to me a few times, said goodbye on his way to his office "to do a little work while nobody's there." Eventually I went across the street to play with Kenny and Nancy Myers, neighborhood friends. Several hours went idly by, until I heard Mamie's frantic voice calling, "Toni, Toni, Toni, come home, come home." Running down the three sets of concrete steps to the street, I saw my mother standing at our screen door, her eyes wild, wringing her hands, and barely controlling hysteria.

Once inside the house, I felt fear. Daddy was lying on the bed in the backroom, breathing very harshly, and Betty was talking jerkily on the telephone. Between half-sobs, Mamie tried to tell me what had happened: "He came upstairs through the basement ... cutting wood ... breathless ... went to lie down ... now just listen ... what will I do?" At one point, she stopped and rushed to his side because of his increasing difficulty in breathing. Betty said in a taut voice, "I've been trying to find Dr. John, but it's a holiday so he's not anywhere to be reached. I've called an ambulance. Don't go into the room and upset him any more. Stay out here in the hall with me."

I was stunned. No one had ever been critically ill around me before. Mamie had had spells of arthritis, Daddy belched a lot, Betty and I had had an occasional headache, but nothing more dramatic. The idea of having an ambulance come to our house and take my father away terrified me. All the movies I had seen had taught me that ambulances were last resorts, that people in ambulances often died en route to a hospital or shortly after they arrived, amid red flashing lights and rushing nurses and doctors. How could all this be happening to my father, who only a few hours before had chosen to play ball with me on a mild January day?

The ambulance arrived. Two men rushed in, reeking of whiskey, speaking in falsely hushed tones. They lifted Daddy gingerly from bed to cot, covered him with an unnaturally white sheet and a beige blanket, and rushed out into their long, low-lying vehicle. Mamie went with them. Their siren was turned to full volume as they sped down our hill. That sound, utterly different from police cars or fire trucks, became synonymous with death and dying, and was capable of producing a rush of adrenalin and an instantly dry mouth.

Leon drove Betty and me to Lloyd Nolan Hospital, the "company hospital" that Mamie had always shunned as shoddy and impolite. We were forced to go there because, not being able to locate our family physician, we had to follow ambulance policy: take the patient to the nearest hospital to be admitted through the emergency room. As I waited with my sister and brother-in-law, I kept thinking about foolish things: "Here I am inside the hospital right up the steep alley hill from our house; this is where I cut through on my way home from high school for lunch." "In the fall, leaves are prettiest here because they are protected from traffic." "I remember that afternoon when I was ten, when Betty and Leon were courting, and we spent a Sunday afternoon on Lloyd Nolan Hill, picnicking. Leon took a picture of me running with both feet off the ground down the sloping hillside."

Once we had parked and found the correct waiting room, we were told that no one could go into his room. He had been placed under an oxygen tent with Mamie at his side. My mother stayed by my father's side, alone, until a doctor brought her out in the hysterics that signaled Daddy was dead. In that instant, I blamed her for his dying. He had been alive when I last saw him, even talking to me a bit. Now he was dead, and she had been there. I felt she had let my father die.

Numb, I rode silently home in the back seat of our Plymouth. Everyone was silent except Mamie who sobbed and moaned continuously. Neither Betty nor I cried during the funeral preparations, the event itself, the aftermath meal. It was a long time, years afterwards, before I grieved. We all agreed not to mention his name in our waking life, lest doing so should rekindle Mamie's uncontrollable feelings. I was forced to confine Daddy to my dreams. In the most recurrent of them, he was standing at the foot of my bed, looking sad and lonely, never calling out or speaking but letting me know by a raised eyebrow or a beckoning hand gesture that he wanted me to join him. I would wake frightened but expectant—I never found him at the foot of my bed or anywhere else, though often at play or when I was hanging up clothes outside I felt a presence and turned quickly to see if I might catch him before he left.

The first night after Daddy's death, I sat up in his favored padded armchair in the living room, enraged but silent. I listened in shock as Betty sent telegrams to relatives and talked with the funeral director. Mamie spent most of the evening sitting on the edge of my bed, holding on to one of my canopy posts, rocking herself back and forth, keening. At some point, Dr. John appeared with his familiar black bag and bedside manner. He sat with my mother trying to calm her, giving her a shot of something to help her sleep. I suddenly saw Daddy yelling at Mamie about "all your damn-fooled visits to that doctor." He was convinced that they were engaged in some kind of flirtation and suffered periodic flare-ups of jealousy.

My rage was at my father for abandoning me. I needed someone to comfort me, but between funeral arrangements and Mamie's state, nobody had much time. Since I pretended to be in control, I was delegated to answer the door, be courteous to callers, keep all but the family and closest friends away from Mamie. Lots of men, mostly black, all poor and working at menial jobs at the mill, came to pay their last respects to "Mr. Mac," whom they so obviously had loved.

One older black man stands out in my memory. He refused to come up onto the porch, preferring to stand on the stoop with his hat in his hand: "Mr. Mac, he fished me out the jail once or twice, and he wrote out my taxes free, and he signed papers to keep the garnisheer from taking our things up to the house. And Mr. Mac, he took me and George, my oldest boy, to a doctor who'd let us come in the back door and he saw to my boy when the rest of the doctors didn't take coloreds." It was typical of how my father did things that I had never heard this story. As the man spoke, he kept looking anxiously over his shoulder, obviously ill at ease to be talking with a young white lady in the daytime when some shotgun-carrying thug might see him. But he admired my father more than he feared thugs. As more and more men came to share their simple, moving respect for my father, I understood: no wonder he never played with me; he was always too busy doing things for strangers.

The coffin arrived that day about noon, closed, so that I never saw my father dead. My last visual memory was of his being rolled out of the house two days before. As the ambulance attendants had passed me in the hallway, Daddy motioned them to stop. They did, and he said, "My wallet and keys are on the dresser. Take care of them." Flattered and angry to be chosen when he had a wife of thirty-five years and a thirty-three-year-old daughter who might better carry such responsibilities, I made no response. I did not even have a driver's license, and he had yelled every time we had gone out for a lesson, "You're stripping the gears," "You're grinding the brakes." But before the end of the day he died, I had gotten into the relatively new, sea green replacement for our ancient black Plymouth, driven down our hill, around the corner into a narrow alley, and into the even narrower garage in which the car stayed. The following week, I fantasized I was a chauffeur, needing to take a refresher test for a higher degree of license. Sufficiently psyched up, I went to an agency where people tested, executed the basic maneuvers as if in a trance, passed everything, and got a temporary permit followed by a real license three weeks later.

Imagining how my movie idols, Gary Cooper and James Stewart, would act under similar circumstances, I remained stiff and silent throughout the funeral. I hoped that by doing so I would please my father who lay inside a flower-draped box over which our minister prayed interminably.

The only person I talked to during the funeral was a young man named Earl, who came with my favorite relative, Aunt Carrie, Mamie's step-aunt. Earl wore a black patch over one eye and seemed exotic. His voice was lower and slower than those of the other neighbors and relatives. I considered speaking to him because he seemed able to listen. He came over to me as I sat rigidly in Daddy's chair and perched on a footstool nearby. I made no answer to his first "Want to talk, Toni?" but gradually decided to trust him.

"What subjects do you enjoy most at school?" he asked, as if we were at tea instead of a wake. Surprised, I answered. I talked first about my sixth-grade math teacher, Miss Gray, who had read poems at the end of some class periods, who told me I was quick at all my calculations, even long division and equations.

"And a special favorite was chemistry last year because Mrs. Fiquette let us pour one chemical over another to make beautiful colors in the bottom of a test tube. Her son plays football at the university and she treats me like a grownup, like you're doing now. I only blew up my experiment twice all semester. It went all the way to the ceiling once, and strange-colored spots are up there still to prove it. I want to take more chemistry when I go to college. How did you hurt your eye?"

Earl answered quietly, "In an accident years ago that messed up the retina. They tried to fix it but it got worse. Eventually I lost my sight. I bet you must have lots of friends in this neighborhood."

I hedged because I had almost none. Finally I mustered, "Well, there's Kenny Myers from across the street, we play pitch together, and his little sister, Nancy, but I mostly help her with her arithmetic. On Easter, the three of us, along with Ward, a boy whose father is my father's supervisor, have an egg hunt and someone always takes a picture of us in our new clothes." Then Earl said, "It must be wonderful to live with "Tee Tee" (the nickname he and all of Aunt Carrie's children and their children had for my mother). I muttered something in agreement and fell silent again, not wanting to say how lonely and isolated I felt without Daddy.

Earl got up from the footstool and built a fire in the fireplace. We sat there together until finally I felt like lying down. Next day, I ate a tiny serving from the mounds of food brought by neighbors and friends. How could people sit and consume plates full of cold ham, cold chicken, endless hot dishes, lukewarm overcooked vegetables, rolls and biscuits, and every imaginable kind of pie and cake topped with vanilla ice cream? "Mamie won't have to cook for a week" kept going through my mind; maybe all this was a gift to her. But the scene seemed ghoulish, and I refused to participate. My father had died, and I resented the world's going on as usual. Earl understood and told me it was all right not to eat or sit at the table with the group. When he and Aunt Carrie left, I felt empty all over again.

I stayed home from school for three weeks, not wanting to talk or hear commiseration. Two or three fellow students dropped by the house to say how sorry they were and they hoped I would come back soon. When I eventually did return, every time a hall bell rang, I fairly jumped out of myself. That late winter and spring were my last in high school, and some events were mandatory: I was to deliver the valedictory address; attend a gala senior prom where I would only dance twice; pass the one senior exam from which I was not excused because of high marks. Six weeks before graduation, I contracted a severe case of whooping cough and stayed home another month, unable to speak more than a few words without hacking convulsively. Grinning and bearing it like the little soldier I was sure Daddy wanted me to be, I got up from bed to attend rehearsals for the commencement exercises. On the appointed night, I rendered the commencement address without a single cough, only to be racked with spasms for the next hour. Mamie, Betty, and Leon tried hard to be festive at the small gathering of friends for champagne in our dining room. Aware only of the hollowness of the occasion, I felt bitterly alone.

In the first year after Daddy's death, I put one foot in front of a semitruck only to pull it back in the next moment, gained thirty pounds to hide myself, dreamed that Daddy was at the foot of my bed, and withdrew even further from my family. Mamie's need for silence meant my need for talk went unmet. Because she had by then convinced me that it was not appropriate to discuss private affairs outside the family, I did not speak of my father to anyone for two or three years. When college classmates asked idly, "And what does your Dad do, Toni?" I replied, tight lipped, "He's dead." No further inquiries were made, and my isolation was insured.

# *Into the Cauldron*

While I grieved for my father, the NAACP formed a strategy for integrating southern schools. Fearing the murder of their children if they sent them to grade school or even high school, they focused on state universities as a beginning. For whatever reasons, they picked the University of Alabama first, followed the next year by the University of Mississippi. For whatever reasons, they picked a female to enter the University of Alabama, followed by a male at Mississippi. What that meant to me was that while I prepared to go fifty-five miles down the road, a young black woman named Autherine Lucy was making her own very different preparations to arrive at the same campus at the same time.

I was more fragile at the end of that summer than I knew. My father's death had left me feeling outside the primary relationship between my mother and sister. If I was in touch with my own sexual or erotic feelings, I did not let that reach my consciousness. On those rare occasions when I had a date, the boy avoided all but absolutely necessary physical contact. I attributed my failure at heterosexual social life either to my weight gain (boys preferred girls with large breasts, tiny waists, and no hips—I had medium breasts, a thick waist, and ample hips) or to my intellectual acumen (boys preferred girls who could converse lightly on a variety of subjects—I knew too much about too many things).

That summer, I had engaged in a barbaric institution known as "prerush." Over 70 percent of the students at Alabama belonged to sororities and fraternities and my mother was insistent that on this occasion I be in the majority. Prerush began in June before a person's freshman year and lasted right up until we packed our bags to go down for rush, a week before school started. It involved being invited to coffees, lunches, swim parties, and teas. It was supposed to be a more relaxed atmosphere than the near-frenetic round of parties during rush week. At the gatherings I attended, I usually felt bored and awkward. But two unforgettable events occurred, one of which might have helped bring me out as a lesbian. The first of these was reported to me by my mother and involved a conversation she had had with a friend whom she told about a sorority's suddenly dropping me after several warm invitations. The friend informed Mamie of the reason: they had found out about my being Jewish. Understandably surprised, since I had been going to the Episcopal church all my life and had never met anyone Jewish except a couple of store-owners with whom my mother routinely flirted, I asked her about this newfound heritage. She told me that I was indeed one-eighth Jewish, that her German great-grandmother had, with her husband and family, fled some early persecution.

The other moment was my initial visit to Pi Beta Phi, a sorority with a high reputation at the University of Alabama. They had asked me to a small luncheon in the home of a young woman who lived in the right part of town, where we used to drive on Sundays to look at houses with big yards and high, thick hedgerows. I went to the lunch assuming I would feel the same as usual—too serious, awkward, incapable of social small talk. That was not the case. One of only three rushees, I was surprised to find myself excited to be talking with the members. One woman in particular, Carolyn, was studying to be a civil engineer so she could design bridges. She was tall and angular, wore severely tailored clothes, had a low voice the sheer sound of which thrilled me. She asked me what I thought about things, places, books, and people in the news. The women in that room talked about ideas and their careers, and expected me to do the same—heady stuff for someone whose family discoursed primarily in abstractions and whose peers talked of football and lipstick shades. I did not want to leave—her or the lunch or that group who seemed unlike any girls I had ever met. I wanted to belong to that sorority more than anything, except perhaps to have been the son my father could not have. Though I had never seen or heard the word "lesbian," I felt newly vulnerable to these intense women who focused their attention on me.

After I had been to the Pi Phi's night party on the last day of rush— an event tantamount to pledging—the membership had a nasty fight. It seems I was in competition with a genuine southern belle who lived on the south side of Birmingham: she would bring them a good address and sweetheart pins from three fraternities, including Sigma Chi; I offered intellect, seriousness, and loyalty. The faction of which Carolyn and the other summer luncheon companions were part walked out of the meeting, but the invitation went to the sweetheart. My heart broke for the first time in my life. I loved those women, at first sight and passionately, and I was angry with my parents for living somewhere that made me less than acceptable.

I dropped out of rush, refusing to accept an invitation from my second choice. If I could not belong where I most wanted to, then Mamie would have to adjust to having her daughter be an independent, the term for those few poor souls who could not get themselves pledged to some Greek group. At that moment, I might have agreed that my mother was a failure for not being able to have debutantes for daughters. Later, during open rush (an event staged for those unfortunate enough not to be pledged during rush week), I relented under pressure from Mamie and my own loneliness. I joined a group that wanted me more than I wanted them, with all the ambivalences of such a choice.

But I determined to be friends with Carolyn's group and began speaking to them whenever we passed on campus. They invariably looked down or away until one day I stopped Carolyn near the student union and forced her to tell me what was going on. "We had a big split that last Saturday night and couldn't win for you, but we so much want you to be part of us and don't know how to ask you." Without any hesitation, I began spending more hours at the Pi Phi house than at my own sorority. We talked about physical education, bridge building, law school, medical school, college teaching. One by one and inevitably, these stunning women who so spellbound me graduated. Several married, asking me to be a maid of honor. I recall how sad and pained I was at each wedding, how much champagne I drank, how abandoned I felt by each exit. Years later I would read letters by Emily Dickinson in which she spoke of someone in "boots and whiskers" taking her women friends away from Amherst, Massachusetts, to a state called Holy Matrimony. I understood perfectly her feeling that her precious circle was dying off, one by one. The women in whose weddings I participated were being similarly stolen, going to places far from Alabama, the Pi Phi house, and me.

Bruised and unsure of myself, I needed comfort, a friend, a buffer, a hero. She presented herself in the person of the new dean of women,

Sarah L. Healy, newly arrived from Michigan—a state I knew was up near the Canadian border. Though I could not have said so then, I fell in love with Mrs. Healy at the first freshman orientation meeting. She talked about "women," not "girls"; she said a university could not be our parents, that we had to begin to take responsibility for our own lives; she tried to soften some of the restrictions on female students, such as being in dorms by 7:00 P.M. on weeknights, a puritan rule that successfully prohibited use of the library while trying unsuccessfully to prohibit sex. I attached myself to Mrs. Healy instantly.

During the opening days of school, I was vaguely aware that a "Negro" student had been enrolled. I had read about it in a newspaper article but not paid much attention. Once I had my room in the dorm, however, it was an unavoidable topic. Students talked about her in shocking ways, calling her crazy, an hermaphrodite, retarded, a nymphomaniac, just plain uppity. They had fantasies that she would attract all eligible dates, sleep with teachers to pass her courses, have diseases they would magically catch by walking in the same quadrangle. I learned that she was not in any of the dormitories but was housed at the only black motel in Tuscaloosa, some ten miles from campus. I learned that it was the dean of women's responsibility to drive her back and forth to campus and that endeared Mrs. Healy to me even more. It meant she did not think like my dormmates. I imagined that, since she came from Michigan, she had played with black children too, a possibility that made us blood sisters.

In 1954, Tuscaloosa, Alabama, had two major industries besides the university: a large paper mill and an even larger rubber plant. Both places resisted hiring blacks and feelings were raw among the lower-class white men who worked there. They earned far less than any national minimum wage, had no union, could find no other job if they lost this one. They knew that integration would replace them with better-educated black men. They were fighting for survival.

On the day classes were to begin, the managements at both mills declared a paid holiday for all their employees—an unprecedented move in that town's labor history. When I walked out of my dormitory, fresh in my skirt and sweater and little white collar that kept slipping askew, with new books for courses that I prayed would challenge my mind, I was met by a sight I have never forgotten. Lined up at least four deep, along the main street of campus, were approximately fifteen hundred men from the paper mill and the rubber plant. I had never seen so many men at once, and my instant emotion was fear. They carried a variety of weapons—bricks, bottles, baseball bats, rocks, sticks, billy clubs, brass knuckles, wide boards. I froze in horror when I saw their faces. They snarled, showing yellowed teeth or blank spaces where yellowed teeth had been. Their eyes, squinted almost shut, glared with hate and anger. Their mouths spewed obscenities that cursed deities, human elimination, and women. I was terrified as I made my way toward English 1A.

At first I did not know what they were doing there, though other students seemed to. All those men were there to protest Autherine Lucy's attendance. I felt they were there to "kill a nigger" for knowing how to read when they did not. As I stood behind them, waiting too, though not sure for what, it dawned on me that these thugs were waiting for Mrs. Healy's car to drive by, since she had gone to get Miss Lucy. I felt angry and protective, so I began to watch the same direction the men were. I saw her car turn into sorority row, where we were all milling around. It was unmistakably hers—the big, silent Olds 88, white with forest green trim, license number 1A 2097, a magical car in my eyes because it belonged to my hero. As it drew closer, I noticed a black woman in the front seat with Mrs. Healy. At home, our maids always rode in the back seat, even when no one else rode in front. I had asked why on more than one occasion, only to be told that that was the way things were, that everyone was fine with it, that I should just go out and play.

Autherine's presence in that front seat incensed the men more than anything else. They also were furious with the "white bitch northerner" who let her sit there. They shouted the same obscenities at both women. Suddenly a big dirty man near me threw his brick at Mrs. Healy's car; it missed the back window and glanced off the fender. I threw my English 1A book at him; it missed his ear and glanced off his fat shoulder. I lit out across campus to the Episcopal chapel, ran in, and found a corner pew where I sat and shook for an hour. I had acted without thought, and my stunned brain and body were filled with excitement and terror. I acted to protect the white woman I adored. But no one would have known that, least of all the fellow I almost hit on the ear. He would have branded me a "nigger lover," when more accurately he was dealing with a fledgling dyke.

Though nothing more serious occurred than a broken window in Mrs. Healy's car, classes were totally disrupted by the white working men. By late afternoon, we huddled inside our residence halls, peering out windows. The deans of women and men issued an emergency bulletin cautioning us to remain inside, due to "unusual circumstances" on campus. We all laughed at deans who could think we had to be told to stay inside. No one wanted to go out into that hotbox. The fifteen hundred men hung around even after sunset.

Next morning, the campus was quieter, most of the white plant workers having returned to work. But the diehards took the day without pay and came back, still with their hideous faces, their homemade weapons, and their hate. Classes were scheduled, and we walked in groups to feel safer. I was calm enough to wonder what would happen if one of the men made a move toward Miss Lucy. There was one of her and still a couple hundred of them. All two hundred could not possibly beat up on one black woman, and I knew from reading *Julius Caesar* in high school that mobs need targets once they unleash their emotions. If this mob began to act, it would inevitably hurt white students. They were all men, their language was nasty about women, Autherine was a woman, I was a woman. I believed that if they ever got started, their rage would spill over to white women students rather than to campus men.

That day I recognized something central about being a girl in the world. I felt closer to Autherine Lucy than to my white male classmates, and I felt afraid because of my anatomy and gender. I cried out of what seemed fear but must also have been the relief of identification. Though it would be twenty years before I used the word, I probably became a feminist that day.

By the third day of class, the men from the paper mill and rubber plant were gone from campus. Mrs. Healy continued to drive out to the motel in the morning to collect Miss Lucy and back again in the late afternoon to deposit her. I had prayed a lot during those three days, and now I felt that my prayers were answered, since Autherine was going to classes and Mrs. Healy was not hurt. But nearly every day I heard snatches of ugly conversations among students or between students and faculty about how unfair it was to all of us to have to put up with "her." No one ever called Autherine Lucy by any name, and I flashed to my alley playmates, wishing I had at least learned their first names. I never interrupted those bigoted exchanges to state my own views about having a black classmate or my feelings about what was being said.

In the months that followed, I saw O. C. Carmichael, the university president, forced to resign because he would not lie about Miss Lucy. During that first violent week, some of us learned the board of trustees pressured him to expel her because of the tensions set off in the town by her presence. Dr. Carmichael told them flatly that the town would have to figure out something to do with its tensions. Then the board told him to say that she did not do well enough on various aptitude tests to be admitted. Again Dr. Carmichael refused, pointing out that Miss Lucy's scores were better than the whites from rural school districts, and that, after all, Alabama prided itself on open admissions for "all the sons and daughters of our fair state."

Finally, in a fit of desperation, the board unanimously ordered the president to issue a press release saying that, though Miss Lucy had the intellectual qualifications, she had shown up as mentally unbalanced on the psychological tests we all had been forced to take during orientation week. Dr. Carmichael stood his ground, went to a special meeting of the trustees, and said that as long as he was president, Miss Lucy would be a student, since there was no conceivable reason to ask her to leave except that she was black.

The board took him at his word and sent him a hand-delivered letter, giving him forty-eight hours in which to resign or else be summarily fired. They said that his views were "incompatible with state policies and local custom." Dr. Carmichael took only twelve hours to decide: he sent a curt reply, announcing his resignation effective January 1st, adding that he could not in conscience carry out "state policies and local customs." That happened two days before school closed for Christmas vacation. A small but vocal band of students, of which I was one, was very sad to see him go. We went to the president's mansion with its elegant pair of curved staircases, its second-floor balcony, its French doors. We wanted to sing carols for O. C. and his wife. As I stood on the finely ground gravel of the driveway, shivering from damp southern winter cold and from the loss of this strong male figure in my life, he stepped out onto the balcony with Mrs. Carmichael. They sang with us, and then he spoke, sadly and warmly. He told us the truth: he was sorry to leave his post because he believed education was the only hope for improving race relations; he had not wanted to give the board the pleasure of firing him, so he had resigned. He had not hedged about why he was leaving. He would miss us. They cried, and so did we.

I cannot remember when Autherine Lucy stopped attending classes, but it was not long afterward. The NAACP advised her to drop out during fall semester, while the board of trustees set about its vicious campaign to get her off campus, and to reenter in mid-January when the courts would have upheld the Brown decision. The Alabama Supreme Court supported the autonomy of the university and its trustees, saying they had acted in the best interests of the student body. I wondered silently about Miss Lucy's best interests.

I only saw her a few times, but the memories remain sharp. Once she was walking alone up the steps of the library. Once she was getting into Mrs. Healy's front seat late one afternoon, to be whisked back to her cell for the evening. Once I passed her on the mall and smiled broadly but kept on walking to class. There was no student or faculty outcry to keep her in school. There was never a word about her exit in the school paper (the *Crimson Tide)*, the *Tuscaloosa Journal*, the *Birmingham Post* or the *Montgomery Herald*. I asked Mrs. Healy toward the end of my freshman year, which would also have been Miss Lucy's freshman year, what had happened to her. Mrs. Healy looked into the distance, I thought back toward Michigan, where I was naively sure things like this never happened. Finally, in a tired voice she said, "It just didn't work—the university and the state aren't willing to obey the law yet."

The trustees installed a new president who signed a letter saying that Autherine Lucy was mentally unfit to attend classes and, therefore, for her own welfare, the university was suspending her "with no prejudice for future success."

My remaining undergraduate years included virtually no contact with blacks, but two experiences off campus burned their way into my brain to lodge for many years, unresolved and unassimilated. Both took place on Sunday afternoons in the public park next to the Birmingham Public Library, where my sister worked as head of the popular literature department. Both took place when I was nineteen.

It was the summer of 1956, a year or so after the Supreme Court decision. The NAACP felt the time had come to integrate more than downtown department stores, which, after all, wanted money even from blacks. The organization decided to focus on outdoor places where whites went to relax and be cool. They chose a large shady park next to the library's main branch. The previous year, they had systematically infiltrated the library itself. I remember Betty's story of her arrival at work on the morning after the court's decision. All chairs had been removed, stored no one knew where, whisked away in the night by evil spirits. The white people in Birmingham hated more than anything to sit down next to blacks. I was shocked that people who ran a library would behave the same as drugstore-counter owners. Betty reported that not a single white patron complained about having to stand up to read the *New York Times* or the latest novel or travel book or story about baseball's hall of fame. They would rather be inconvenienced than sullied. The chairs miraculously reappeared about a week later, and the tiny number of blacks who went to the library got to sit down if they chose.

My sister had to work one Sunday afternoon a month, and I often went with her. One Sunday we arrived about 12:30 and I noticed a group of people milling around on the fringes of the park. Since I seldom read newspapers or listened to the news on radio or TV, I had no idea that this was the Sunday chosen by the NAACP for black families to bring picnic lunches to that park. After Betty opened up her room, I went into the children's literature department where I usually read. I chose that spot because it had a side door that opened onto the park, where I could sit in the sunshine or stroll on the paths. That day I went outside almost as soon as I was settled at a table.

What I found froze me in horror. About thirty black people—fathers, mothers, and children of walking–talking ages; no babies, teenagers, or really old people—were having a group picnic after church. They all wore suits, best dresses and heels, the children in miniature versions of the same things. A crowd of rowdy whites, not nearly as well dressed or behaved, had gathered to shout and heckle. One of the men (I later learned that he was Martin Luther King's brother, A. D., the minister at a local Baptist church) started singing, "What a Friend We Have in Jesus" and was immediately joined by the rest. They sang and ate their sandwiches and potato chips amidst the booing and cursing around them.

The whites grew more abusive as their numbers mushroomed. I was scared but could not go back into the library and shut it all out. I stood, mute and paralyzed, as the minutes crept by. I wanted the black people to go home before somebody threw something at them or hit them. Unable to fathom why it mattered for them to have a picnic where they were so obviously not wanted, I also wondered why they had brought their children where they could not protect them.

Suddenly the crowd fell silent, and I heard sirens in the hot afternoon air. Police cars began arriving, first in twos and soon in platoons. I counted fifteen cars and knew there were more down the streets. At first, I was relieved, since I thought the police had come to ask the whites to move on and let the black families finish their picnic.

When I saw police jovially slapping white men on the shoulder, my fear returned. Still unable to move, I stood on the outskirts of the action and watched the big, fat police officers, their dark blue uniforms stained by huge half-moons under each arm and triangles down their backsides, open their car doors and let out unmuzzled German shepherds. Before I could register what was happening, the dogs were unleashed, and the police were shouting, "Sic 'em." The dogs raced toward the well-dressed, hymn-singing blacks, who jumped up and ran. They tried at first to stay together but then broke into little units, catching up smaller children who could not run fast without stumbling. Children cried, and women wailed to the deaf police to have mercy. Black men yelled to "call off your dogs" and Reverend King appealed to the white authority. That man was Police Commissioner Eugene Connor, commonly known as "Bull" because he was thick necked and tough and stubborn. His own men, all white, feared him. Reverend King made his way through the crowd of cheering whites and found Bull, shotgun on his hip and a big plug of chewing tobacco in his jaw. I could not hear their words, but Connor's only gesture before he had four policemen drag Reverend King into the nearest police car was to spit a healthy stream of brown liquid at the black minister. It landed somewhere below his knees, wetting his impeccably creased black trousers.

I saw dogs sink teeth into a woman's buttocks and rip her lovely dress. These angry German shepherds snarled at children's feet dangling from their parents' arms. The children became hysterical, a few even seemed to pass out, falling utterly limp in their protectors' arms. The dogs drew blood from ankles, calves, and, in the case of one rather large man who must have stumbled from lack of breath, a face. The whole event did not last more than half an hour. All the blacks were eventually cornered by the dogs and held at bay until the leering police arrested them. Some of the men stood firm with furious dogs all around them, and when a white cop touched them, always violently, they would relax into lifeless forms and let themselves be dragged off. This dead weight made transport harder for the already sweating police, and I was glad.

As they were carried to waiting cars and jail cells, the black men smiled and sang hymns. One came close enough for me to hear what he said as he faced a triumphant white mob, its dirty work being done by law enforcement officers: "We are obeying the law here, and you are breaking it. God will reward us all accordingly." He repeated this meekly but bravely, like a litany and a warning. I believed him and prayed hard for the next few weeks that God would see that I was not being cruel to those picnickers. I felt guilty and ashamed because, just as with Autherine Lucy, I had decent emotions but no will to act. My silent presence seemed assent.

When it was over, bits and pieces of picnic lunches lay strewn over the park grass. I went inside and only then let myself know how scared I felt, sitting in my straight-backed library chair, quiet and serene on the outside, shaking within. At six o'clock when Betty came in to fetch me, I said nothing about what I had seen. There was no news of it anywhere, and no one I knew talked about it.

Years later I learned that national TV had taped the scene, and people all over the country had seen Alabama's finest police force once again restore law and order, assert state's rights, and deny humanity to keep the race pure. Large dogs bit me in nightmares for the next few weeks, and until fairly recently I feared dogs and never wanted to live with one. I also hated police and cowards like me.

The next time Betty worked her Sunday shift, I went with her again. A large crowd of already angry whites circled the park adjacent to the children's room of the library. Betty seemed not to notice them. We went in, and I settled into my usual chair near fairy tales and mythology. But I went out into the park as soon as the doors opened to the public, noticing that virtually no one had come in.

There they were again—a group of very dressed-up black families, sweltering in the summer humidity but sitting proudly on bright tablecloths for their after-church picnic. Some of the adult faces were the same as the month before, and once again Reverend A. D. King was their leader. They must have come earlier this time, since the level of hostility was already pretty high by the time I arrived. There were more children. Had someone in charge thought their presence might appeal to the white women who taunted them? If more little children were along maybe even white police would think before turning loose dogs trained to be vicious. All these thoughts flew through my mind as I stood within the safe shadows of the granite building. In the middle of my fear, I felt strangely drawn to the scene and the blacks who were making it happen. I thought they were brave and I thought they were foolish. I watched the scene in the park as I would a horror movie, feeling relief at some deep level that punishment was being visited on someone besides me. I became a voyeur, not merely a spectator. I felt no allegiance to the white bigots who tormented the blacks; my sympathies were with the victims. But a contorted sense of relief, born of my unacknowledged privilege, was undeniably present. I was not glad that these quiet, peaceful people were being persecuted and hurt, only that it was not I.

Shortly after I took up my post, I heard the familiar sirens close and insistent. Fire trucks, rather than police cars drove up. Where was the fire? The only passenger car was Bull Connor's private, unmarked one, which arrived last. He emerged, minus his shotgun, and began to talk very quietly with the firemen, who in turn began to unroll their hoses and screw them to several hydrants nearby. They turned on the hoses, full force, and walked slowly toward the blacks, who were eating their sandwiches and singing hymns. I have no idea how many pounds of pressure are behind water that comes out of a fire hose, but it is enough to knock over a full-grown man. The group panicked as it had not done the month before. The barrage of water was somehow more terrifying than the dogs. Or maybe it was simply unexpected.

If the firemen trained their nozzles on adults, Bull caught them up short and yelled, "Do what I told you!" Then hard streams of spray tumbled the children, dressed in their Sunday best, head over heels. They were knocked up against tree trunks. They were driven down sidewalk paths, the skin on their legs or arms or faces grated off by contact with cement. They were sprayed directly in the face, which choked and blinded them. Their mothers went crazy at the sight and at their cries of terror and paralysis. I hid my eyes.

This Sunday's horror show was shorter than the first one but did more bodily damage and caused more spiritual pain to the blacks. Men tried to run in front of the hoses to absorb the water's force, but the firemen worked too fast for them. Mothers tried to throw themselves over children's bodies, but again the firemen proved too skillful. Those years of training hoses on a fire's center had been perfect preparation for this afternoon. Within fifteen minutes, they had satisfied themselves, turned off the water, neatly rolled up their hoses, climbed back into their mammoth trucks, and driven off, led by Bull with his hidden siren going full blast. No white person had made a single move to stop this atrocity, including me.

I retreated to the library, much more shaken by this experience than by the earlier one. When I left the scene, a small group of weeping, enraged blacks were trying to calm terrorized, water-soaked children. They swore at bands of whites who laughed and spat out phrases like, "That's what you jigaboos get for coming here and trying to take over our place. Why don't you just stay where you belong?" At first I was glad to hear the victims fight back at least in words, but when I realized that those curses included me, I felt guilty and scared. Six years later, while a graduate student in Madison, Wisconsin, I read John Milton's sonnet, "On the Late Massacre at Piedmont." This poem expresses the poet's rage at hearing of a battle in which people he saw as barbarians "rolled mother and infant down the rocks" of a cliff in order to win the day. The park scene leapt into my mind, and I had to stop reading and go for a long walk.

The second incident made the white papers on Monday morning, and I read about a "minor skirmish" in the park, "quickly handled by Police Commissioner Connor in his usual efficient manner." The story claimed that the only injuries were a "few skinned knees and stubbed noses." I never told anyone what I had seen.

At the same time that racism was becoming a tangible reality to me, I was struggling to keep my own special creativity alive. When I realized that I would not attend Chapel Hill or Duke because my father's unexpected death eliminated the requisite financial security, I let myself get excited about at least one aspect of the University of Alabama. Roy McAllister taught piano in the music department. A wonderful teacher and performer who studied every summer in New York with Madame Nadia Boulanger, he also happened to be my brother-in-law's brother. I had gone to a few of his recitals and been attracted to his patrician nose and deeply wrinkled brow. He and his family had visited us on several Sunday afternoons. On one of these occasions, Roy and my mother had fallen into a violent argument about the relative superiority of Rubenstein and Horowitz. Mamie was sure that Rubenstein was the finer because of the soul that so obviously poured from his hands. Roy found that soul marred by technical errors and preferred Horowitz, whose execution he found flawless, never mind that he played with less emotional investment. In the midst of their fight, Roy yelled something like, "Oh, you only speak from uneducated taste, whereas I'm a serious pianist and know the difference." Leon rushed his brother out of the house as quickly as possible.

This fracas occurred several years before my arrival on campus, but it may well have remained in Roy's mind; it certainly lingered in Mamie's. Naive in the ways of such feuds, all I thought about was having him as a teacher. When he agreed, though reluctantly, I was overjoyed. My weekly lesson was on Thursday at 12:30, and I looked forward to my hour even though I was being reintroduced to Miss Plosser's purists, Bach, Scarlatti, and Clementi. Roy's intensity pervaded the very air of his studio. Whenever he played a particularly difficult passage, I was excited by the contained emotion in his veined hands.

I very much wanted to please Roy, but that almost never happened during the year and two months I studied with him. From his point of view, work devoted to my advanced English class or my premed chemistry labs two afternoons a week signalled a lack of seriousness about the piano. Often, he interrupted my attempt to render a three-part invention with an impatient "You've been doing something besides practicing piano this week." But one day I played several pieces Bartok composed for his children in such a way as to win unadulterated praise. When I finished the fourth tiny étude, Roy paused before saying in a tone I would never hear again: "Well, Toni, Bela himself wouldn't have found fault with those." For days, I played that sentence in my mind as I walked to the library or fell into sleep.

Most days, however, we labored through the hour, he wincing at my obvious rustiness, I vowing silently to do better next time. At the end of our last lesson in May, Roy sat me down and tried to be fatherly: "I want you to spend the summer seeing how you really feel about the piano—try to set priorities, let yourself know how you feel when you play well and when you don't. We'll talk about it in the fall." While that summer after my freshman year is shadowy, I know I did not do any of those things. I never thought of talking about it with anyone, not even my roommate with whom I talked about most things. The topic seemed too intimate, like my sex life or my dreams—parts of me to be kept utterly private for fear of ridicule or rejection. In September, I returned to Tuscaloosa and told Roy I wanted to continue and that I was determined to practice more diligently.

That same fall, a friend of my sister, whom she had met at the library where he went for books about resorts on the Mediterranean, had returned to college on the GI bill. Wealthy and aimless, Tim Phillips told army stories about leaves in the Yucatan where he picked up Rita Moreno in a rented red sports car. He began driving me back and forth to campus, since my family trusted him. We enrolled in the same physics class and signed on for the same lab periods. Not liking labs, we talked openly while the assistant wrote equations on the board. After my glaring failures at dating all through high school, I was vulnerable to any friendly male. I went along with whatever Tim suggested, turning away from Toni the serious student, who had performed so beautifully for so long. Afternoons we rode around town looking at fancy houses, and, in defiance of college precautions, visited one of the several black barbeque outlets after dark.

Needless to say, my resolve about piano practicing faltered. As I was stumbling through a Bach three-part invention in early October, Roy jumped up from his armchair and yelled angrily: "You're betraying your talent. I won't go on watching you do that. You're good enough to become a concert pianist. I want you to decide by next week whether you're willing to work for that. If you are, fine, I'll help all I can. If not, I can't go on teaching you. Leave now and make your decision."

Concert pianists had come to Birmingham, and Mamie had taken me to hear them. Because I had seen females on the stage—the male/female teams of Vronski and Babbin and Lubaschutz and Niemenoff had played in town—I even understood that a girl could become such a person. Beyond that, I knew nothing about what Roy was asking me to decide. I told myself, "Concert pianists would not be home very much, might not even have homes. I want a house full of children and friends and holiday warmth." The seven days slid away.

When I walked into Roy's studio the next Thursday, I said with honest regret, "I guess I'm not going to work to be a concert pianist. But . . ." I was not allowed to finish my sentence expressing real love for the piano as a part of my life short of a major career. Roy snapped, "I thought as much. Well, it's pointless to sit down and go through another painful lesson. This is the end of your study with me. Good day."

That was on a Thursday about 12:45. On Saturday, I went down to the river flats with Tim, where we sat in his front seat with the car light on, playing gin rummy and drinking half a fifth each of warm bourbon. Before that moment, the only alcohol I had tasted was Mogen David, served in tiny, faceted wine glasses at Christmas. The bourbon burned as it went down but smoothed some of my raw nerves.

That evening was the first of countless spent on the river bank or similar spots. Though Tim continued to recount scenes of his picking up and flirting with models or actresses all over the southern hemisphere, he seemed completely oblivious to my body. His wanting to spend so much time with me suggested that something about me pleased him, yet we never got any closer than we could have in my living room in Fairfield. In fact, Tim seemed to prefer my mother and sister as ladies to whom he could pay court. I kept saying "yes" to his invitations, at first out of simple loneliness, but soon out of a fascination with how effectively alcohol deadened my feelings about not studying the piano any longer. If Tim used me as a convenient chum who provided entree into our house, I used him as a supplier of decent bourbon.

After a fall and winter of four nightly visits a week to the river flats with Tim and a bottle, I recognized a fearful dependence on alcohol. Spring was a little late in 1956, but when it came to Tuscaloosa, I could not distinguish the yellow-green buds on the trees that filled the quadrangle. Since watching them unfold had always been special, I panicked at the haze that kept me from them. I tied that hazy vision to my drinking and with characteristic speed, between eleven in the morning and dinner, I decided to stop. Since alcohol seemed inseparable from Tim Phillips, I concluded that I must also stop seeing him. When he came for me at the appointed time, I leaned in his open car door window and sputtered, "I'm not coming with you tonight or any other night; I'm giving up liquor and you." In the remaining months of his stay at the university, I remember only passing greetings when we found ourselves in the same place. My mother and sister inquired about his absence, and I lied, saying he had lost his heart to a sweet sophomore and had no time for mere friends.

Tim was the first male whom I found attractive and who wanted to spend time with me. Though we never so much as held hands, I turned our card-playing drunks into a fantasy sex life. My sorority sisters believed that I was finally doing the "normal" thing, and some even became concerned about the amount of time I was spending with "an older man." Up to this point, I had been valuable as someone whose grades were guaranteed to drive up the house's average. I did nothing to correct their impressions about the nature of our relationship, and when I suddenly stopped seeing Tim, I got a lot of sympathy about the "break-up." They included me in plans for movies or jaunts to the nearest fried chicken hut, attentions that went some distance toward filling the void created by Tim's banishment.

# *Awakenings*

*A*s I made my way through college, I became progressively less sure of myself except as an intellectual. My thirty extra pounds reinforced my conviction that I was not sexually attractive. Simultaneously, I had several close male friends, all of whom were gay. As a voyeur of their love lives, I learned about infidelity, rejection, passion returned and spurned, enthrallment to the beloved. They conveyed an image of sexuality shrouded in secrecy, threats of exposure with dire consequences, and the certainty of each great passion's lasting no more than a few months at best. Their stories never shocked me, and I took the seriousness of their feelings to heart. My sympathies were with them as suffering victims of a cruel society that refused them daylight relationships and expelled them for doing what every coed believed was part of a normal campus weekend. These young men's stories were my first knowledge of love between persons of the same gender.

Though as I moved into my twenties I was not surprised to learn of my male friends' sexual activity with people like themselves, I certainly made no connections to my own life. I knew of no women who loved other women; I had never seen or heard the word "lesbian." Nevertheless, I developed close friendships with some of my own sorority sisters and with those magical women in Pi Phi, and had my first extended friendship with a woman.

We met in English 1A, taught by Miss Locke, a staunch supporter of smart women. An achiever like me, Jean spoke long and clearly about Conrad and Keats, so I started walking out of class with her, prolonging our conversations. When we moved into the same sorority house, we chose to room together. Though most beds were housed on a vast sleeping porch, our room had a cot on which we spent idle hours, rubbing backs, dozing, talking about the meaning of life, crying or laughing about some event in our day.

In our romantic poetry course, we read Coleridge's "Christabel" and decided we were very like the two women in that gothic tale of evil and forbidden fruits. Our nicknames became "Chris" and "Gere" (the other character is called Geraldine), and we developed a private language around them and that poem. At another point, we listened constantly to a popular song called "The Green Door," whose refrain was, "What's going on behind the green door?" Our sorority sisters harbored various feelings about our three-year friendship, ranging from envy to downright spite. When we went into our room, closed the door for hours, and ignored the social life in the adjacent lounge, generous members worried, and the rest were infuriated. Once we came in from classes to find a sign tacked to our door. THE GREEN DOOR, it read in large, angry letters. We further enraged and alarmed our sisters by leaving it there, embellished with pencilled flowers and sketched-in windows. What went on behind that magic door excited me and left me without frustration since I never dreamed that I might want to take my amorphous feelings in any specific direction. We talked long and hard about poetry and plays, about why people did what they did, about our own dreams. We gossiped about our sorority sisters, sure that we were the most sophisticated among them.

In some way Jean and I were innocents: two girls who had led sheltered lives, groomed to become proper southern ladies, wives, mothers, churchworkers. Since the basis of our attraction was mutual intellect, it was only after I had made love to a woman that I fully grasped the complexity of what we had. Later such nonsexual primary friendships would leave me miserable, confused, and angry. But with Jean, I knew a warmth and closeness, an ability to rely on her that had been previously absent from my life.

During her senior year, Jean found an older man who had been a pilot in the Korean War. She dated him, went steady, married, had two daughters, and eventually, twenty-four years later, divorced him. When she asked me to be a bridesmaid, I of course agreed. Her decision left me feeling afraid and lonely: I was about to lose someone precious. Any day, at the slightest provocation, I cried. At one of the rehearsals, I met Jean's cousin, Wayne, who was to be a groomsman. Several years younger than I, Wayne was tall and skinny and full of acne. But he was Jean's cousin, so I liked him. When he offered me a ride home, so that the couple could be alone, I agreed. Before that night was over, we had engaged in some pretty heavy petting. We continued doing that, in spite of my mother's growing anxiety about my seeing him. Wayne and I had very little to talk about. He was anti-college, while I was busily applying for scholarships to graduate school. But I felt closer to Jean when I was with him, so I was willing to put up with boredom and a certain distaste for his boniness and bumpiness.

Shortly after Jean's wedding, I graduated. Having nothing I particularly wanted to do, I accepted a scholarship to complete a master's degree in nine months. I liked the free money and the challenge, since everyone said a master's degree took at least twelve months. Deciding on Vanderbilt as my academy, I made plans to drive to Nashville. It was the fall of 1958, and Wayne had decided to go to the University of Alabama and try to learn. He proposed that I come to Tuscaloosa before I headed north. Cut off from all my emotions except a dull missing of Jean, I went along with his plans. I lied to my mother and left for Nashville seven days early, ostensibly to "help with rush week." Though I officially stayed with a woman friend who lived in town, except for one sorority party, I spent most of my time with Wayne in his already messy apartment hardly big enough for him. Since we still had almost nothing to talk about, I read a lot while he pretended to be settling in, a process that involved moving piles of clothes and books from one side of the apartment to another. I fixed lavish dinners and tried to feel romantic about my escapade, but much of the time I just felt nostalgic, remembering long back rubs and endless talks I had always had with Jean. I kept wondering why Wayne could not be more like his cousin.

When he suggested that I stay the last night before my exodus north at his place, I offered no resistance. Understanding his request to include intercourse—a step we had always carefully avoided—I mustered the courage to ask him to take precautions. He answered, "Oh, yeah, I have some condoms in my dresser drawer."

Suddenly I was ten again, standing in my sister's room a few months after she and Leon had gotten married. As I opened her underwear drawer to put in some clean laundry, my eye was caught by a box that had a Greek warrior's head in profile and his body in armor. It read, "Trojan condoms," a phrase that filled me with some unnamed excitement. Sensing that the box had to do with Leon's being in our house with Betty, since I was sure the box had never been in my sister's drawer before, I took it out gingerly and opened it just enough to see a bunch of rubbery tan things that puzzled me. I never asked Betty about them, since I did not want her to know I was rifling her private things.

Wayne and I did indeed have intercourse, or what he called that. It lasted no more than fifteen minutes and took place in the pitch dark. I was disappointed: I had long wanted to see a man's body and had some notion that he might want to see mine. Wayne seemed utterly ashamed and in a great hurry. Consequently he was awkward and rough about the anatomical details that led up to his release. The instant that occurred, he was out of me and into the shower. No words were exchanged then or the next day about what had happened; no questions were asked about how I felt (this was, after all, my maiden voyage, and he knew it). As I lay awake in the moonlight, listening to late summer crickets and Wayne's interrupted breathing, I thought of novels I had read about first love and high passion. Inside my head, voices vied for supremacy: "You ought to be ashamed of yourself— not waiting until your wedding night." "I'll bet Harold Smith would have wanted to be gentle and playful before and after, maybe even have lain on the bed and talked about how magical it all was." "What a letdown—why does everybody make so much of something that hardly even happens before it's done with?" Next morning, an awkward silence hung in Wayne's apartment as we collected strewn clothes. I hurriedly threw clothes into my suitcase, saying, "Oh, don't bother with breakfast, I'll pick up something on the road." We both carefully avoided any exchange about what our being sexual might "mean." As I drove away to graduate school, Wayne mumbled something about having "forgotten" to put on his condom.

My rage lasted all the way to Tennessee and for the next three months. It was joined by terror when, days after my period was to have begun, I realized that I might be pregnant with Jean's cousin's child. That was 1958 in the South and abortions were done in back alley walk-ups by unlicensed, seedy "doctors." I did not know a soul in Nashville and could not think how I would find such a butcher. All the money I had was a modest weekly allowance; I knew the process was expensive. For the two months I did not menstruate, and the few immediately following my eventual bleeding, every young male I saw, in class, on the streets, in church or the grocery store, reminded me of Wayne and his awkward, silent, thoughtless attitude toward something about which I felt inherently positive, which I had anticipated for years.

In the months preceding my going to Vanderbilt, I had persuaded my mother that I was old enough at twenty-one to live in one of the official residential houses for female graduate students. We were about ten women of widely divergent backgrounds, studying everything from English literature to speech pathology and pharmacology. The woman who wanted to be a pharmacist was Kolinde Schroff, born in Bombay. She wore saris made from exotic materials: cotton for everyday use; a voile-like material when she wanted to look formal; silk for elegant celebrations. On her birthday, she asked several of us to wear a sari to the park where her party was to be held. That park was on the edge of town and housed an exact replica of the Parthenon, an edifice of which Nashvillians are terribly proud. Feeling distinctly international and luxurious, I glided along the grass in a teal blue sari flecked with gold thread. I felt more graceful than I could remember, and distinctly less vulnerable to men yelling compliments or obscenities from their car windows.

As we were dishing up the ice cream, a police car stopped near us. Its two occupants left the car and began sauntering toward our gathering. "What can they possibly want with us? We don't have beer and aren't making noise to disturb any of the families here." It seems we had crossed some invisible line of acceptable white attire—the officers said we were in "inappropriate" dress and would have to leave the premises immediately or be arrested for vagrancy. We agreed even as I remembered another park on another Sunday when police had forced people deemed inappropriate off the grass reserved for whites willing to conform to codes.

Kolinde cooked her own food in our communal kitchen and soon the house was redolent with the odor of cumin. I loved the pungency, but most of the other women complained that "Kolinde's food stinks." She smiled sweetly and kept right on making her curries. In all my vocabulary work, I had never come across words like turmeric, cumin, coriander, cardamom. Now I was not only learning to spell them but to distinguish their special aromas and particular tastes. And rolling them off my tongue—turmeric, cumin, coriander, cardamom—gave me distinct pleasure.

Kolinde was very dark brown with jet black hair worked into a single braid that reached down to the small of her back. She and I were half of a group that formed early in the fall and became inseparable.

One of the other two women was studying speech pathology even as she was preparing herself to become a Methodist minister's wife; the other was in animal psychology, which meant to me that she did studies on Siamese kittens whose feet were kept in test tubes to prevent them from having sensory experiences.

One Friday night in late October, we four decided to go to a movie. It was a major event, the first time we had stolen so long away from our studies. At the ticket window, we lined up with the speech pathologist first, me second, Kolinde third, and the psychologist last. As Martha Jo and I waited for Kolinde and Beth to move up, it happened. The young woman inside the ticket booth said in her deepest Tennessee accent, "You have to go to the line that's for coloreds. This here is the white line." She was talking to my friend Kolinde from India. Kolinde fell mute, so I stepped up and said, from the depths of my racist heart, "Oh, you misunderstand, Miss; Kolinde's not a Negro, she's from India." Unimpressed, the young woman repeated herself. We whites felt insulted for our friend. Martha Jo and I forced the ticket seller to give us back our money, saying, "If Kolinde can't buy a ticket here, we don't want to go to your old movie."

I was humiliated that Kolinde should be mistaken for an American black but oblivious to the racism that lay behind that response. Not understanding about hierarchies of oppression or competitive rankings within groups of color, I wanted to separate my friend from the ticket seller's prejudice. Because I still had not analyzed my attitudes toward blacks, I failed to learn the lesson presented at the box office, just as I failed to grasp the implications in the phrase "colored people." Kolinde was some color, not white; as such, she was inadmissible.

Nashville is the home of several colleges, among them Fisk University, one of the few all-black universities in the South. I had heard it was a good school, patterned after Vanderbilt, its students "clean middle-class Negroes from professional homes." During the fall semester, the English department at Vanderbilt got an invitation for graduate students to attend a foreign film festival at Fisk. The first thing that caught my eye was the alliteration. I decided to go, since I had seen such films in Birmingham and was curious to hear languages and see faces different from my own. Four other classmates wanted to go, so we planned to have dinner together before driving across town to the school.

The series began on a Friday with an open house before the film showing at 8:00 P.M. Curious about more than the foreign films, we decided to get there about 7:30 and meet some of the students. We talked animatedly at dinner about how exciting it would be to meet "educated Negroes," since we had known only servants who had little or no schooling. Because of late afternoon classes, we met at the cafeteria in school clothes: skirts and sweaters, socks and loafers for the three women; blue jeans with nondescript shirts and pullovers for the two men.

We arrived at the administration building on the Fisk campus at precisely 7:30 and walked into the designated hall. We were the only whites in a room of over a hundred blacks of all ages. The series was open to the community, and everyone was in formal attire: men in dinner jackets, bow ties, polished patent leather shoes; women in long dresses or short cocktail length skirts with filmy silk blouses, spiked heels, and gloves. They were all drinking punch from crystal cups, eating petit fours, and chatting.

I felt tacky because I looked tacky. I felt visible because I was. As we were standing on the outskirts of the group, cringing inside and wondering if we could escape before anyone saw us, a tall, handsome stranger walked over and introduced himself in tones I had never heard from anyone in the South. I later learned that he had spent a year at Oxford and now taught philosophy at Fisk. He laughed off our muttered embarrassments, brought us into the circle, put a punch cup and a little cake in our hands, and introduced us to the assembled company.

After what seemed hours, it was eight o'clock. We were ushered to seats, and the lights went down, hiding our gaucherie. I breathed for the first time since entering the room. I have no recollection of the movie because I spent the hour and a half trying to make sense out of what had just happened. What I knew most strongly was that I had been treated entirely differently as an outsider than I had ever seen blacks treated by us. No one turned angry dogs or fire hoses on me; no one called me degrading names or ordered me to leave. I was so moved by their civility and warmth that I went to all the movies in the series, wearing clothes that could serve for formal or informal occasions. I met women and men with vastly more interesting lives than my own or my friends'. I talked about racial politics and learned something about how educated blacks perceived the white world of Nashville and Vanderbilt.

Spring semester, the English department at Vanderbilt organized a film series of old American movies starring great actors. No invitation was sent to Fisk graduate students. I felt crazy: I had been taught from earliest childhood that the code of the white South was chivalry, civility, and hospitality; I learned that in Nashville, Tennessee, the persons exercising that code were black.

In addition to expanding my awareness of racism and coping with my terror over a possible unwanted pregnancy, I spent my early months at Vanderbilt trying to concentrate on Chaucer, Shakespeare, English ballads, and a history course. I also met a man different from any I had known. Adam liked to talk and, furthermore, was articulate on any subject having to do with art or culture. I was determined to avoid silent men, since the last one had almost cost me my future. Adam was tall, gently handsome with a fuzzy beard and a crew cut, soft-spoken, and shy in some way I instinctively trusted. I fell in love and spent that year at Vanderbilt pining for what I could not have. At our initial meeting, he had been quick to tell me about his fiancée in Louisiana: "Anna's wonderful—she plays the piano masterfully— we're totally committed, I want to spend my life with her, we are going to marry just as soon as I get my master's degree and a teaching job to support us." In an odd way, Adam was safe: I could fantasize to my heart's content, risking no more unwanted babies or painful hit-and-run incidents in dark apartments.

We spent endless hours together, and a loneliness I had known since my father died gradually eased. We climbed church towers to find dead pigeons in the belfry; we drove out into the country around Nashville to ogle sleek horses and smell bluegrass; we spent whole nights in the Episcopal church student lounge, talking intensely until we fell asleep on two long couches facing each other across a large expanse of carpet. Only once did we come close to unleashing erotic or sexual feelings. We had been at a late party and were both a little drunk. At the party, we had improvised at an upright piano, making a special kind of love. Riding home in the back seat of a friend's car, I sat on Adam's lap because we were too many for the space. As the driver swerved around a corner, our mouths touched and stayed longer than the maneuver warranted. During that suspended moment, I knew I would marry Adam if he asked me. We never spoke about that night, and we never repeated it. But it erased a nasty taste that rose in my mouth when I thought about my two or three unsatisfactory attempts to be sexual with men. My man-hating softened, I let myself experience vague and specific sexual feelings that never went beyond fantasies but that served to connect me with my body in ways that would eventually help me become a lesbian.

I left Vanderbilt for a teaching job in Mississippi, at an Episcopal girls' boarding school. I went there ignorant of two important facts— one about me and one about the town—both of which I would learn within weeks of my arrival. I did not know when I began working at a school attended by 150 girls, ages fifteen to twenty-two, that I was a lesbian. And I did not know that where I would live for two years was the last place to fall to General Grant.

# *Sure and Certain Knowledge*

$As$ I drove from Birmingham southwest into Mississippi, I marveled at how lush the country was and how soft the wind that came into my car window seemed. The closer I came to my destination, however, the more anxious I became. Eager to begin what I believed would be my career, I was worried about being so young. Barely twenty-two, I fretted over the fact that my students, never younger than fifteen, would sometimes be as old or older than I.

These worries vanished as I turned into the long boulevard leading up to my first job site. The school was situated in a Civil War memorial park in a sprawling colonial building where faculty and students lived, ate, studied, went to classes, had sexual fantasies, spied on each other, and fought for privacy. My room was on the third floor; the window nearest my bed looked out onto a large cannon pointing directly at me. Because there were no movies worth seeing and only one decent place to eat fried chicken, I spent a lot of time driving or walking in the many-acred park. I learned that each state fighting in the Civil War had been awarded a section in which to erect a memorial to the event. By allowing northern states to have space, the town fathers could pride themselves on their liberalism. I discovered, however, that blacks rented shacks in the sections assigned to the North, while wealthy Mississipians held large tracks of land in the southern portions. Streets were unpaved in the northern sections but mowed and planted with day lilies along the shoulders of southern sections. The war was being prolonged at the levels of civil engineering and landscaping. It felt ludicrous, since in a moment of largess, designers had jumbled up northern and southern states. The result was that I could drive on smooth asphalt for the two miles designated for Alabama, only to fall into mammoth mud holes while maneuvering Vermont's five hundred yards.

During the two years between 1958 and 1960, when I lived in that park, I saw very few black people and met none. They were never on downtown streets when I shopped and seldom were seen outside their park dwellings during the daytime. I never found out where else the town was allowing them to live. Not even the school's kitchen or grounds crew were black. The longer I listened to local residents, the more logical the blacks' invisibility became. The town still talked about General Grant as a monstrous firebrand. I was taken to river bluffs from which the brave men of Mississippi had defended their land and other miscellaneous possessions (wives, children, darkies, cattle) for 131 days. They were finally defeated by cleverness—a Yankee trait. It seems the general concluded that he would never scale the bluffs from the river, so he sent battalions around back of the southern troops, surprised them, and won. That in itself was seen as cowardice, since no "real man" sneaks up on his enemy.

Because the town fell on July 4th, every year merchants took down their American flags and installed black ones as a sign of mourning. Not understanding this symbolism, but knowing of the use of such flags by European anarchist groups, I once asked a drugstore owner if that was their meaning. He walked away enraged, constrained from attacking me only by virtue of my being a "southern lady." I decided that in such an atmosphere black people in 1959 stayed under cover because they could only remind the white townspeople of General Grant and the collapse of slavery.

That first job was the hardest I will ever have. I was the English department. That meant I taught three high school classes, in addition to freshman and sophomore courses in the junior college wing. As a perfectionist, I believed each student should write a theme a week. So every weekend for the two years I worked there, I graded and commented generously on some seventy or eighty papers. Many students found their voices in my classes and went on to good colleges, all out of the South at my urging.

The students stayed in my classroom after school to talk about eternal verities and other equally unmanageable topics. And they worked hard at reading, memorizing, writing about literature by all the major white male authors. I did not teach a single female writer. Out of class, we spent idle hours walking in the lovely woods surrounding the school or shopping in the tiny town on Saturdays, when students were allowed off campus without an official chaperone.

My car was the subject of one of their many projects. It was a baby blue Volkswagen, the first car bought on my own, though I had only made one payment before my arrival. The girls decided it had to have a name and for days worked on possible options. Finally they settled on "Beatrice Portinari," which combined their fascination with my story about Dante and his ethereal love, muse, idol, and their loose Latin coining of a word to mean "that which carries McNaron," "porti–nari."

One of the high school seniors, April, began spending late afternoons talking about music and nature and how much she adored whichever writer we were studying. She was tall and willowy with silky-looking dark brown hair that hung down around her shoulders. Her deep set brown eyes looked questioningly at me until I was not sure what to do next. She liked French almost as much as English, and gradually I began reading French with her, telling myself I needed to keep up my skill since I was on my way back to more graduate study.

When her teacher assigned Saint-Exupéry's *Le Petit Prince* as optional reading, April jumped at the chance, suggesting that we read it together before compulsory evening chapel. After a day or two of reading at adjacent desks in my classroom, I proposed that we retire to my room on the third floor where we could be more comfortable. Once there, I realized that the way to do that was to sit on my single bed, since there was only one chair at the small desk provided for letter writing. So tall, willowy April and I began translating a story about a strange and wonderful attachment between a little boy who has fallen from the sky and a fox, a story about taming and being tamed.

Since my dormitory room faced west, our late afternoon sessions were framed by breathtaking sunsets, which we interrupted translation to watch. Kneeling on my narrow bed, we stared out my little oval window, commenting on colors and rays and the beauty of it all. We tried to ignore the cannon on the hill. After one such hiatus, April lay down on my bed instead of sitting back on its edge to continue Saint-Exupéry. "Looking at those last rays of sunlight has made me drowsy," she said. She napped for the fifteen minutes before chapel, while I sat uneasily in the lone chair watching her. Unfamiliar pleasurable feelings were periodically erased by waves of fear. What did it mean that I looked so tenderly at this student who trusted me—or she would not be napping on my narrow bed in the growing dusk? None of my gay male friends' stories entered my mind as I searched frantically for some mooring onto which to pin my strange emotions. It never occurred to me that April might be having similar feelings or even be acting in ways that elicited mine. Since I had never asked her about her past, I had no idea of her sexual history, though she was not at all surprised or awkward when we first made love.

At the end of fifteen minutes, I realized that I had to awaken her or run the risk of missing chapel and being turned in. Attendance was taken of both students and faculty by the dean of women, Agnes Crane. She stationed herself at the back of the church with a clipboard and several alphabetical lists. If a girl missed once without an excuse, she was called in to chat with the rector. If she missed a second time, she was denied her shopping or dating privileges for three weeks. Three times and her parents were called for consultation preparatory to asking her to leave. If faculty were absent, Agnes cornered us somewhere inappropriate like inside a cubicle in the ladies' room. Standing over April as she slept, I broke into a cold sweat. I called to her softly but she seemed not to hear. When I knew that I was going to have to touch her, I gingerly shook her left shoulder with two fingers and saw her eyes open slowly and a shy smile spread over her face. My impulse was either to enfold her in my arms or to run out of the room. Doing neither, I hurried us off to chapel where we arrived as the rector was saying the Sanctus. Agnes erased check marks on two pages, and I registered that she not only knew we were late but that we were late together. I felt instantly cautious, angry, and protective.

Within a week of her initial nap, April and I had lain down side by side on my single bed. Sleepy from translation, she had once again reclined for the half-hour before chapel. Tired myself from a long night of paper grading, I joined her, not consciously suspecting what could so easily happen. Again April seemed to drift into a sound sleep, while I lay wide awake, my mind filled with thoughts and my body with new desires, not present when I had slept with Wayne or even when I had felt passion and tenderness for Adam. Over the next month, our progress on the bed went from long soulful looks to seemingly innocent hugs to a day when we kissed. As a girl, I had experienced mild discomfort at 1940s movies when Clark Gable and whoever was his current flame filled the silver screen with their French kisses. Their lips seemed too parted, too moist, too hungry, especially his. But when April and I kissed, all I felt was excitement.

Not surprisingly, we became lovers shortly after that first kiss.

Neither of us felt awkward or shy about how to make love, but I cannot remember what we actually did or how that felt. I remember my experience with April as incandescent, although I have no language with which to describe it.

Our initial setting was the logical place: my bed. But not even faculty doors in the dormitory had locks. We began to feel anxious and to interrupt our delight when we thought we heard footsteps outside or someone turning the door handle. Once we were barely able to spring up and rearrange our clothing before a student came in to ask me about some poem by Alexander Pope. She had not bothered to knock, and I felt the same way I had as I saw Agnes Crane erase her check marks in chapel: watched, suspected, guilty without quite knowing of what. After that narrow escape, I determined to find a more private, preferably lockable place for us.

But before I could locate such a haven, I was called into the rector's office. The head of our school eventually became presiding bishop of the Episcopal Church of America. That morning in 1958, he tried to preside over my dismissal, but I refused to cooperate. He told me that a student had come to him with a "sickening story" of having seen me the previous evening kissing April in the back of chapel. My immediate response was, "Call her in and have her say that to my face." Maybe I had read of such melodramatic scenes in novels and remembered the stoolie's collapsing in the face of the virtuous accused. Whatever my model, I was reversing the scene: I was asking a young woman in one of my classes, where I insisted that students name whatever reality they saw in literature, to look me in the face and deny that she had seen what she had indeed seen. April and I had taken to staying at prayers until everyone else had finished. Then we met quickly in the foyer for a few words, some small gesture of endearment, and a goodnight kiss.

The rector agreed to the meeting but stipulated that April be present as well, hoping that she would betray us. While he sent for the informant, I rushed to the student lounge, which was in a separate building fondly called the Play House. Finding April smoking with her choir friends, I pulled her aside and told her of our plight, that she would have to submit herself to the interview with the rector and the as-yet-unknown informer. Once we gathered in his office, the student looked at me, burst into tears, and stammered something about being mistaken or just exaggerating again. Stymied, the rector's anger flared, his face reddened. He sent us all away, shutting the door loudly behind him.

The rector continued his accusations over the next year. Steeled against what was to come, I would enter his office and hear the door shut firmly behind me. I waited for him to lock it, since his office did have that capacity for privacy. Usually we were alone, though sometimes Agnes was there with her ubiquitous clipboard. Twice we were joined by the dean of academic affairs, Henry Hyde, who not only liked me but thought me a superb teacher. The rector opened each of these grillings with the same phrase: "Toni, I'm going to have to ask you to leave if you don't change your behavior. You're corrupting the young and I can't allow that." His fantasies of how I was doing that must have upset him a great deal because, by the end of this brief opener, his face would be covered with ugly red blotches. My responses were pretty uniform, too, ranging from "I don't understand what you're talking about" when he was general in his condemnation, to "But you have no evidence and so you can't fire me" when he mentioned April specifically.

Once when the rector was particularly vicious, Henry intervened, reminding him of my excellent work with the students, bringing hard evidence in the form of their devotion to literature, their memorization of endless lines by numerous poets, their long, cogent papers written and copiously responded to every week. He also reminded his boss that I was the only English teacher they had, and it would be impossible to replace me mid-year. The rector sputtered and fumed but backed off for that interview. My gratitude to Henry was expressed in renewed efforts to do my job superbly; my students thrived while I consistently gained weight, drank too much, and slept poorly.

My initial confrontation with the rector heightened my sense of urgency about finding a private place for April and me to meet. A place presented itself within the next week. My classroom was across from the library in the basement of the main building. It opened onto a narrow corridor that led to piano and chorus practice rooms. Sounds of students playing Chopin or Bach and of young voices lifting hymns of praise comforted me on evenings when I sat alone at my desk grading yet one more student theme. In that corridor were two doors: one to a toilet and the other to some unknown space. Inside the second door, I found a tiny room full of trash, part of an oil furnace, and a small metal box just inside the door in which lay a lead key. A security system comprised of several of these little boxes was strategically located around campus. Evenings, an aging watchman patrolled the grounds, checking in at each watch box by inserting its key into a round clock slung over his shoulder. I never figured out how that activity could possibly alert him to anything amiss, but the watchman was quite faithful. In order to determine his interaction with the empty space next to the bathroom, I observed him for four consecutive nights. His habit was to reach around the corner of the door, bring out the key that he inserted into his clock, perform the requisite ritual, and then return the key. During this period, I also registered his schedule of rounds, so I would know precisely when he would need to be able to reach into our room.

At no point in his proceedings did he do so much as shine a flashlight into the abandoned space, so I decided to make that little room our everywhere, though it had neither lights nor a window. Every night for two weeks, I went directly to my classroom after supper, ostensibly to grade papers. Part of each session was spent filling my two wastebaskets plus the ones in each empty practice room with as much trash as I dared without raising the janitor's suspicions. Finally, the room was empty of debris. I cleaned it as best I could, installed a padlock on the inside, gave April the second key, and hoped for the best.

When I felt all was under control, I invited April in for our first evening in privacy. I bought flowers, though it was too dark to see them. There, in that literal closet, in constant fear of the curious or fatal knock, my gentle and loyal first lover and I talked and cried and made love.

By and large, my scheme worked, though we had a few narrow escapes. The worst was the appearance of the watchman fifteen minutes before his appointed time. We were lying on our clothes making love; I was experiencing as I always did the sheer luxury of that, compared with our contorted squirming amidst skirts, hose, garter belts, underthings, blouses. I recall April's having just laughed softly at something I said about her body's resembling a flower—we both referred often to the other in terms right out of the English romantic poets. Suddenly the door was pushed hard, the padlock jangled ominously; after a few seconds, the watchman pushed even harder, assuming perhaps that something had mysteriously gotten wedged against the door. I motioned for April to grab her clothes and get behind the door. I threw mine on, talking to him all the while about having bought a lock for the room so I could have a little hideaway from all the students wanting to sit in my room and talk after hours. By the end of this outlandish tale, I was more or less dressed and could let him in. He pushed open the door, little aware that right behind it stood a stark naked student who might at any moment break out into a sneeze or cough or laugh or uncontrollable cry of sheer terror. His motions with the lead key were reluctant, as if he sensed my lie. But he finished clocking our station and must never have spoken to the rector about this strange occurrence or even about my use of the room.

Once he left the furnace room, I waited to hear the side door open and close on its slightly rusty hinges, indicating his exit from that part of the building. Then I drew April from her hiding place, and we collapsed into tears and laughter. That near miss happened in February, and I never really relaxed again, though we continued to meet when our schedules allowed. We never spoke of our escape any more than we spoke about any part of our relationship. But the scene of our touching and kissing and of my discovering something new and powerful about myself in a dark hole intended for garbage haunts me.

My closest friends at the school taught art and music, and were very good at it. I remember the art teacher's invitation to her dormitory room for late night tea, where she looked me hard in the eye and asked, "Is there anything I can do to help, Toni?" I was not able to answer her. Too much was understood, too little had been articulated. The effort fell flat, and we both sat awkwardly with our cups and our mutual pain. I found out, after neither of us taught at the school any longer, that she had been fired from her previous job for exactly the same "offense" as my own. Even more frightened of the real topic between us than the art teacher, the music teacher simply tried to love me and show support. No one of us ever said a word about what was going on. When I first read Adrienne Rich's "To a Woman Dead in her Forties," I wept twenty-year-old tears for the three of us trapped in that hothouse environment, singing, painting, and speaking about poetry, unable to touch any of our personal scars or to name any of our real joy.

Because it is still easier for me to blame a man or men than it is to acknowledge the depth of patriarchal thinking in all of us, I want to talk about Agnes Crane. She and the rector were old church friends, and she and the academic dean hailed from the same town in Arkansas. She had five grown sons, though no longer any husband. Her energies went into flirting with the male staff and fussing over "her girls," as she called the students. My popularity undoubtedly caused her pangs, since she had been chief confidante before my arrival.

Even before April and I became lovers, I had discovered that Agnes could not be trusted with any confidence. Once I shared my early impressions of the college freshmen, usually young women unable to attend prestigious schools but embarrassed to go to a local public junior college. One of those freshmen confronted me shortly after my talk with Agnes: "Mrs. Crane says you prefer the high school girls because they are quicker and more verbal and because they adore you. Is that true?" Though twenty-one-years old, I felt eight again, coming home from school or play to hear my mother questioning me about a confidence I had just risked sharing with a playmate's mother or a teacher I thought I could trust.

From the moment in chapel when I watched her erase checks by my name and April's, I guarded myself in Agnes's presence, understanding that she was against me in some intangible and significant way. About a week after my first scene in the rector's office, she waylaid me after supper and insisted that I "come have some tea" in her room. Her room was filled with photographs of her children at every age, engaged in every conceivable ultramale activity: little boys on ponies; slightly bigger boys in their Little League ball uniforms; teenagers playing football; older boys holding up large dead fish or sitting in speed boats grinning into the sun. No image of her husband existed. Our decorating tastes were antithetical, with Agnes's running toward pinks and frills while mine leaned toward wood or rough-textured burlaps and corduroys. Being in her apartment reminded me of home; every surface was covered by ornaments. I felt once again that I had to keep myself as narrow as possible or I would upset some valuable and appear clumsy.

Agnes was all smiles and solicitations, asking about my classes, my family, friends back home. The crunch came early: "And is there someone special back in Birmingham waiting for your letters and visits?" I knew she did not mean my mother or best friend, Jean. Agnes was fishing about the men, or more hopefully, the man in my life. My sparse "no" concerned her. What followed was a tortuous recital of the need for heterosexual bonds and most especially for children to "steady" us women and "give us a focus." I listened politely, noticing the wings of sweat fanning out under each arm of my blouse, wondering when I could go. April was waiting in my classroom, and we only had forty-five minutes until the student curfew bell sounded. I finally excused myself "to prepare my classes," but as I was opening the door, Agnes sidled over, put an arm around my shoulders, and assured me that I could tell her anything that was bothering me. Smiling weakly, I thanked her, saying nothing was troubling me. As I left, she said for the first time a sentence I was to hear often during the rest of that nightmarish year: "Toni, you'll understand all this better after you've had five sons." At the time I assumed she meant I would be fine if I were just like her, since that was the size and gender of her brood. More recently, I have wondered if she was admitting to some love for women in her own background, which she forcibly stamped out by producing a brace of boys.

In the months after that awkward tea, Agnes made me her project. Evenings found her skulking around my classroom, offering ever slimmer explanations for her presence. Suddenly my room became attractive to her, and she would burst in without even a soft knock, saying, "Oh, I was just up here [on the third floor] and thought I'd stop in your room for a view of the river." Cannon you could see from my window—the river, only in the dead of winter when all leaves were off the trees, and this was early November. When I became as cool as I dared, she backed off and convinced lonely students to spy on me. I bore Agnes very hard feelings for her infringements, probably displacing my own guilt about my earlier trick with the student informant. We were all caught in a web that necessarily comes to surround personal lies, secrets, and silence. The necessity for my relationship with April to remain hidden was bound to mean complicity, unseemliness, and base actions on all sides.

The most hurtful part of the dean of women's campaign was her determination to force me to see the ill effects my friendship was having on April. Always tall and thin, she had lost weight by spring, what with trying to live a regular student life and her clandestine one with me. The strain of juggling and lying showed, and I worried. Though I bought special treats that would help her gain weight, no amount of malted milks or candy did the trick. My lover simply began to look peaked by late March. Agnes noticed, of course, and thought she might reach me through April, since her more direct efforts were failing. I remember one especially grim interview where the only topic was: "Have you noticed, Toni, just how bad April looks?" As she listed the signs—loss of weight, circles under her eyes, increased cigarette consumption, jittery nerves and poor temper, inability to sleep well—I felt myself sinking under the sheer onslaught of data. I agreed to having noticed some of these symptoms but insisted that she had occasion to see April in more settings than I: "After all, Agnes, you're her dorm mother, and I am only her teacher." Both of us knew my comment was a particular lie.

After that dreadful scene, I had a long talk with April, trying to be sensible, saying that she was not the cheerful, happy person she had been in the fall. I suggested we stop meeting in the dark room. Flatly refusing to stay away and assuring me that she would cut down on cigarettes and get more sleep, my lover stuck it out until graduation day. We had talked in the final weeks of school about my coming to visit her in Georgia, where her family lived. Setting a date for the end of summer, we agreed to write twice a week and to call periodically.

Graduation arrived and all the parents and siblings of the seniors invaded campus. They brought trade to local motels and hotels but put a strain on the school's kitchen staff, who had to feed a couple hundred more mouths. I was anxious to meet April's parents; she had written them about her "keen English teacher," saying we had become friends outside class. They had responded either with positive remarks or neutrally, so I felt I had a good chance to be liked. Her father taught English literature at a southern university, and I assumed her mother would be like my mother's friends in the neighborhood and at church. I felt no qualms about conversing with either of them.

What I omitted from my fantasy was the extent of the rector's anger. As I would learn from Father Hyde, the rector felt it his duty to have a private chat with April's parents before they met me, telling them in unimaginable terms about my dire influence of their daughter, urging them to get her home as quickly as possible and to discourage further contact with me. Unaware of this interview, I approached the meeting with a strange eagerness. The academic dean did the honors, saying something very complimentary about me. I extended my hand to April's father, only to find it dangling in space for the first time in my life. I was shocked and crushed. Her mother was cooly polite in a way southern ladies are taught to be in awkward social situations. Only her little brother smiled. He had not attended the private meeting and so did not know I was a monster.

Excusing myself as quickly as possible, I fled to my third-floor room and wept bitterly. I drank too much that night with my friends in art and music, and left for home the next day depressed and fearful. I wrote April immediately, trying to be casual, hinting that maybe my summer would be too busy to get to Athens after all. I waited in agony for her reply, only to wish it had been longer in coming once I read it.

She wrote briefly and stiffly: "Thank you, Toni, for all you've been and done for me this past year. I really appreciate it and you a lot." Then came a brief paragraph that confirmed my sense that the entire note had been dictated by the man who had found it impossible even to touch me. "My father forbids me to receive or send any more letters to you under the circumstances. All my phone calls will be monitored, and I am to have no visitors from All Saints' this summer while I regain my health and color." It was signed, "Sincerely, April."

That letter was more devastating than the year of office run-ins with the rector because it seemed a betrayal of me and of the reason for our suffering. I spoke to no one about my pain and spent a lonely summer that ended in a six-week vacation with my mother, up the Atlantic seaboard to Washington, New York, Quebec, and the Gaspé Peninsula. Every day I thought of April and the warmth and closeness we had gone to such lengths to achieve and maintain. To have all that snatched away left me isolated and bereft. I would return to the school and its distinctly southern ghosts for a second year and be as coldly aloof from students as I had been accessible. I would be celibate because it was simpler than finding my passion only to have it denied me. Someone had slammed a heavy door in my face, and I did not want a repeat performance.

On the surface, my second year in Mississippi was quiet. I taught well, left my classroom when my last class was over, and retired to my room to read. I had been given space where only faculty lived; the doors had individual locks, and students were not welcome. The authorities allowed me in, ignoring their own waiting list, in hopes of "containing" me and keeping me away from "their girls." I was happy with the privacy; it helped me live a hermit's life fit for the pervert the rector's lectures, Agnes's condescension, and April's father's disgust had named me. I was best kept away from impressionable youth unless a literary text and a lot of distance lay between us.

All that year I continued to gain weight, to drink far more than I should, to stay up late grading endless student themes I had assigned to guarantee myself no free time. The art and music teachers and I continued our Friday night vigils at the local chicken emporium, but I concentrated more on the food and bourbon than I did on conversation. The one purely positive fact of this year was my confirmed sense of myself as a teacher. I loved my work, no matter what whirlwind of pain and confusion raged around me. I remembered my four months of practice teaching at the end of college. Working in the local high school, I discovered my gift for catching and holding students' attention. Refusing to wear high-heeled shoes ("After all, how else can the students distinguish between themselves and you?" our supervisor intoned), I found countless ways to stand out as the teacher. Even boys who generally booed when it was suggested they read Shakespeare came to my sessions prepared and eager to talk about why Brutus could not just feel good about killing Caesar or why Pip had to be brought to his senses after he comes into his inheritance. I was one of the lucky ones, as I would come to understand. Not only did I enjoy my work, but I had found it on my first try.

In the midst of my malaise, I met Harold, a senior at the local public high school. His English teacher asked me to tutor him in poetry and playwriting. He actually wanted to be a painter, so I was less helpful than his school had hoped.

He began coming over several afternoons a week to sit in my classroom, just as April had. Since his presence helped me to display an acceptable self, I left the door open for all to see. By the time I met him, I was lonely, so I also welcomed our time together, especially when we went to a movie on those rare occasions when something worth seeing played at the local picture show. He sketched me once in colored chalks, and I carried that drawing around for years. I must have figured in Harold's erotic fantasies because one night, under the porch chandelier, he leaned over to kiss me. I did not resist but rather thought, "I hope Agnes Crane and the rector are looking." While I may have used Harold, I also had great ambivalence toward him. Still confused and mute about my own sexual development, I was flattered by his attention. Finally, after all those years of trying to date, I seemed attractive to a boy. Part of me had always assumed I would marry and have children, so Harold's adolescent courting "fit" my expectations better than my previous year's underground passion with a woman. The fact that he was satisfied to hold hands, be affectionate, and occasionally kiss coincided with my need to give and receive warmth while avoiding sexual passion.

At the same time that this young man was drifting around the edges of my life, I was helpful if not friendly with the girls I taught. From verbal clues, I guessed that several had understood all that had happened the previous year and wanted to befriend me. Unable to tell them anything, I was distant with them. One senior in particular, Nella

Day, tried to talk with me after class about writing and poetry, but I snubbed her. She was very bright, lived in the Southwest with wealthy parents, and had scars on her face from too many x-ray treatments prescribed as an acne cure. I liked her and knew that I could depend on her.

Most of the students were willing to forgive and forget whatever feelings of neglect or jealousy they had harbored while I had ignored them for my lover. In fact, the senior class dedicated the school annual to me over the fierce objections of the rector and Agnes. It must have galled them to have someone they considered a pervert honored in so public a manner. I cried when the students presented the first copy to me at assembly and marveled when many parents expressed appreciation for my insistence that their daughters work hard and for my belief in their abilities and creativity. In particular, Nella's father thanked me effusively, inviting me to visit if I could get away during the summer. The contrast with the previous year was startling.

As I packed to leave my first job, a knock came at my door. I opened it and found Nella standing somewhat shyly outside, asking, "May I come in and say goodbye, Miss McNaron?" After some standard remarks, she said she hoped I would accept her father's invitation. I held out my hand to shake hers only to have her smile and embrace me. That summer we wrote every other day and talked several times by long distance. At the end of August, I went to the Southwest on my way to Wisconsin from Alabama over loud protests from my mother that it was miles out of the way. I knew Nella and I would become lovers during my visit.

She was a good choice because she was open about her love of women and because she obviously relished her body and my own. I first heard the word "lesbian" from her. Before that, I had known only what I felt and understood that society deemed it wrong. We sustained our relationship over the next two years, while I went to graduate school in Madison and she attended a good university in Texas. The day my doctoral prelims were over, I got into a friend's old Nash Rambler and drove nonstop to see her. I stayed near campus, visited a few English classes and met her professors, toured her dormitory. The rest of the time we made happy and continuous love in my motel room.

As I was about to leave, Nella shyly told me that April had gone to school at her father's university under his watchful eye, been selected sweetheart of some fraternity, became engaged to the captain of the football team. That was the last I ever heard of my first lover.

I paid a second visit to Nella at her home. It was financed by her father who insisted that I accept his help since I was on a meager fellowship. Wanting very much to see my lover, I accepted this bizarre offer. The visit went along without incident until one morning when Nella, her younger sister, and their mother decided to motor to the nearest town to shop for clothes. Not included in this outing, I planned to read Tennyson for my next week's classes. Mr. Day (K. C., as he insisted I call him) asked me to lunch at his dining club, where women could come only as guests of the all-male membership. But before we went to that club for elegant plates of chicken salad, fruit slices, and a parfait, he tried to have intercourse with me.

Feeling the specialness of the occasion, I had dressed in my nicest dark blue skirt with a blouse embroidered along the neck and sleeves. When K. C. pulled into his drive before lunch, I gathered up my gloves and purse, eager to be escorted to so fine a place by so fine a man. But once inside, he wanted us to chat a bit, since his reservation was not for forty-five more minutes and it took only ten to drive to the club. He went into his daughter's bedroom, motioning me after him. Standing too close to me, K. C. suddenly drew me into an awkward embrace, and I felt the pressure of his big hands urging my body backward toward one of the twin beds. Feeling simultaneously terrified and safe in his strength, I offered no struggle. After considerable fumbling with my clothes, he moaned, "Let me put it in." I refused, and he did not force me; he settled for rubbing my vagina with his fingers. After what seemed an interminable period, he stood up so I could get off the bed and arrange myself. He had never even taken off his lightweight summer jacket or loosened his tie.

What I remember most clearly is how red K. C. got and how deeply his breath came and how much hoarser his voice was than usual. Stunned, I had let him fondle me. Part of me even thought I had achieved some new level of acceptability if a mature man was attracted to me. If he comprehended the relationship between Nella and me, part of the price of his acceptance was granting him this seamy favor. When we were both presentable, he drove us to his club where I met several of his cronies. He felt no need to tell me to keep our secret since he assumed I would never mention the incident. I never spoke of it, indeed stopped remembering it until about ten years ago, when, listening to a woman talk about her uncle's sexual abuse of her, I suddenly was propelled back to that morning, full of shame and rage.

Nella and I separated before she graduated from college. I lost track of her until recently, when I located her in a nearby midwestern city, living with her successful doctor husband and their one biological and two adopted children. Children had been the stumbling block to continuing our relationship: she desperately wanted them. She preferred women for her emotional and sexual pleasure, but being a mother seemed more important than either of these. So we parted, and she found a kind man with whom to live out her life. Once, in about 1984, we saw each other briefly when she and her husband were in Minneapolis for a medical convention. After a strained but civil lunch and before a tour of my house, Nella asked me somewhat cryptically if being with women was "enough," if I might not be "lonely."

# *Advanced Studies*

*A*fter a long, solitary drive north in my second Volkswagen, forest green this time and packed to the roof, I arrived in Madison bone weary. My blind date and old friend from Tuscaloosa, Joe Wheatley, miraculously was getting his Ph.D. at Wisconsin and had eagerly agreed to ease me into the local culture. When he met me, however, it was with changed plans—he could not host me around town that first weekend because he needed to drive to Mundelein, Illinois, where his lover taught high school. I was to stay at his apartment while I found one of my own; I knew no one else. Not wanting to abandon me completely, Joe had asked a good friend to stand in for him. So it was that I met Barry, a short, fiesty man who held radical political and literary ideas and had small tolerance for those who did not.

Barry offered to take me to some of the local beer gardens on State Street, the heart of the student quarter. Grateful for companionship, I quickly agreed. At about eight o'clock we set out on what would be an amazing evening. At our second stop, I had barely accustomed my eyes to the near total darkness when I saw a sight that stopped me in my liberal tracks. Seated at the bar was a couple: she was white; he was unmistakably black. My expression must have given me away because Barry touched my elbow and said, "So what's up, Toni? You look like you saw a ghost."

The ghost was from my southern background. While no one in my immediate family had ever railed against mixed-race dating or couples, the very air I had breathed for twenty-four years had been fouled with that nameless terror, "miscegenation." I thought I had rid myself of my racist roots by speaking positively about Dr. King, by loving Josephine dearly, and by driving north. "I've never seen a mixed-race couple, Barry, and it's just a shock, I can't help it." I could not say more since opening my mouth to say anything made it clear that I was about to be nauseated; instead I rushed to the ladies' room.

Before that evening was over, I had drunk a lot of Wisconsin beer and told a comparative stranger my feelings about the South—all negative. Several times I had to say the word "Negro," since we were talking about black–white relations and "black" had not entered our vocabularies. Barry told me toward the end of our talk that I had to do something about my pronunciation. Defensively, I snapped, "But I'm very careful to say 'nigra' as my mother taught me—she forbade me as a young child ever to say 'nigger'—it would have hurt our maid's feelings."

Patient for one of the few times in my experience of him, Barry informed me that in the North, people who wanted to be understood as antiracist said "negro"; if anyone at the university heard me say "nigra," they would brand me a redneck bigot whose father probably belonged to the KKK. For the next few days I practiced in front of a mirror making my mouth form the longest "e" imaginable. By the time I was in conversation with other graduate students, I had mastered the magic vowel that could save me from disgrace.

Though I continued to see black students on campus, none ever took graduate English classes with me or was in my freshman comp courses. Gradually I learned that many of the dark faces were African, exotic and therefore less threatening to the status quo than American Negroes. Eventually I understood that my discipline would be one of the last places such students would ever risk being found, since "correct English" was a weapon used against them. Moreover, in my three years of doctoral study, I was never asked to read any literature by black writers.

Going to Madison, Wisconsin, had felt like a deliverance from things southern. I had received chamber of commerce materials that included proud statements about the city's history of liberal politics. Brochures boasted a wide variety of persons at the university (40 percent from foreign countries) and a metropolitan atmosphere without any metropolitan problems. Progressive schools nurtured the whole child, and Jews and Christians had a long tradition of working together harmoniously. One sentence even went so far as to advertise Madison businesses as refusing to discriminate on the basis of race, creed, color, or religious affiliation.

I arrived in this shiny place in early September, 1961, and, following an old custom, bought a newspaper. Madison was in the midst of a full-scale housing war. Blacks were moving into posh neighborhoods, and residents were up in arms—the very same arms I had seen so often back home, never mind if the objections were phrased in multisyllabic, polite terms. Hired counsel for the white residents had drafted a petition delaying the integration of residential areas until more studies could be conducted to show the impact on children and real estate values. Midwestern rhetoric was opaque rather than inflammatory, but I still felt tricked. Madison did not want "coloreds" in their parks or restaurants or libraries, but having let them into those places, they were up against a wall of their own making. From such a vantage point, these liberal midwesterners looked sadly familiar.

During the years I studied there, I was putting down new roots in a part of the country that would become my second home. I tried to have friends my own age, something that was quite foreign and not a little scary. Also, I used those three years to weigh men and women in terms of my own sexual direction. By the time I left, I had moved away from marriage fantasies and into a life centered around women.

Like most graduate students in English, I read late into the night after spending evenings in some part of the library stacks. I wrote endless short reviews of critical articles, did longer papers at the end of each semester, and took what seemed interminable tests staged every three weeks or so throughout the year. Recreation often centered around bratwurst and beer, the cheapest way to eat and drink out. I even remember going to St. Patrick's Day parties where genuine green beer was ladled from the bathtub of our Boston Catholic hosts.

Unlike most of my peers, I still attended church. In fact, the only other friends who did so were the Roman Catholics among us for whom Mass was still important. I found a small Episcopal church within walking distance of my apartment, where not only was there Communion every Sunday but each Wednesday at seven in the morning, and every day during Lent. Going to all these services, I quickly discovered that I had found a so-called "high" church, where the only real difference between us and the Catholics seemed to be obedience to the Pope.

My love for ritual was so satisfied that in gratitude I taught an adolescent Sunday school class. Though we seldom read the Bible, we talked a lot about situation ethics and how to be both moral and sexual.

They seemed to like me, and the class grew from three or four a week to an unprecedented ten. In addition to the usual flowers and candles, this church was permeated with the faint odor of incense, used for early morning Communion on Wednesdays and for high holy days like Ash Wednesday and All Souls'.

The priest preferred to be called "Father" and was known to hear confession without the anonymity of a closed booth. When I later learned that the good father was sexually involved with two of my friends, I tried valiantly to reconcile this behavior with his extreme piety. Failing, I shrank from the church altogether, attending only on Sundays and occasionally during Lent. But I stayed with my class of teenagers until the year was over, thinking they were the least appropriate target of my anger at this man's hypocrisy and misuse of position.

I loved taking classes in a great sprawling building on top of a steep hill. By the second week of school I understood that Bascom Hall was the locus of campus agitation. Protests in front of "my" building occurred at least weekly. Graduate teaching assistants protested their treatment at the hands of tenured faculty and organized a union; undergraduates picketed over everything from poor dorm food to the Bay of Pigs invasion; we all attended rallies decrying the U.S. military presence in far-flung places.

But the single event that brought out almost the entire university and caused classes to be cancelled was the assassination of John F. Kennedy. It was about 4:30 P.M., and I was at Cecil's Shoe Shop. Cecil was a fixture around campus, beloved by me for welcoming me to his shop and talking to me when I felt lonely. At least twice a month, he insisted on taking me to breakfast at the local diner; on Saturdays when he went fishing, I minded the store. Each spring, Cecil brought me morels from a special woods known only to him.

This particular November afternoon, we were listening to a country western music station while we talked leisurely. Suddenly the program was interrupted by a man speaking in a shaky, frightened voice: "The president is down! The president is down! We don't know more, but he's been shot in the head in Dallas. Oh, no; oh, no; oh, no ..." Cecil and I looked at each other, too stunned to speak. We stayed by the radio, silent, waiting for more news. The next comment was the final one, "John F. Kennedy is dead; our president is dead from an assassin's bullet in Texas."

I wandered around back onto campus, eyes unwilling to focus and head beating. When I passed other students and faculty whom I recognized, we had absolutely nothing to say. No one seemed to know what to do, so we gravitated toward Bascom Hall. A priest had been pressed into service and was conducting a silent vigil for Kennedy's soul. I had no qualms about his soul but was terribly worried about the country's and felt sick within my own. We stood around even when it began to drizzle, reluctant to leave the cold comfort of the group.

Next morning I went to a friend's to watch the funeral. All day I sat frozen, staring at the black-and-white images proving that the first public figure about whom I had ever felt passionately was gone from my life—vanished as surely as all the private ones before him. At lunch and dinner time, I put sandwiches into my mouth and drank tea or strong ale; I left the screen only to go to the bathroom.

For the rest of that week, no one went to class, and no one cared that we didn't. The faculty was probably relieved not to have to go on with business as usual, since most were liberal Democrats. I called my mother long distance, and we quietly cried together for a long time. I drank too much beer and ate too little food. I avoided Cecil's Shoe Shop, unwilling to stand in the space where the horrible announcement had found me.

Though Wisconsin's undergraduates had energy to protest outside the English building, they seldom wanted to take risks inside. Many of the students I taught had come from secure upper middle-class homes, lived in expensive dorms, and were preparing themselves to be medium-range executives or their wives. I was used to students who worked long and hard, who inquired about everything literary. Most of my freshmen wanted to do the least possible to get by. But then, so did I, since my primary purpose for being at Wisconsin was to get the ticket necessary for admission to the professoriate. I taught with only half a heart, though I taught well enough by everyone's standards.

All freshmen composition instructors were required to teach the same novels—one year it was *Barchester Towers,* hardly exciting fare for eighteen year olds; the next, *The Forsythe Saga.* Try as I might, I could not make my students care about dotty country parsons and their female relatives or generational development and intrigue, even when they involved money and power. My self-styled blasé radicals were bored to tears.

In addition to teaching the same literary texts, we were supposed to use standard handouts on construction and grammar as we molded better expository prose writers. I can still remember those handouts, carefully prepared by the woman who ran the program: printed on variously colored paper, they seemed deadly dull to me. One series, on a washed-out blue background, had a string of statements in each of which was embedded some syntactical or grammatical error. In the exercise, students were to spot the mistake and revise the sentence accordingly. Sometimes, I did not know what the mistake was; other times, it seemed so obvious as to be insulting. The worst aspect was the content: not quite at the "See Spot run" level, it was certainly no more advanced than eighth grade. Not only were my freshmen self-styled radicals, they were also self-styled chic. My blue sheets were sure to evoke their scorn.

In a gesture partly of defiance and largely of desperation, I said as I distributed the sheets: "I have to hand these out. Use them as scratch paper if you like." Though I gained some small degree of credibility with my classes, I went around for the next week in utter dread that the program director would find out and call me in on charges of insubordination.

If my life as a freshman composition teacher was less than successful, my world as a student made up for that. I had chosen Wisconsin because of the presence in the English department of a woman named Helen C. (for Constance, one of the dearest New England virtues) White. Miss White had an international reputation for her work in medieval and seventeenth-century literature, and I wanted to write a dissertation on John Donne. When I was accepted into the graduate program, I was ecstatic: not only could I flee the South, I could work with my academic hero.

My first semester, I enrolled in three classes and taught two sections of freshman English with fifty attendant weekly themes to grade. Finally I was in a learning situation in which I had to perform at levels not automatically easy; the pressure excited me. I was determined to prove to the university registrar that my southern A's were genuine. In my acceptance letter, he had written: "Though your record at the University of Alabama is excellent, 'A's' from southern colleges are viewed as 'B's' until you demonstrate that you can receive the same marks at Wisconsin." Though I slept very little that term, I made all A's and was never late in handing back freshmen themes.

Miss White herself taught the graduate lecture course on metaphysical poetry. Twice a week, I sat spellbound as this six-foot plus, large-boned woman dressed invariably in purple burst upon the lecture hall and opened her file folder. As she spoke with knowledge and passion, interweaving lines from poems with facts and anecdotes about the various poets' lives, informing everything with stunning critical insight, I hardly breathed. When the lecture was over, she closed her file folder with certainty, smiled benignly, and strode out as if she knew she had just given a stellar performance. So completely did the work of the metaphysicals enter my consciousness that I once actually went out onto the mall after reading Andrew Marvell's garden poems and embraced a tree. Later, when I discovered Henry Vaughan's mysticism, I convinced myself that I too had seen "eternity the other night like a ring of pure and endless light." Richard Crashaw's extravagant stanzas seemed a bit too baroque for my taste, though I valued his insistence that his relationship to God be erotic like St. Teresa's. John Donne and George Herbert won my heart. Donne knew sin intimately and treasured love above almost everything; Herbert's simple faith caused him to worry about usurping God's role by creating lyrics even if they glorified the deity—a conflict I found terribly moving.

On the first day of Metaphysical Poetry, Miss White said that different forms of literature were classified into something that started with a "g." No one at Alabama or Vanderbilt had ever spoken that word; I puzzled over whether it might just be a northernism. Unable to spell whatever Miss White had said, I wrote in my notes what I thought resembled its sound; that night I spent a very long time with my dictionary until I found "genre." Though this was an extreme case, I often encountered totally new concepts that stirred me to know more. *Hermeticism* was one such term, and I was greatly disappointed when Miss White leaned over the podium and said, I was sure only to me, "Now, students, don't ever toy with hermeticism—either embrace it entirely or leave it alone—it can be dangerously attractive to the dabbler." It was not until a few years later, when I first taught Marlowe's *Dr. Faustus,* that I more fully understood what she had been cautioning. But, loyal to her every word, I did not pursue the hermeticists.

Miraculously, since she had her pick of each year's graduate class, Miss White agreed to be my dissertation advisor. Her exact words were, "Now, Miss McNaron, you have already been out in the profession as a teacher. I want you to finish your dissertation and leave school just as quickly as you can. That will be my main goal in looking over what you write—to help you become your own mistress." Good advice, though I frequently longed for fuller commentary on my chapters.

I wrote on John Donne's sermons—all 170 of them. After using the library's copy of volume 1, it became clear that if I were going to complete my project I would have to own my own books. There were seven large volumes, costing over thirty dollars each in 1963. My dissertation fellowship barely paid for food and the rent on my apartment, the entrance to which was from an alley later named Clymer Place. I wrote a pleading letter to the publishers, outlining my straits and asking for the privilege of paying small amounts over many months. It was the sixties and they agreed, sending me all seven tan volumes with gold lettering on the spines. When they arrived, I promptly installed them on my primary bookshelf and began making copious pencil marginalia.

The professor who touched me most deeply, after Miss White of course, was Alvin Whitley, expert in romantic poetry and vintage sherry. Because my M.A. had been on Keats, I was deemed "prepared" in the Romantics and hence barred from his courses. But I visited on the days he talked about the odes, and I was sure that he identified completely with the melancholy young genius, that he believed his life was equally doomed and so had remarkable insights into the meaning of the works. Whenever I read or teach the odes, I still picture Alvin standing in front of us in his black three-piece buttoned-down suit. With the slightest lisp, he delivered piercing truths about these great poems.

He could also be piercing about undergraduate frivolity. On one occasion, a young man came into lecture late—something sure to infuriate Alvin. Rather than taking an empty seat in the front row, the student crept up the risers to the row in which his assigned seat was located. As he was sitting down, somehow the change in his pants pocket began falling out. Coins clattered onto the wooden floor, and several rolled loudly down steps until they finally stopped, one of them almost at Alvin's feet. He had stood utterly still during this excruciating scene and when the last copper was silent, he looked up at the devastated young man, smiled a lethal smile, and said, "Bring your tambourine?"

When I heard that he had come to my rescue during the evaluation of my doctoral preliminary examination, I was deeply touched. I did not quite pass the eighteenth-century exam. No wonder, since I found that material the least stimulating of any for which I was responsible, and since I had not understood one of the two questions asked. As a reader of the nineteenth-century exams, Whitley knew my performance there. When the readers met to assign final marks, my failure was reported. In a conversation with the reader of the medieval essays, Alvin had learned that mine was perhaps the best of the lot. He argued that my excellence in his century, together with my extraordinary comprehension of the middle ages, should offset my weaker handling of Pope, Swift, Fielding, and epistemology. The committee bowed to his suggestion and gave me a low pass for the entire exam, requiring no retakes. Because I knew all this from a confidential source, I never was able to thank Alvin.

The other men who taught me seemed trapped by something I could neither see nor comprehend. One paced from one edge of the podium to the other throughout every lecture on the early moderns. Another had never quite adjusted to civilian life after having served as a major in World War II. A third sweated profusely from a bad case of alcoholism. The only happy one was my Anglo-Saxon teacher. Newly from Harvard, he had bushy red hair and a tall chunky body, reminding me of an oversized teddy bear. I caught his enthusiasm for Anglo-Saxon poetry and culture, feeling that if I had taken my *Beowulf* requirement sooner, I might never have made it into the seventeenth century.

Though Wisconsin's English department had several distinguished male professors, it boasted a troika of powerful women at a time when most universities employed them primarily as secretaries. Miss White was one; the other two were Madeline Doran (authority on Shakespeare and Renaissance poetry) and Ruth Wallerstein (giant in late seventeenth-century prose and poetry). Several years before my arrival, Miss Wallerstein had been driving her sports car in the Alps when she had a fatal accident. Rumors had it that she may have intended that accident because a great romance (with another woman, we constantly wondered?) was ending. Miss Doran had flown to the scene to claim the body since no one had been with her, and there seemed to be no available kin. Miss Wallerstein's presence hovered over the other two grand dames, and she came into their conversation often. When either Miss Doran or Miss White spoke of her, their tone of voice sank to a lower, more intimate level. Though they never called her "Ruth" in front of us, their devotion was obvious and marvelous to witness.

Miss Doran was about ten years younger than Miss White and a sterner presence altogether. Shorter by several inches, she had dark hair with gray wisps at the temples. She wore it pulled back severely from her face. Her eyes, also dark, drove into you until they turned away in some kind of animal terror, like a startled deer or a rabbit caught in headlights. Her style of dress was tailored and fairly drab—the antithesis of Miss White's marvelous shades of purple, lavender, and pink.

Though I shied away from Miss Doran's Shakespeare seminar, I sought her out for readings of Sidney and Spenser as I began preparing for my Renaissance prelim. Her office walls were wrapped in books, many old velum volumes of secondary and tertiary figures from the sixteenth century. Beside her large wooden desk and her own chair on rollers was one straight-backed chair placed for the student lucky or brazen enough to get beyond the door. Miss Doran led an almost reclusive life in a little house located on the grounds of the university arboretum. She was a passionate bird watcher who reputedly arose at dawn to station herself with binoculars on her secluded deck, waiting for the day's parade of winged creatures.

Like Miss Wallerstein, Madeline Doran was also supposed to have had a great and failed romance, the gender of the other party remaining a subject of speculation. By the time I knew her, she was well insulated from students, seeing only such long-time associates as Miss White and a sweet beanpole of a man working in the late middle ages. Several of us latched onto a story that she and Miss Wallerstein had been close and that after the alpine catastrophe, Miss Doran had sunk into a personal decline.

My visits to her office had an intensity that fairly seared my nerve ends. I would go in timidly with my question about *The Faerie Queene* or *Arcadia;* Miss Doran would begin responding with total concentration on the question and me. As she talked, she inched her chair ever closer to my face until by the end of some exposition she might be within a foot of me. Suddenly, she would return from somewhere purely intellectual, realize her proximity, and literally wheel herself back to her side of the room, making clear as she went that further exchange was unthinkable. Sensing her discomfort, I would hastily end the interview, leaving her with tiny beads of sweat on her upper lip and forehead—beads that reminded me of Christ's agony in the garden of Gethsemane. Like him, Miss Doran was struggling with some phantom capable of diverting her from her determined purpose.

In my last weeks in Madison, before going to the University of Minnesota where I had accepted an assistant professorship, an extraordinary event occurred—Miss Doran invited me to lunch at one of the several Italian eateries on State Street. She had a small antipasto salad but insisted that I get some of the splendid spaghetti for which the restaurant was famous. We talked awkwardly during the meal, since I certainly felt it inappropriate to ask her anything, and she shied away from personal inquiries. Most of our comments ran to birds and flowers—safer subjects than ourselves. Just as she was figuring out the tip, she looked up at me with her startled deer eyes and said so quickly I almost missed some of the words: "Toni, when you arrive at Minnesota be careful, don't try to change the system; it's like a broad brick wall, and if you do, you will only hurt your head." Before I could respond, she had scooped up the check and was fleeing the cool, darkened interior for the brightness of a late May afternoon on the pavement.

Many times during my first years in Minneapolis, I recalled those urgent statements. I knew there was a personal story behind them that I would never hear. I also knew she was profoundly right since my increasingly frantic efforts to change the structure and workings of my department, college, and the larger university were leaving me depleted and lonely, often with a headache that I numbed with generous quantities of bourbon.

When Miss Doran retired, she spent time in California with her ailing mother; when her mother died, Miss Doran spent time in her retreat house with uninterrupted bird watching. At some point, she published a book of nature essays reminiscent of Loren Eisley. When I read them, I wept for the wasted passion in her life. Some human being could have been made joyous in the aura of Madeline's magnanimity. No wonder her lectures about the concept of greatness of soul that flourished in Renaissance Italy and England moved us so. Like Alvin Whitley, she thoroughly identified with her subject, talking about herself the only way she knew how—in deep code and through someone else's text.

Miss Wallerstein was lost to me by death, and Miss Doran was largely absent, I thought, through her fear of what attachment might mean. But Miss White had a warmth and accessibility that quite amazed me. I decided the reason lay in her active spiritual life—she wrote novels (under a pseudonym) about such saintly figures as Francis of Assisi and had received the Roman Catholic church's award for outstanding service by a lay person. As I ferreted out how someone as worldly as she seemed could remain so devoted to a church whose doctrinal positions were far from her own, I comprehended something that proved invaluable: Helen White took from the church what she loved—the spirit of prayer, the example of Jesus, the sheer aesthetic glory of the liturgical calendar—and let the dogma go.

It took students very little time to figure out why she was nicknamed Purple Goddess. All her clothing was either purple or a color that went easily with it: flowered blouses in magentas, ochres, pale greens; entire dresses of soft lavender wool set off by a paisleyed scarf of red violet and navy; luscious purple skirt suits accompanied by spotless white blouses with Peter Pan collars. Once I steeled myself to ask why she seldom deviated from her color. Her reply missed the point of my question, perhaps intentionally: "Well, my dear, it's so much easier just to get out of bed and take something from the closet knowing it will match." I wanted information on why that particular color, not an argument from expediency. My own theory ran to one of two connotations: purple is the color associated with women-loving women; it is the color used in liturgical churches (and monarchical governments) to connote royalty. "Goddess" had been added because of her stature—she resembled an Amazon gliding from office to class to the ladies' room nearby.

I remember going into that ladies' room on one occasion and spotting Miss White's unmistakable black brogans in the stall next to me. I held my breath, excited to be so intimate. Rather than speaking through the partition (which would have been invasive and, besides, would have let her know that I was making a careful study of her footwear) or even hurrying with my own activity so that I could just happen to be washing my hands when she was, I sat very still and listened while she let herself out of her cubicle, ran water to wash her hands, pulled out and used a paper towel, perhaps touched her cornsilk white hair at its edges or arranged her clothing before meeting the public, pulled open the eternally squeaking door, and vanished.

Yes, I had a crush on Helen White. She was the most exotic woman I had ever seen off the silver screen. To come into such close and frequent contact with one's hero is usually not desirable; our need for giants demands distance. But I wanted ever more personal closeness and went to exorbitant lengths to get it. For instance, Miss White always walked up Bascom Hill on her way to work from her small apartment off State Street. After weeks of trial and error, I determined almost to the minute when she began her ascent. I began arriving at the beginning of the sidewalk precisely as she did, acting surprised to see her, falling into step beside her. I still can hear her even breathing as she took the long, slow incline deliberately, pausing midway to tell me about the architecture of the Law School or to show me the periwinkles as they progressed from glossy-leafed shoots to a luxurious ground cover full of tiny blue–violet blooms. Occasionally Miss White would give in to my repeated offers to carry something—two or three reference books from her library at home, a plastic bag housing her brogans for wear inside. (When it snowed, she wore short booties with the merest hint of a heel.) Once or twice I even carried her overnight bag, brought to work because she would taxi directly to the airport and fly away to speak at some conference or to a major university where she would consult with others of her rank and station, though I was convinced there were no such individuals.

The Purple Goddess protected her doctoral candidates from bureaucratic harm and other forms of academic harassment. One summer she found work for the not-as-bright husband of a brilliant woman working on the influence of things medieval on metaphysical poetry. Another summer she helped me stay in Madison by hiring me to alphabetize her library. Every morning I arrived at her apartment promptly at nine. It consisted of a smallish living room, a dining area used as a library/workroom, a tiny kitchen in which she ate breakfast, a tinier bathroom, and her rather large bedroom with its single bed always unmade. Some days I felt bold enough to make it, wash her dishes, bring in fresh flowers for the table—I fantasized being Helen's partner, taking care of the one who took care of so many of us. When I did these domestic things, I always got a little scribbled note in her miniature handwriting. I kept these tiny sheets for years, inflating them to the status of billets-doux, reading and rereading their few words of gratitude and warmth: "You're so sweet to tidy up"; "I prefer my bed made but am just too lazy to do it"; "My dear, you are too kind." A few mornings she left out crackers and a clean tea cup with a note to fix myself midmorning tea; once she prepared a light lunch of cheese slices and rounds of caraway bread, lovingly covered with waxed paper.

When all the books (literally hundreds) were in perfect alphabetical order within specified categories such as "medieval romances," "pre-Socratic philosophers," "Donne criticism," I could no longer prolong my visits to my idol's private quarters. On my last day, I cleaned the entire apartment. For her part, Miss White had left the last of a series of checks for more than my hours warranted. When I had protested early in the project, she had written feeble excuses: "Oh, my dear, I must have misread your figures"; "Oh, yes, well, we'll fix all that in the next check, won't we?" When it became clear that she had no intention of paying me what I had actually earned, I decided that she had probably invented the entire scheme to have a gracious way of giving me money. My suspicion was confirmed when I received a late night call two days after I had finished my work. It was the Purple Goddess saying, "Now, my dear, I'm so sorry to disturb you, but could you come over in the morning and find some books for me? You have my library in such wonderful order, I'm terribly afraid I can't locate what I need, being so disorganized as I am." In a flash I knew that the activity had been for my benefit not hers, that she would probably have to revise the order to find what she needed quickly.

We devotees endlessly speculated about why Miss White was "Miss." The more conventional among us were sure that her deep participation in Catholicism encouraged her to be a kind of secular nun. The more romantic believed she had probably had a "great love," and when he jilted her, she had shut off her sexual self, sublimating that energy into writing and teaching. Those of us who stood outside heterosexuality had a different version. If there had been a great love, it most certainly had been a she, perhaps even the elusive Ruth Wallerstein of the alpine car crash. My private fantasy was that sometime in her far distant past, Helen White had invested too heavily in some female graduate student who had then left her for career or husband or both. This story reflected well on me, since I fancied that Miss White felt some special bond with me. Certainly I would never forsake her if she would only speak the word to draw closer.

While I am relieved to say that the word never came, Helen White did save me on one crucial occasion. During the second year of my studies, just as I was formulating my dissertation topic, my mother became seriously ill. Under and between the lines of her letters, I heard her wishing me closer. More overtly, my sister told me Mamie's health was worsening, that Mamie missed me, that my absence was increasingly hard on Mamie's nerves. Bowing to a guilt I already felt for leaving home in the first place, I wrote that I was applying to graduate schools closer to Alabama so we could see each other more often. Since that process entailed getting letters of recommendation, I of course asked Miss White for one.

In no time I received a note from the departmental secretary asking me to make an appointment with Miss White at my earliest convenience. The minute I stepped into her inner office, I knew she was serious. After telling me she would be glad to write a strong letter, she sat quietly, pensively, indeed I even thought, sadly. Not daring to disturb her, I waited uncomfortably. Finally, she turned her swivel chair until she faced me and began telling me an autobiographical story. She was from Boston, one of four children (two girls, two boys), none of whom had ever married. She described her mother as the matriarch of the family and her father as rather shadowy. Gathering herself up in her chair, she came to the climax: "Well, my dear, there came a day when my father called me into his room and said, 'Helen, leave Boston now or you'll never get away and you'll end up like me.' I understood him to mean that all of us were so involved with Mother that, without a physical break, we would simply submerge ourselves. I left that fall and have thanked my father ever since. I could not have done what I have without his words. [There followed a long silence in which I watched her struggle with some complex range of emotions.] Toni [my heart leapt inside me, for she'd never called me by my name before—"Miss McNaron" or "my dear" had served], I've told you this because I fear for you now. You love your mother so very much, but if you say yes now, you may never say no. Of course, I'll do whatever you ask about your future."

When she finished, she sat staring out her window. The effort of sharing her life, even at this great remove, had obviously tired her. I think her silent response to her own words made as much impression on me as the words themselves. But I was not strong and that evening I phoned home to tell my mother and sister that I would come closer if it were necessary. My mother rose to the occasion: "Honey, I want you to stay there. My health is improving and I just know you will get far better instruction at Wisconsin than you could at the University of Texas or Colorado [places I had been tentatively accepted]. Now promise me you'll call them and cancel your application."

I made a feeble protest that I did not mind returning, which in turn let Mamie insist that I stay. We both saved some face. I hung up in tears of relief and sadness that my life was taking me further and further away from a woman whose love I both wanted and feared. As I sat on my bed across the one room of my apartment, looking at the decaled refrigerator, I remembered Miss White, gazing wistfully out her office window. That night I lay awake listening to the hum of that refrigerator, feeling grateful to my mother, who had decided that it was important for me to stay in Wisconsin without guilt.

During my last year there, I was freed from teaching by receiving a much-coveted dissertation fellowship. As Miss White had promised, she hurried me along with the writing: "You need to finish and go be an adult somewhere," she told me kindly. When the chapters came back with such brief comments as "Fine; keep going," I sometimes resented her pushing. When she did make a marginal note, I valued it far more than I might had she been more copious in her responses. My favorite came in her spidery hand on the first page of my second chapter: I had remarked that language could be used to mask as well as to reveal; she had written in the lightest pencil: "Very well put and wise too."

My last fall in Madison, Helen C. White asked me to accompany her to the local grocery late one afternoon as we both were leaving school. She had agreed for the umpteenth time to entertain a small group of honors freshmen at her apartment. Every year, this internationally famous scholar chatted with eighteen year olds while serving them cider and cookies. This year's crop was due in a few hours, and she had neither food nor drink.

Ecstatic, I assented, and we hurried down Bascom Hill to her place where she swapped her ancient leather briefcase for a large string bag she had picked up in Italy on her last visit to the Vatican. Once at the little grocery, she set about with dispatch, and in no time had three boxes of mixed cookies and two gallons of cider paid for and ready for transport. She put the bottles into the string bag first, then the more delicate cookie boxes, and turned to me: "Toni, my dear, can you just take one of the hoop handles and I'll take the other?" So I grabbed the left-most handle in my right hand, while the Purple Goddess took the other in her left, and we walked briskly up University Avenue the five blocks to her apartment. I was supremely happy to be so fully involved with her, even if in so mundane an activity. We said little but were drawn together as the evening closed around us. Once at her building, she took her bag in her own large hands, smiled warmly, murmured a good night, and slipped inside.

Though ostensibly working toward a Ph.D., I found myself plunged into a period of intense emotional growth. I struggled to form friendships with peers, fell seriously in love, and received my last marriage proposal. Having learned in Mississippi that I was neither a sexual nonentity nor a sexual failure, I could no longer pretend unconsciousness. My first job had also taught me how it felt to be rejected and in danger because of my erotic feelings. So crushes on Miss White or fantasies about Miss Doran were safer than having lunch with some woman in my James seminar toward whom I might develop an unmanageable attachment. I made easy connections with the men in my classes or with whom I shared an office. With women I maintained polite distance.

The men I gravitated toward were usually married or gay, hence less likely to have romantic expectations of me. The exception was Michael O'Hara, close friend of my favorite people, Jim and Mary Kilroy. I met Jim in a graduate course my first semester and soon he had invited me to dinner at their apartment. Mary was one of the sweetest people I had ever met, and we often saw each other for long talks over several cups of tea. When they had to rush to the hospital one predawn morning because their second child was insisting on making an appearance, I was the person they woke to come stay with their first.

To one of their dinners, they invited another friend, thinking we might like each other. Michael was a Catholic whose mother's family had come from Italy in the not-so-distant past. He was volatile and easily wounded. A bit shorter than I, he had beautiful dark brown eyes that looked out under heavy black brows. Opera and Victorian prose writers were his great passions, with good food and Boston University, where he had been an undergraduate, taking a close second. A worrier, on one occasion he ordered tickets for a famous string quartet a year in advance.

The four of us spent many slow hours over Italian dinners talking about God and literature. I felt secure and calm with Michael, not romantic, though I must have given my family to think that I did. In a letter written in response to my concern about possibly leaving Madison to be closer to Mamie, Betty wrote that she was so happy that I was in love with such a nice-sounding young man. I seem to have been worried that I would lose my last opportunity to find a husband I loved and made Michael central in letters because my relationship with him was "normal." What I needed most was someone with whom to talk about my increasing passion for an older woman at the university, about the confusion that was causing me. Betty assured me that other suitable men would present themselves since I was embarking upon an academic career that guaranteed interesting and sensitive colleagues. I was considering whether someone teaching at a major university could live with a woman lover and keep her job.

When it became clear that Michael was also misreading the time I spent with him and was thinking in terms of "our" future, I stayed awake calculating my options: I could marry him, have a pleasantly companionable life, and be safe and cared for; I could be honest and move more wholeheartedly into my lesbian self, even though that carried with it all manner of unforseeable troubles and punishments.

Trying to act differently from my past, I discussed this major decision and my dilemma with Joe Wheatley. Himself engaged in a closeted, commuter relationship, he talked about the futility of suppressing "homosexual leanings" if I had them. He cautioned me against using a man and marriage to buy social respectability, tempting though that was to many of "us."

Joe and Mary Kilroy were true friends through it all, exerting no pressure on me to fall into Michael's arms, although they would have liked nothing better than to be our witnesses at a quiet little ceremony at the local Catholic church. After a month of deliberation, I decided to tell the truth. This was rather ticklish, since Michael had never formally proposed, though we both knew he meant us to marry. He was disappointed and probably angry, and avoided me for a long time after our stilted conversation. Several years after we had both left Wisconsin, I heard he had married, and when next I saw him at our professional meetings, he seemed simultaneously uncomfortable introducing me to his wife and smug to have one to present. I wished him all success and meant it.

Nella and I had split up because she wanted children more than anything, and, in 1961, that was not possible within a lesbian relationship. After smarting under distinct feelings of inadequacy and remembering my contorted attempts to become my father's son, I had begun to adjust to single life. At the same time, I was falling in love with the most interesting and unusual woman I had ever known. We both were connected with the university, though in quite different capacities; we were separated in age by more than fifteen years; and she was still in her marriage. I simply did not care how complicated things were or might become; I was powerfully drawn to her. Not since I had played Liszt and Rachmaninoff had I been so absorbed. The fact that we had to be clandestine felt unfair to me, but the frustration was minor compared with the intimacy. This relationship had all the power of a fully realized attraction, but the seeds of its eventual doom were implicit in her reluctance to sever her marriage bonds—when we first became involved or many years later. To speak more specifically about our time would be self-indulgent, since she would wish fiercely to preserve anonymity; not to acknowledge her at all would be false to the overwhelming emotions I originally felt.

Though our eight years together were anything but placid or easy, I felt more alive and in touch with what I now understand to be my essential self than at any time in my life. I learned to appreciate the outdoors and the life of the mind as we drove out into the Wisconsin country, spent long weekends in northern Minnesota, and roughed it in the Pacific Northwest. Our conversations ranged from Elizabeth Bowen to Democratic politics, from which perennials could survive midwestern winters to how a kind god could allow children to die and countries to wage war.

Perhaps it is fair to say I grew up in my relationship with this woman. The process included betraying and feeling betrayed, a recognition of just how hard a virtue clarity can be; but it also affirmed me as a vital, physical person whose thoughts and desires could stimulate and please someone with remarkable faculties for self-exploration and engagement with the world.

Around the edges of these two intimacies, I developed a special friendship with a woman named Katherine, whom I met in a class. A graduating senior, she seemed far more worldly and self-reflective than I. As had been the case with my college roommate, Jean, so many years before, we began by liking the same British writers—Thomas Hardy and Wilfred Owen in this case. Gradually we formed a pattern that greatly pleased me: as soon as Professor Wiley, the pacer who grew progressively more caged during the semester, finished lecturing, Katherine and I went for tea. The longer we did that, the more I wanted to talk about other things, even ourselves. She met my interest with her own, and our friendship developed to a level of closeness that frightened me because I feared I would lose her as I had April. But I stayed put and waited.

As Katherine took me into her confidence about the man in her life, I became keenly aware that I never spoke about my sexuality. No one at Madison "knew" except Jim Stathis, and I planned to keep it that way. Now I felt this woman searching with her eyes and inviting through her trust. Dare I tell her who I was? Would she not vanish in disgust or at least retreat to the safety of war poets and the Wessex landscape?

While I was agonizing over whether to disclose, Katherine was introducing me to her old friend Jane, with whom I wound up sharing an apartment my second year in Madison. Always expecting the best from people, Jane was often disappointed but never lost heart. We lived together for a year in genuine amicability, splitting chores, shopping, cooking. She loved my southern grits and fried ham with red-eye gravy; my favorite was her English boiled dinner: big peeled potatoes, some cheap cut of beef, a few carrots, and a whole green cabbage simmered for hours in nothing but salt, pepper, and water.

When she and her fiancé married, I drove from Madison to Elmira, New York, taking them something far too expensive for my budget—a large Orrefors vase—but feeling glad for my sweet friend and her happiness.

One of Katherine's favorite things to do when Jane and I were roommates was to come over for supper and then fall into hours of deep talk at the end of which she'd be too tired and it would be too late to go home. She would then curl up on our couch and stay over for breakfast. Once while Jane was visiting her parents, Katherine proposed that we have one of our evenings. I assumed she meant just dinner and perhaps an abbreviated talk, since without Jane's presence, she would not choose to stay over.

After a dinner of fish bought on sale and delicately poached, steamed broccoli topped with warm mayonnaise, and fudge ripple ice cream with coffee and tea, we settled in the living room to discuss Buber's notions of I-Thou. About midnight, we were too bleary eyed to care about the distinction, and I suddenly blurted out, "Katherine, I've wanted to tell you something for a long time—I love women and can't seem to find men appealing anymore. I know it may be wrong to you with all your Christian background, but it's the truth."

Not waiting for her response, I began to pick up cups and fetch her jacket—it was March and evenings still got cool. Looking surprised and a little hurt, she said, "But, Toni, I always sleep over when we have these marathons; can't I do that now? And, besides, I can't just leave after the gift of your telling me about yourself—we have to talk, I want to know more, my 'Christian background' just makes me love you more for being so honest. Sit down and let's keep going."

Amazed at this acceptance from a heterosexual woman, I sat back down and cried. Katherine held me, which puzzled me even more: she was not afraid of physical contact even though she knew my deepest secret.

Knowing I was a lesbian seemed to let Katherine talk even more freely about her own love life—something I had not expected, since she was in love with a man. I had no understanding then that being specific about myself made it easier for her to do the same. We grew closer, and when she moved away to attend Union Seminary, I genuinely grieved. I gave her a hardback copy of one of her favorite theologians, and she gave me a delicate nightgown. Falling just below my knees, it was pale lavender with a scooped neckline edged by a tiny bead of lace. The card read, "For a dear woman who deserves all the softness she can find. I love you, Katherine."

I cried and cried over that nightgown. In 1958 when I had discovered my sexuality, all I knew about lesbians was that psychology books said we all wanted to be men. I did not want to be a man, but without any other ideas, I was no longer sure that I was a proper woman. By presenting me with that nightgown, Katherine affirmed that, in her imagination at least, woman and lesbian could be one. I had always worn either pajamas or longish t-shirts, believing diaphanous sleepwear was reserved for some other kind of woman. Though at first the gown crept up around my neck during the night and felt very sparse all the time, I slept in my gift with pride and curiosity.

Long after Katherine's gown was frayed at the edges, I persisted in wearing it. Then for years I used its fragments to dust my most precious possessions. Finally, the material melted into almost nothing, but the meaning remained intact. I had been seen, heard, and loved anyway—my healing had begun.

# *Alone*

$H$ow to love my mother without getting lost: I struggled with that dilemma from early childhood. My efforts at independence and privacy worked best when they took place out of Mamie's geographical sphere. Try as I might to define privacy at 5130 Holly Court, I invariably found myself drawn back into communal space where my mother held sway. Yet, from the moment I went the fifty miles away from Birmingham to Tuscaloosa, Mamie supported my movements further and further away, coping with whatever sense of loss she felt. So the final story is a complicated one.

It is too simple to say she wanted me to stay at home—of course, she did, but she also wanted what was best for me out of her great love for me. Letters frequently said something like, "Multiply how much you miss me by 100 and you may approximate (nearly) how much I miss you—but my love and my thoughts are with you constantly." On my birthday in 1960, she wrote:

> Waked up this morning at seven o'clock and thought of my baby, as I do every morning—But—this was a very special morning. At seven o'clock twenty-three years ago—you were born—I was filled with a sense of relief from pain—and a feeling of anxiety as to your welfare—*But* when they brought you to my bed—and told me that you were a *perfect* little girl—and put you in my arms—*my first contact with you,* so precious—so warm—and so completely dependent upon me—*that was pure delight!!!* You know what a joy you have been to me—I realize what wonderful daughters I have, and I am very grateful to you both—How could anyone who loves as deeply as I love my babies and is

loved as deeply as I know they love me—not believe in eternal love—and a Divine Being?

For my part, I wanted her approval at the very same time I wanted to be my own person. When I first went away from home to the University of Alabama, Mamie and I agreed to write one another every day, even if only a brief note. Most of the time I kept my part of the bargain, but when I did not, I got a frantic phone call from Fairfield asking if I was sick or tired of writing. I always assured Mamie I was just overwhelmed with schoolwork, avoiding the real issue—sometimes I did get tired of writing. Often I scratched off a hasty note late at night just to have something to put into an envelope. Looking back at some of her letters, I understand that she must have done the same: often I have a single sheet of relatively small paper, in her largest hand, telling me she is too tired or sick or busy really to write, but "just want to get a word off to my Baby before the day ends."

By the time I began my Ph.D. work, we had come to a tacit agreement that three letters a week were enough, though Mamie still commented if one was late. My correspondence must have been longer and more interesting at that time, because her letters are full of obvious replies to things I have initiated: discussions of movies, books, politics, the complexity and power of human relationships, and lots about spirituality. Though her poor health and worries about not being asked to do enough substitute teaching to earn the money she needed pepper this correspondence, for the most part my mother seems fully participatory in an inner life and in the world around her. She tells me of concerts attended, plays and movies seen, art galleries visited—all with a relish she seemed to have for new ideas as long as they occupied some public space and did not require direct changes in her daily life.

These letters are also full of cautionary notes about my hair, my finger picking, my long-term weight problem, my grammar and spelling, my general state.

Fall 1962: How is your hair? Rolling it? I had a topaz rinse put on mine and it looks lovely—not brassy—just "highlights."

Spring 1962: Gary, my poor, stupid little pupil—picks his fingers which reminded me of you. I'm afraid that your poor fingers have suffered during *this* [I was preparing for my German exam]

—Won't you use the Nivea and Band-aids? I'll be glad to pay for them—Don't think a *teacher* with *no fingers* would be very apt to acquire a good post. Really worry about your fingers—Understand (really I do) how nervous you are—but couldn't you develop *another* habit—not biting your mouth for Heaven's sake [I had done that until a doctor terrified me by telling me that if I persisted, I would have to have the sides of my mouth and perhaps my tongue removed]—that would *mutilate* something beside a part of your anatomy—Please try, honey . . . .

Fall 1962: All of the eating that you write about *must* be putting pounds to your already overweight body—Why don't you do without one meal a day—I know it is hard but I hate to see my lovely Toni gain *so much* weight. Please try—I am going on my starvation diet again—Want to get down to 139 before you come home for Christmas—think it is impossible but I shall try.

Spring 1963: (*Your* saying, darling) remember the gerund takes a possessive pronoun? [I must have used "you" in my previous letter].

Late winter 1958: "Pushed up" [I had used this phrase in a letter] is a very poor choice for an English major getting her Master's— and Watch your grammar—vocabulary—rhetoric—syntax— wish *we* were near to help with that—Your *knowledge* is remarkable—your perception—ability—keenness of mind—expression—ability to write—*but I do find fault/criticize/condemn/disparage/disapprove/lament* your grammar and rhetoric.

Spring 1962: Poor Easter eggs *died* instead of *dyed.*

Spring 1963: I *will* see, young lady, that you attend to your lovely teeth when I get there [written shortly before her visit to Madison the spring before she died]. Do you want to wear dentures? Makes me angry to think that I did everything and ate everything that would prenatally be of value to you and now you are *abusing* the very thing that I was and am concerned about—teeth . . . and *gums* (hate that word)—but your lovely soul and spirit, are a joy to behold.

Mamie's vigilance about my appearance often drove me away; I felt her concern as nagging and did everything possible to avoid certain subjects. I also eventually tried to avoid going home, since in her house I was under her rules. The summer after my first year in Madison, I went home for about a month. After a year truly on my own, I was not looking forward to resuming my place within the family; to protect myself, I militantly outlined what I had to do to pass my preliminary exams coming up the next March. "It's absolutely *imperative* that I cover everything in medieval and the Renaissance this summer or I'll never be ready by next March. That means rereading and making study notes on the most important of *The Canterbury Tales*, plus outlining Malory and 'Sir Gawain' and the Pearl poet. And that's just for the fourteenth century. Then I have everybody from Barnaby Goodge to Thomas Hooker to review for the sixteenth. So I just don't know how I'm going to be able to get it all done in time." Mamie agreed to my modest request to retire to study one hour in the morning and another in the afternoon, showering me with, "Oh, honey, I'm so proud of you; you're at such a triumphant point on your intellectual journey. I don't know anyone else's child who has done what you have." Just underneath this effusion, I felt her hurt and sense of neglect. She also wanted to say, I was sure, "Since you're home for so short a time, can't you just suspend study—after all, it's eight whole months till that test; can't you study on your time and not mine?"

I had long suffered from the oppressive heat of southern summers, finding it impossible even to read for more than about twenty minutes at a time because sweat ran down my legs and arms, and I stuck to whatever I sat on. Using this as a defense, I set up a study space in our basement. Most days, as my hour neared its conclusion, I would hear the upstairs door softly and slowly open. Determined to have my agreed-upon time, I would act as if I had not heard the squeaky hinges. In a minute or so, Mamie's footsteps would then ease down the first two or three steps. There would be a long pause, while I continued with my head bent studiously over one of my several outsized texts, and then she would say, "Toni, your study time's over and I won't see you again till Christmas; surely you don't begrudge this little time with me."

One of the most significant things my mother and I ever did together was to take that unique vacation, just the two of us, during the summer of 1959. I had finished my first year of teaching in Mississippi, where there had been nothing to spend money on but Friday night dinners and the one movie worth seeing that year—*A Room at the Top*. Since room, board, and laundry were included under my contract, I banked the majority of my salary. I proposed to Mamie a driving trip from Birmingham over to Atlanta and from there up the Atlantic seaboard to Williamsburg and Washington, D.C. After a week in New York, we would drive to Quebec City and then due east to the tip of French Canada, a place called Perce because it boasted a huge rock from which an arch had mysteriously fallen out during the late nineteenth century. A few miles out into the sea there was Bonaventura Island, home to thousands of ocean birds, even the elusive puffin. We would be away almost six weeks; I had never been alone for that long with my mother.

Williamsburg's reproductions of products and people from the revolutionary era bored me after the first hour of sauntering along falsely cobbled streets, and trying to drive around D.C.'s monuments and government buildings when I had never been near a freeway made me frantic. But New York was a sheer delight. My mother's enthusiasm for antique shops and Broadway plays knew no bounds. No inch of Seventh Avenue escaped our scrutiny, and we saw ten plays in seven days. We sat in the front row for *West Side Story*, and Mamie was enchanted by the young men dancing so close that their sweat fell from the stage into her lap. We seemed to understand the inside jokes at *The Tenth Man*, sat glued to our seats through electrifying performances of *Five-Finger Exercise* and *Toys in the Attic*. We even braved our way to the off off Broadway original production of Genet's *The Balcony*, staying afterwards to speak with the actors who came out from behind the arena stage to mix with the audience.

In Quebec I put us up at the Chateau Frontenac, paying exorbitantly for room service at breakfast, complete with a waiter who brushed off the tablecloth in between toast bites. Mamie relished every minute of our stay because it reminded her of her Selma girlhood with its grandeur and elegance.

In Perce, we relaxed. Absence of neon came as a welcome change from the Big City, and we walked on the beach for hours every day, picking up magic shells or just watching the tide creep up the sand toward our bare feet. If we felt energetic, we toured one or two of the ubiquitous shops displaying local artisans' work—images in every conceivable medium of seagulls, cormorants, puffins, and the big rock with the hole in its middle. Our hotel was a throwback to an earlier, more leisurely era—spacious rooms with huge bathtubs, a dining room with glass windows on all sides so no one missed the gorgeous view at any meal, a porch across the entire back facing the ocean and filled with outsized cane rocking chairs. Guests were assigned their own table for the duration of their stay, so Mamie and I got to know our waitress and were advised to wait and tip her after our last breakfast in the dining room. The food was primarily French: beautiful vegetables augmented by piquant sauces of mysterious composition; perfectly broiled and absolutely boneless fish; bread so crisp on the outside you could hardly get teeth through it to the still-warm softness of the middle. The desserts made even Mamie envious—giant éclairs with the least rubbery dough we had ever tasted; layer cakes whose fillings were sweet but not in an American saturated way; homemade sorbets and ice creams that soothed away any slight perturbation from the day.

One of the high points of our week in this place at the edge of the world was an afternoon trip out to the famous pierced rock and the bird sanctuary. Little boats motored small groups of tourists to within a few yards of the face so we could see bird nests and colonies. The trip out was leisurely enough and the display of bird life spectacular: miniature gulls nesting on ledges so narrow they seemed no ledges at all; bigger gulls with their young still screeching frantically for food; cormorants hanging onto sheer rock; even a puffin or two comically holding fish in their bills, just as on the postcards in every shop in town. As the boat swung around to head back to the dock, winds suddenly came up causing waves to spill over the edge of our tiny craft. A nonswimmer, I panicked, sure we would capsize any minute. The driver kept assuring us, "This is nothing, ladies and gentlemen, sit back and enjoy; we'll soon be tied up, snug as a Canadian bug." Before we reached such safety, our boat was half-full of sea water, and the helmsman looked more worried than not. Mamie seemed to love it, however, holding her hand out to catch the spray, licking her salty fingers, comforting me with words about our "seaworthy" boat and her superb skills in the ocean. That night we ate the speciality of the house, telling ourselves that we had earned it from our adventure on the high seas.

We both loved our time together, but when either of us talked with friends about this trip, we tended to recount the worst aspects. For Mamie, those were my getting lost trying to get out of Boston (and driving over the Mystic River Bridge five times until the man in the toll

booth recognized us) and her conviction that I wished I were somewhere else with someone different. My story involved asking for a
morning alone after our first night on the shore of the St. Lawrence
River en route to the Gaspé Peninsula. We had been together virtually
every moment, in hotel and motel rooms or my tiny Volkswagen bug.
I needed some breathing space. Though Mamie accepted my withdrawal, she subjected us both to a day or so of hurt silence. Perhaps
neither of us could acknowledge how wonderful it had been to sneak
away from responsibilities and stare at rows of serene gulls for hours
or eat French delicacies at every meal.

My motives for taking my mother on that trip were complex.
Having just completed a difficult first year of teaching, punctuated
most dramatically by my growing fear about what it meant that I
wanted to make love with women, I needed not to spend three months
sitting idle in Fairfield. But as much as I needed that movement, I was
led to propose our getaway from some deep sense of loneliness for my
mother. The facts are that my mother spent a great deal of time with
me when I was growing up and was extremely generous in giving me
things and opportunities that enriched my life tremendously. But I
always felt outside, that her relationship with her husband and first
daughter, my father and sister, overshadowed my chances for genuine intimacy. To "have her to myself" for six weeks seemed a rare and
important event, worth the inconveniences it might cost me.

The summer before she died, Mamie came to Madison with Betty.
She stayed with me in a friend's home; Betty audited a summer session
class and chose to live in a dormitory. For my part, I was trying to get
history courses out of the way quickly, so I had registered for two,
which proved an almost disastrous miscalculation. I introduced my
mother and sister to my friends who were uniformly charmed by
Mamie and impressed by Betty's verbal prowess and eclectic knowledge. Most afternoons, they sat at teas or elegant extended lunches at
one of Madison's luxury lakeside hotels, while I tried to cram pages of
information into my head before dinner time.

I could tell Mamie was not well because of glaring somatic and
psychosomatic symptoms. Several times while on shopping outings,
she was seized by attacks of bursitis or extreme shortness of breath,
forcing us to take her home or to a doctor. Partly out of a terror about
her health and partly from overexposure, I tried to deny the reality of
these "spells." After all, I had been coping with them since childhood

and knew that occasionally they were ploys, albeit unconscious, to get me to do what she wanted. Somewhere deep inside, however, I knew things were more serious this time, and I supported her trying to slow down Betty's desire to experience everything Madison had to offer in the way of culture.

Because of my own academic schedule, I felt mostly torn between wanting to show Mamie my world and needing to find a carrel in the library and study seventeenth-century English history. But we had long breakfasts in the usually cool summer mornings—tea and toast in front of my friend's huge picture window that opened on a beautiful garden. I also remember vividly my sudden fear the day we had all three walked up Bascom Hill so Mamie could see where the English department was. Once the tour was over, we were to walk back down, but her face told me we could not do that. It had turned ashen, her generous application of rouge notwithstanding. Little beads of sweat had popped out through the French powder on her forehead and upper lip, and her breathing had become labored. Betty seemed to be blocking out all these symptoms: was she even more afraid than I? I stepped in, "I'll just go get the car and pick ya'll up and we'll take Mamie right home to lie down and rest before dinner."

At the end of that summer, I drove back to Alabama with them in Betty's Volkswagen. We had planned to have lunch in Nashville with an old friend who was to meet us at a Holiday Inn on the outskirts of town. After a lively meal, as we were ordering dessert, Mamie announced she was having an attack and could not breathe. While Betty rushed to the reservations desk to get a room for the afternoon, I said hasty goodbyes to our friend and went in search of ginger ale. Sometimes, having that over shaved ice helped to calm Mamie's system enough for her to stop hyperventilating. After a few hours of utter quiet in a tightly curtained motel room, she felt better, so we set out at dusk and arrived in Birmingham by nine that evening.

I stayed home for the next week, watching Mamie switch from proposing we all go to a picture show to lying on her bed trying to catch her next breath. When she felt more herself, she lectured me about my susceptibility to my friends, my need for continual vigilance about food and finger picking, and my tendency to speed on the highway.

When I drove away from Holly Court in early September of 1963, waving gaily and expecting to return for another lavish Christmas celebration, I little thought that I would never see my mother again.

Late in the afternoon of December 12th, I had finished a seminar on John Donne, on whom I was beginning my dissertation. I was to spend that evening with my lover and was excited to get home and straighten my apartment. When I walked in the door, she was standing in my dining room, looking grim. I panicked that she had come to tell me it was off because her husband or employer or some other authority had found out and was threatening dire consequences. Before I could ask, she put her hands heavily on my shoulders, looked me hard in the eyes, and said all in one breath: "Betty called me at the office. Your mother's dead. I've made an airplane reservation for a six o'clock flight with a changeover in Chicago. I'll help you pack and drive you to the airport."

All I remember about that trip to Alabama is the changeover in Chicago. I was supposed to have an hour to get from one flight ramp to the other, but we were kept circling over the city interminably. Once in the airport, I had seven minutes to go up the terminal causeway, across the main circular building, and onto another causeway that would take me to the southerly routed planes. It was 1963, and I was in high heels, hose, and girdle. I was carrying a suitcase, overnight bag, and purse, but I ran harder and longer than I had since I used to race around my backyard until I dropped, my wild energy momentarily spent. Somewhere along the way, I became aware of pain in my hands from the weight of what I carried and pain in my feet from running in pointed-toed shoes. My chest hurt so badly and my breath was so short that I felt dizzy and nauseated. But I made my connection, amid various statements of concern from passengers, red caps, and stewardesses. I smiled weakly or thanked them, but spoke to no one, preferring to have three stiff bourbons and ginger ale with no dinner.

My carefully disguised drunkenness was met by Betty's obvious state of shock. I remember how ravaged she looked and my awkward attempts to comfort her. But she would have none of it, needing to stay in control as we drove to the funeral home. As we went, I asked her repeatedly to tell me how Mamie had died. My questions were met with silence, comments such as, "How can you ask me that now?" or sobbing. At the funeral parlor, I was outraged by the piped-in organ music playing maudlin tunes and the dark, flowerless hallways with their trapped gardenia scent. I think I saw the coffin then—closed, not to be opened—again denying me the physical reality of a parent's death.

Mamie's funeral was a replay of Daddy's. Betty fell apart; I held myself together on the surface and dealt with visitors, this time shielding my sister from all but the chosen few. Her husband was in Endicott, New York, learning about a new IBM machine. He arrived unmet at the airport several hours after I did. When he entered our living room, he burst into tears. He broke down again at the cemetery, where I sat dry eyed and stony, full of emptiness and guilt and a sense of final abandonment.

I flew out of Birmingham a few days after Mamie was lowered into the ground, returning to Madison and the care and comfort of my lover. Ten days after my mother's death, I repacked my bags and returned to Chicago for the annual meeting of the Modern Language Association. If I wanted employment that next fall, I had no choice but to endure the interviewing process. Still in shock from Mamie's death, I ran up and down the stairs of the Palmer House hardly aware of who or where I was, much less of what I was saying to questions that seemed too trivial to be endured. My head pounded without stopping during the entire three days, but some protective angel kept me from drinking, and I survived the seven interviews scheduled.

At the interview with the University of Minnesota, where I eventually took a job, Samuel Holt Monk, renowned scholar in eighteenth-century literature, revealed that he was from Selma, Alabama. Through a chain of questions that brought me close to fainting, he determined that he had thrown the *Selma Gazette* onto my mother's family's front porch when he was a little boy. Tears almost surfaced, but I was trying to appear professional and sophisticated. I pushed them back for the second time that month. It would be many years before I let them spill, before I even began to grieve my loss of this primary woman in my life.

# Part III

*Top right:* the author, 1990; *center left:* the author and Susan Cygnet, 1980; *bottom left:* the author and her sister, 1987. Courtesy of Toni McNaron.

# *Finding Self, Finding Words*

The next ten years bleed into one another like Madras cloth in the wash: one ten-week course after another in Shakespeare or Milton or English literature from *Beowulf* to Virginia Woolf with from thirty-five to sixty undergraduates; one passionate nine-month relationship after another with a woman ten to fifteen years younger than I; one evening or weekend after another full of too many bourbons and ginger ale or on the rocks.

On an external level, I accomplished a lot during this muddled decade: I won promotion to associate professor after only three years, billed as one of the bright new stars in Minnesota's crown; I won two competitive awards for outstanding teaching; I became one of the most sought after faculty to serve on policy-making committees. Efforts at writing were less than satisfactory, though I began many projects. The closest I came to publication was the acceptance of a book manuscript on Shakespeare's late romances in which I argued that forgiveness and continuing to live were more valued by the older bard than heroic deaths or the senselessly violent pursuit of vengeance. Mouton, a publisher in the Hague, liked it and was about to put it into press when their budget and my project were slashed. My severe depression over this catastrophe only deepened when I heard that one of my colleagues had probably written someone he knew at Mouton to sabotage my work by claiming it was actually the product of my graduate research assistant. Jack Daniels profitted enormously from this reversal, and my writer's block worsened.

Social psychologists are fond of hypothesizing the ill effects of precocity and perhaps that partially accounts for my slump. Certainly, I had sailed through school, college, and graduate school with assorted A's, fellowships, and awards. But it had only been partly a joke that I was best with children and stray animals: I was not adept at making human connections, and people my own age tended to silence me unless I had had several drinks.

As a new assistant professor, I was invited to dinners and cocktail parties held in the homes of older members of the English department. Unable to refuse and unable to take my lover to such gatherings because we had convinced ourselves that we had to live in one of the darkest closets imaginable, I hovered at the drink and food table hoping no one would try to make conversation with so obviously unsocial a being. Inevitably someone did.

"Well, Toni, and how are you finding Minneapolis/your students/the winter/our art galleries/the symphony/your neighborhood?"

"Oh, just fine, thank you," gulping my drink or sandwich in a frantic gesture to buy some time while I thought about what I could say next to the person trying so hard to set me at my ease. I certainly could not return the gambit, since whoever was in front of me had lived in the city for at least a decade.

"Are you making friends, meeting people, or are you lonely for someone special back in Madison?"

Utter panic. My "someone special" was at home studying the MMPI or Rorschach blots or theories of personality development and deviancy while we lived a life my conversational partner might well see as an example of the latter. So how was I to answer so innocuous a question? "No, I'm not meeting people—it takes all my spare time to manage my lies and secrecy, thank you."

Gradually, I began to refuse such invitations, preferring to stay home where I could drink uninterrupted. If I did go to a colleague's for dinner, the pattern was set: I arrived exactly at the appointed hour and either refused any predinner alcohol or sipped something tasteless. Once at dinner, I nursed a single glass of wine while other guests went for seconds and thirds without seeming to give it a thought. The moment dessert was over, I excused myself, offering class preparations or my habit of arising at 5:30 in the morning or a headache from a hard day at the office to my confused and at times irritated hostess. Back in the isolated safety of my apartment, I began to drink in earnest, drinking until I fell asleep or drifted into a blankness that passed for sleep.

By my early thirties, I certainly realized that I was in trouble with alcohol, though that realization made no difference either to my drinking or to my efforts to get help. I promised myself routinely that I would stop on the first of the next month or when the current bottle was used up, on New Year's Day or my birthday. Such promises and their attendant "wagons" lasted anywhere from a day to six months on those rare occasions when I was more frightened than usual about not being able to read as long as I once could or not being able to get letters of recommendation done on time or at all.

Working in the English department during the late sixties and early seventies was poles away from present conditions for incoming assistant professors. We taught three courses for each of three quarters, almost all of them different from one another. That meant that nine times a year I faced new students, strenuous preparations, hefty sets of mid-quarter exams, papers, and finals. We were expected to serve on at least two department committees a year, attend at least one professional conference, and somehow miraculously progress toward being famous scholars in our fields. The longer I escaped into alcohol and remained unable to speak about my personal life, the less well I did at any of this except classroom teaching. For some reason, the moment I entered one of the uniformly dingy spaces in which learning was to occur, I dropped my shyness, lost my fears of being apprehended as a criminal, and spoke—passionately and convincingly—about "The Wanderer," with whom I identified completely as he waked from his lovely dream of some good old days when he sat at his master's feet after having served him loyally to the cold reality of old age and loneliness, or about the Romantic and Victorian poets, who again appealed to my growing melancholia and *Weltschmertz*.

When anti-Vietnam protests reached my campus, I was one of the first faculty to participate. The students struck against a university with heavy investments in the Honeywell Corporation, which was busily making antipersonnel bombs just across town. Out of fierce sympathy, I held classes off campus, hauled my Milton students in my little red pick-up truck from one to another of their nearby apartments. We read *Areopatigica* and grasped censorship in a way not possible in previous quarters. When a graduate student friend and I were maced, I realized that there were all sorts of reasons the authorities might turn against their own—not just sexual difference—and understood coalition for perhaps the first time. Bob and I rushed into the nearest classroom building where other students stood at water fountains with wet cloths for burning eyes. Once we could see again, we decided to proceed as quickly as possible across the bridge that separated us from my parking ramp and the quiet of home. As we were about to go up the stairs leading to it, a large, angry policeman stopped us with, "Just where do you think you're going? Can't you see we've got a situation on our hands with these stupid kids rioting?" After I showed him my faculty identification card and assured him that Bob was my assistant and not a "stupid kid" even though he had very long hair, he grudgingly agreed to our passage. But when Bob put his left hand on the stair rail, the officer became suddenly incensed. In a split second, he brought down his billy club with full force just inches from my friend's hand. When I saw how close Bob had come to having his five fingers pulverized, I grasped just how furious certain Americans were at other Americans.

When students on the Kent State campus were fired at and killed, I marched with outraged students and faculty in Minnesota. When similar events occurred at Jackson State, I watched liberal colleagues straining to feel what had come so naturally when white students were attacked and killed. During this time, I renewed my acquaintance with the only black person I have known at all well since moving north. I had met Anna years before when she took a train from Mississippi to Minnesota to attend a community college where my lover worked as a counselor. She came to our apartment once for iced tea. Though we were all pretty stiff, she and I did talk about Mississippi and her grandmother. When she decided to transfer to the university, I was her initial contact, but we had not seen each other for some years.

A rally marking the deaths at Jackson State was held atop the steps and between the Doric columns of our large auditorium. It turned out that Anna and I were both scheduled to speak: I to demand action from the university about another academic assault; she to demand action from whites. I was cynical, and Anna was bitter. While an assistant vice-president for student affairs was droning on, we made rather loud fun of him from the sidelines. When he tried using black language, Anna and I broke out laughing. For the next few minutes, we talked urgently about what it meant that we had both grown up in the South. We acknowledged that for the moment we were closer to each other than to white or black northerners; we shared a common culture and language even if we were on utterly different sides of southern tracks. That scene on the stoa of Northrup Auditorium remains incandescent in my memory, though my bone-deep racism continues to haunt me.

In 1983 my partner and I were vacationing in London. Friends had told us to be sure to visit the public baths near our flat, assuring us that they were antithetical to their American namesakes. We made appointments for "Ladies Day" and had a two-hour adventure in water and steam heat. My only anxiety turned around the significant numbers of black women who were also there. I had never seen a black woman naked and kept catching myself staring at their bodies. Swinging from amusement at my own fascination to awkward embarrassment, I especially recall an older woman, wiry and strong, with salt and pepper hair on her head, under her arms, and at her pudendum. She talked with us as if we were just some more people at the baths: "Oh, it's just so invigorating to go quickly from the sauna to this cold water. I jump in all at once and swim to feel the most tingling possible. You must try it, really." Other black women advised us about which saunas were the best temperature that day, where it was safe for us to put our towels, and how to sign up for a marvelously nurturing soap massage during which whole buckets of tepid water were thrown over one's back. No whites spoke to us. I was drawn to and afraid of black women up close, unable to relax in their presence, unable to imagine caressing or being caressed by them without feeling either too excited at breaking a taboo or just a little squeamish. Later I admitted to myself that I would have deep trouble making love to a black woman. In that instant, I tasted the southern poison running in my veins at a level seemingly untouched by intellectual, literary, or even emotional change.

My experience of the Vietnam War combined with fledgling conversations beginning to take place about what would later be called feminist pedagogy taught me a permanent and invaluable lesson. I comprehended that the classical lecture format in which one person is supposed to have all knowledge while many others are convinced of their ignorance if not stupidity was academic colonialism. If I was willing to risk my vision and safety protesting such a policy in Asia, I surely needed to rid myself of my own comparable practices.

As so often is the case, I careened from one extreme to the other. In the early seventies, I stopped lecturing entirely, saying to each new group of students, "Coming in here every class and beginning to lecture about things you may not have the slightest interest in hearing is like intellectual prostitution, and I won't do it. I will arrive and wait for questions from you on matters of urgency in this play/poem/

story." Naturally, my students were stunned into deeper silence than usual, and we spent many uncomfortable sessions: after all, I was expecting them to know enough to ask me intelligent questions about a subject they had taken precisely because they wanted more knowledge of it.

Fortunately for us all, my innate passion for the literature overcame my rigidity about having academically pure politics. Though I have never returned to unbroken lecturing, I have come to accept responsibility for all I do know that they do not, and remain accountable to them for using that knowledge to empower rather than mystify.

Drinking enough Jack Daniels or Seagram's Seven Crown (depending on when pay day had been), silenced the voices that told me I was somehow inadequate. But by using alcohol to escape them, I also lost contact with my best self. From earliest memories I have seen myself as intense—the four-year old oblivious to anything but shaping animals out of her feces; the child digging tunnels under the oak tree for an imaginary escape in her toy cars; the ten-year old devastated by the brutish foot that smashed her peep show. But I have also understood sabotage from a very early age, how insidious it is and how cunning. While accenting my spontaneous intensity, I ignored or downplayed my need to carry through, to face the consequences of being bright or sensitive or creative. I let out just enough of my interpretive powers to know that at the heart of my often flawed or unfinished products lay a jewel. I fooled myself for years. Somewhere along the way, I began pulling back from full experience or expression of myself. Others' early responses meant too much: "No one draws pink cows and brown people." "That note is way off key and too low for a girl to sing." "If you touch yourself there, your hands will fall off." "Girls don't become orchestra conductors or forest rangers." "Why don't you go out with some nice young man who is appropriate?"

Bourbon numbed my feelings and left me depressed. I swung between heavy drinking and periods of sensing that I could not continue both to drink and develop my intellectual and creative abilities. The first thing to suffer was my critical writing; eventually, I ceased being able to put any words onto paper. By 1968, I had stopped writing letters to everyone except my sister and Josephine.

Evidence of my demise lies in pathetic souvenirs of attempts at creativity. My filing cabinet still has a folder in it full of lists of projects:

subjects for long high-minded poems; topics for scholarly articles; designs for a better world. The tab on the file reads: "Scraps"; "Fragments"; "First Thoughts"; "Bits and Pieces"; "Inspirations."

In addition to these ephemera, I have drafts of articles, first on Shakespeare and later on Virginia Woolf, written when not actively drinking. These were sometimes even sent away to a journal, only to be rejected. On rare occasions when comments accompanied the nos, readers indicated that my piece had a bright kernel lost in opacity and verbiage. Such essays generally came back when I was once again focused on whiskey, in no condition to revise.

For the last eight years of my drinking, I managed only essential schoolwork. Papers that absolutely had to be returned were read; otherwise, they piled up for months, even years, collecting shame along with office dust. Books were somehow gotten through, though sitting still to read became virtually impossible toward the end of my drinking years. I had to resort to teaching titles of which I had prior knowledge. Most of my time was taken up with academic committee service, for I sensed that if I did not want to be exposed as a raging alcoholic, I had to move into administration, where work could be defined less specifically than in the classroom or in the library.

Two tangible outcomes are the existence of several university documents of major importance and a thriving women's studies department. While unable to write literary criticism, I authored a policy for evaluating teaching on a regular basis; a system-wide statement about academic freedom and its less-welcome corrolary, faculty responsibility toward their students and institution; a plan to give students one more credit than the number of hours spent in the class, thereby recognizing that learning takes place outside the classroom. What I remember most clearly about those documents is typing drafts way into the night, always with a glass near my typewriter. Occasionally I would reminisce about 1959 in Nashville, when I wrote a master's thesis about neo-Platonism in Keats's *Endymion* and lived on farm-ripe tomatoes and Jack Daniels Black. It was summer, and my fellowship had run out at the end of May. While my family gladly would have sent me more if I had asked, my guilt over spending so much on liquor kept me from asking. Once a week, however, I cooked for an evening meeting at the Vanderbilt Episcopal student center, always making more than was needed, counting on the charity of the chaplin who insisted that I "take home leftovers or they'll just get thrown out back."

In the case of women's studies, I was approached by a small cadre of graduate students eager to see us begin offering courses with an avowed feminist perspective. Not only did I assist them in drawing up a document to present to the dean, but when a program was established on a three-year experimental basis, I applied for and was chosen to be the first chair. My three years in office coincided with my last year of drinking and my first two of not. While we made tremendous strides as an academic unit, I struggled inside with a growing sense of desperation. In order to perform the groundbreaking functions set before me, I simply transferred my addiction from liquor to food. One of my last acts as chair was to clean out the massive wooden desk we had been willed by a woman retiring from decades in student personnel, who in her last years had consistently rescued our fledgling program from such minutiae as class scheduling deadlines and faculty appointment papers. In one of the side drawers, I came upon ancient crumbs from cinnamon rolls quickly stashed there when I would hear a student or colleague open the door of the outer office.

In all my years of drinking, I never missed a day's work. But I remember waking up feeling as if I would not be able to get out of bed, stumbling through a shower and strong hot tea, driving too fast to school to meet my classes. Once school was over, I drove purposefully home, thinking only of that first drink. I parked my car outside my house, walked quickly up the steps and into the foyer, opened the heavy oak front door, and made a straight path into the kitchen. Out came a glass into which I poured liberal amounts from my current bottle, maybe adding ginger ale, maybe not. Swallowing as rapidly as possible without choking, I downed number one. Only after that reliable streak of fire had cut down the front of my body was I calm enough to speak to my two cats who had come into the kitchen to greet me, take off whatever coat and shoes or boots I might have on, pick up the mail from the concrete floor of the foyer, and get a sponge to wipe up the trail of snow or mud or rain water that I had tracked on the wood floor and linoleum in my frantic need to drink.

The more deeply I sank into my pattern, the less able I became to make positive choices in lovers or to stay in a relationship longer than about nine months. My partners increasingly became women unwilling to face their own involvement with liquor. Our liaisons began in high passion but usually ended with my feeling victimized by younger women whose attention had wandered. Actually my own attention had never been focused on them. To do that would involve time and risk, and I already knew how much energy it took to maintain myself within my secret. Besides, no person could be counted on to deliver exactly what I needed as often and without fail as my beloved bourbon could, so I chose partners who would not interfere with that pursuit. A year or so before I stopped drinking, some brave lesbians opened the Lesbian Resource Center (LRC), housed in a storefront across the street from a popular gas station. When their newsletters began coming to my home, I was shocked and frightened, since "no one knew." But come they did, announcing pool playing, card games, weekly community meetings, occasional dances, special holiday meals and celebrations. I devoured every word, memorized all the dates and times, quickly located the address, and drove by on community meeting nights. Unable to walk in, I tried to soak up something through my car windows and the center's heavily curtained front. I told myself I did not fit in, but the truth was I knew I would and was scared. Being a private lesbian was one thing but identifying with a cross-section of society seemed quite another.

I began to mail the LRC cash donations in unmarked envelopes, telling myself I would be fired if my bank saw a check made out to such an organization. One Thanksgiving, I received a colorful flyer announcing a feast in lesbian space, asking people to bring food and to come share warm company. Afraid to attend, I nonetheless had become increasingly an invisible part of the LCR's activities. After some brain wracking about how to participate without going, I devised a workable if sad solution. I had a neighborhood grocery deliver a handsome turkey to the center the Wednesday before Thanksgiving, and, as I ate a T-bone steak alone in my house, I pictured a room full of women brave enough to go and eat that bird.

The LRC supported a journal, *So's Your Old Lady (SYOL)*, and, from the occasional copies I had seen, I knew I had skills to offer such an enterprise. Simultaneously, I was becoming aware that a couple of political lesbians had opened a bookstore in someone's basement. I tried to convince myself that I could work on these activities or at least publish in *SYOL* under a pseudonym. Nothing happened for another year except that I worried about the idea whenever I was sober long enough to catch a glimpse of where my life was going.

During the summer of 1974 a colleague told me he had been to a wonderful bookstore full of books by women, located next door to a combination pool hall, bowling alley, and bar. His recommendation allowed me not only to drive by but finally to park my car and go in. I told the two women working there about my *male* friend's excitement, hoping that my flimsy excuse would cover my real reason for being there. One of the women was tall and quite thin, the other shorter, more compact, and intense. Both were utterly silent, forcing me to initiate any conversation. They owned a rather large black dog named Sappho, who insisted on being friendly but whose nuzzling frightened me even more than I already was. By the end of an awkward half-hour, I had volunteered to work in the store two hours a week on Saturdays.

The shorter woman, who turned out to be a cofounder of the LRC, was usually on duty when I worked. I had to laugh about getting in way over my head with my first foray into the "lesbian community." Her name was Karen Browne, and I was immediately attracted to her—politically, intellectually, physically. Each week my two-hour shift stretched a little longer, and we slowly developed the literary side of the holdings, since current stock reflected both her and her partner's training in social science and political activism. We undertook an inventory and devised a system for ordering new books. We also gazed at each other a lot, touched hands of necessity as we worked with books, became a bit easier in one another's company. Only as I was driving home would I realize that I had not been breathing very deeply during my shift.

One Saturday, Karen talked about women who sent the LRC anonymous donations but never lent energy to the ongoing life of the place. I called in sick the next week, ashamed of my cowardice. She risked public ridicule so that lesbians could meet somewhere other than dark bars or private homes behind pulled shades, while I sent in my secret money.

The big change in my life came in the fall of 1974 when I was thirty-seven. Karen had a part-time job at the university and, since we lived within three or four blocks of one another, it seemed natural to ride to and from work together. As I fell increasingly in love with her, I realized I had to end my pro forma relationship with the person living in my house. She was a kept woman—kept by me. I paid for elaborate dinners, a plane trip to Denver and the Painted Desert as a celebration of her passing her doctoral examinations, her room and board in my house, a Cordon Bleu crêpe pan so she could fix her friends elegant suppers when I was working late at school. I even let her bring an

English sheep dog into my house, when I thoroughly disliked dogs. That puppy was locked in the laundry room each morning as she left for long days at the library. The combination of his frantic whimpers and the growing smell emanating from my basement drove me to walk him around the block, urging him to "Do your stuff" outside. My two cats looked at me with startled eyes every time he grew another inch, something that seemed to happen every other day. After all my wool carpets were deeply stained by urine, my lover asked if I would buy an outdoor running pen for her playful pup. In a conversation with a salesperson at Sears I learned that the cheapest run cost $1,200. That evening I announced that we were getting rid of the forty-five-pound puppy who made my hardwood floors shake when he careened from kitchen to front porch. That decision was the beginning of my exit not only from the relationship but from the matrix within which it existed.

The summer before, this same woman had sat rocking in my living room, drinking gin and tonic. Suddenly she stopped, leaned toward me, and said calmly: "I miss the excitement of our first six months, 'cause now I feel like I know all there is to know about you; we're not finding out anything new about each other and I'm worried about getting bored." I countered with: "Maybe we've gotten through vital statistics and can now really start getting to know each other on deeper levels." When I saw that my suggestion was not registering, I silenced my rage by falling off a six-month wagon. Under that rage lay a depth of hurt that overwhelmed me but that I pushed down as I tried vainly to think up more exciting tidbits about my past that might catch her attention. What I wanted most was someone to tell what it felt like to live inside my skin, lonely, hung over much too often, scared of being out as almost anything I really was—Southerner, lesbian, drunk, writer, passionate human being with dreams of a feminist world.

That fall was early and violent. By mid-October, most leaves were down on lawns, in gutters, in the crooks of steps. Late on the night of October 22nd, I was driving my car home from Karen's. The wind was throwing wet, dead leaves all over the street in front of my car. I slowed down to watch those leaves rising on the updraft, only to sink back into a sodden heap and be ridden over by someone on their way somewhere.

I decided to write a poem about the leaves when I got home.
I decided not to sleep with the woman who found me boring after half a year.

I decided to a read a book (*Sappho Was a Right-On Woman* by
　　Sidney Abbot and Barbara Love), which I had let sit on my
　　shelf for over a year, not wanting to know what it said.
I decided not to drink while I read that book.
I decided to stay up all night in my living room so both the book
　　and the poem would be done by breakfast.

That night was uncommonly long. Lying about feeling restless, I
found my book, some scratch paper, and a pencil, and went downstairs. I boiled water for hot tea, which tasted bland, harmless, unsa-
tisfying; I wanted a big glass of room-temperature bourbon swallowed fast to quiet the jitters beginning down the middle of my body.
I drank quarts of tea, liking it less as my hands began to shake and my
stomach to draw up into familiar knots that meant my liquor ration
was overdue. But I sat rigid on my couch, reading, fighting against
sleep and panic and pain. About three in the morning, I came to a
sentence late in the book on the right-hand side of the page that burned
its way through my brain just as Jack Daniels had burned my body. In
a long discussion of small ways lesbians lie about how and with whom
we celebrate, the authors asserted that for a lesbian to go to work on
Monday morning and lie about the sex of whom she spent her
weekend with is like committing suicide slowly but surely. I spilled
the tea I was nursing and began to shake from something new; Abbott
and Love were speaking only to me in that living room while the fall
wind whistled and moaned around the corners of my house.

I left the book unfinished and worked on my poem about wet
leaves in a chance wind—it seemed infinitely safer. What I wrote fast
and carelessly did not qualify as a poem, but it had lines, indented
from the left-hand margin, and it told the truth. I stuck it away in my
study where I would not come upon it for over a year. For the rest of
that night, I sat stone still while my cats slept nearby offering mute
comfort and my mood swung from lightheadedness to terror to
something resembling sanctification.

Before the woman upstairs arose, I poured all my bourbon down
the sink and threw the empty bottles into my outside garbage can. I left
the gin since it had never been my drink but wrote a note saying I
wanted it and her out of the house by December 1st. Then I walked toward my neighborhood shopping area, feeling sick from no whiskey
for almost twenty-one hours. I found a café open early, where I devoured a lumberjack special: two eggs over easy, hash browns, toast,

bacon, sausage, lots of very strong tea. Later that day, I decided to tell somebody I was lesbian and picked my good friends from whom I had bought my house. I called to ask if I might stop by after work. That seemed to shock them more than my news: I had never dropped in on anyone or wanted them to drop in on me since I drank in secret. In their living room I was offered a drink. I said, "Thanks, I'm on the wagon," a comment accepted without question. After a couple of stuttered false tries, I blurted out my dire announcement. Martin smiled easily: "I love ya," while Martha quipped, "I was beginning to think there must not be any in Minneapolis."

Nothing magical happened when I sobered up. I simply stopped taking liquor into my body. While that was a momentous decision, my ways of dealing with myself and the world remained essentially unchanged. I transferred many of my compulsive needs from bourbon to Karen, putting far more faith in and strain on our relationship than any such delicate connection can bear. Though we continued to respond passionately to each other, sustaining the dailiness of a commitment was not possible, and we eventually set one another free.

Most of the mileposts along my recovery route involved wanting to make things. The first summer after I quit drinking, I decided to paint the trim on my house. For months, I persuaded unsuspecting friends to "come over for dinner and a little outside project." We climbed ladders, hung from eaves, and fought late-summer wasps. There came a moment when everything was done except three small pieces of gutta-percha pipe sticking up above my brick chimney. Determined that it be perfect, I eventually straddled my chimney and painted away these last traces of fading brown. Having enough sense to grasp that getting up on the peak of my steep roof alone might be a bit foolhardy, I waited until an old friend was visiting. She stood on the opposite side of my house from the chimney and held a thick clothesline, the other end of which was around my waist. We both believed this scheme would magically save me if I fell. Sitting atop my roof on a gorgeous Saturday afternoon, I was alive, able to breathe, happy. A snapshot catches this moment: me grinning against a perfectly blue sky, holding my four-inch paintbrush and my funny rope.

The second summer of sobriety, I dug a small garden in my side yard and planted flowers bought from the local farmer's market. Though my garden brought me moments of pleasure, somewhere around midsummer I forgot the plants and focused on the bright cans of cold beer everyone else in town seemed to be holding. The weeds got ahead of me that year, but every year since I have put flowers into the earth. When I finally bought perennials, I knew I was willing to bank on having a "next spring," that I wanted something to bloom from the year before. Those first tulips and lemon lilies were precious investments in my capacity to care for my own creation. Before signing a purchase agreement to sell my house, I inserted a clause stipulating that I could return the next spring to dig up my lilies and take them to my new yard.

For many years after 1974, my creations were primarily nonverbal. One Saturday when I wanted more than usual to drink, I drilled three-quarter-inch holes in very long two-by-fours instead. I needed space for cookbooks and other volumes that were spilling out of my downstairs study, so I decided to build a bookcase in the hall. Shunning the simple, I picked a no-nail design needing twenty holes for dowels on which would rest welcome shelves. I drilled ninety holes because I knew that as long as I was in my kitchen doing that, I would not go to the liquor store.

As a child, I had loved stories in books; my teenage years were consumed by books, since reading smoothed the edge off my loneliness. Once I was deeply into drinking, however, my ability to concentrate inevitably lessened. While going through a treatment program after I stopped drinking, I heard a lecture that helped me understand and forgive my restlessness in front of a printed page. It seems that each time a person gets drunk, several thousand brain cells die and must be replenished. I had to accept that it would take longer for my brain to dry out than it had for my hands to stop shaking. When, during my fifth year of sobriety, I suddenly found myself reading for a whole hour, my joy was exquisite. Almost every night as I lie in bed with my current book, I give thanks for the return of that gift.

As long as I was drinking, I could not afford to invest very heavily in my ideas or their expression, preferring the predictability and cold comfort of a bottle. But, in 1975, I accepted that I had something to say in words, on paper. After about a year of unsuccessful attempts, I stumbled upon Virginia Woolf's *A Writer's Diary* where she speaks of the function of her journal as a place to loosen her writer's ligaments, comparing journal writing with practicing piano scales before tackling more formal compositions. Willing to try her method, I tentatively chose to begin a journey toward my voice—I bought a journal.

Each volume was titled, which now intrigues me as I wonder what

I might have written inside something called, "A Notebook of Spirals," "Fronds & Tendrils," "Webbings," "Knots." At one point in my recovery of my writing self, a friend suggested that I cull from all those journals salient vignettes and publish them. For a month, I read diligently, marking in red along any margins I thought worth excising.

June 13, 1975: Reading exam papers from a course I just coordinated on courtly love—a thought on the word "elevation" in relation to power. Power is played out on the street level, the pavement as Woolf calls it. By elevating woman, men removed her from contact with power. So when Shakespeare says in Sonnet 130, "My mistress when she treads, treads on the ground," he is doing more than mocking courtly love conventions. His mistress seems genuinely in control, not falsely so by virtue of the poet's participation in the courtly love game. The desire to put woman on a pedestal is a way to keep her off the streets, out of the places where power is played out. We might consider the trap inherent in the myth that power corrupts. Like Renaissance-elite males wishing to preserve their position at the top who argued that ambition was evil, contentment with one's lot good, men may have made up the slogan "power corrupts" to deter the truly moral from embracing it. Power only corrupts if its wielders use it badly. Women could use power in new ways and not corrupt ourselves or others. . . . I've felt so well today, yet still can't stop my current eating binge—I have to do something. Each morning I intend, each night I gorge. I need to get physical exercise—I feel chained to this house.

June 10, 1976: Mary Schultz had her breast removed.

*Losing Weight*

"I'm still a compulsive eater" you say
Even though they've taken your breast away?
Was it white meat, or are we, like ducks, all
    dark?
"I lost in the hospital" you muse
from loss of appetite, you think.
I say your white-masked Shylock sliced his legal
    pound   and then some;

left you lopped and asymmetric/
Latter-day Amazon, take up your bow
against the world of female measurements:
   0–34–38
You sit amongst us eaters, worried that you'll
      binge again
"reward" for losing tissue, skin, and special
      female veins.
Grafting pounds to other places
cannot bring you back your lovely melon,
cannot fill that utter hollow.
So sit and smile your brave, wan smile
and be a bosom cyclops.

I've said I'd make chicken salad for Mary so she won't have to ask others to make so many meals for her. Here I am, in my kitchen, dripping sweat into the bowl—special natural salt—cutting a gelid chicken with big, sharp scissors just like my mother did, covering it and me with grease that will become worse as it warms on my skin. Once all the available meat is in the bowl (tall, super-white metal bowl that held *So's Your Old Lady* money when I read of women's hurts and loves) and some scraps are in my cats, I move to eggs—hard boiled a day ago so the shells fall off from compression in the ice box. Once naked—smooth and super white, like the bowl—eggs go one by one in a childhood gadget that slices them thin and even. Criss-cross I go to make smaller cubes—cold crumbles of yolk stick to my greasy hot fingers and I suck them and revel in that yellow softness on my tongue. Now the celery: greener on the outside cuts, whitish at the center—cut, cut, my knife eats up stalks, making them hard diamond cubes tossed in on top. Suddenly the salad looks like a monotonic mosaic shelf. Mix it up, I think—and do with my bare hands—up to my wrists—the stuff takes me over and my total impulse is to sink my face into the sea of salad and drink it in gulps. Instead I spoon mayonnaise into, around, among ingredients till the whole is viscous, oiled, ready—a mound of chicken salad for a lady with only one breast.

Travels back to my creative self have been slow, filled with relapses into verbosity and abstraction learned in childhood and rewarded by schools. I struggle not to feel either ashamed of where I am at my age or full of grief for the wasted years. Those women who have patiently but consistently urged me to my own speech have given me a jewel that I cannot always accept with open hands but one without which I would still be largely mute.

Every so often, I stumble on some artifact that simultaneously heartens, frightens, and depresses me. These remains share certain features: they do not look familiar to me, yet are in my handwriting; they reveal how much I can draw from a poem or a story when I focus. One of the clearest of these ghostly experiences came in 1983 while I was teaching a seminar on the poetry of Edna St. Vincent Millay, Louise Bogan, and H. D. When I opened my copy of *Helen in Egypt,* I was immediately distracted by marginal comments. Neatly penned in blue ballpoint, they indicated an intelligence keenly in tune with the poet's own. In addition to copious notes, boxes appeared around certain clusters of words having to do with shadows, ghosts, veils, dreams—images that provide crucial linguistic and emotional threads through this epic. I could not recall making the notations, but the handwriting was unmistakably my own. Turning to the front of the book, I found that it had been a birthday present in 1977. Amazed, I realized that though I had been free from alcohol for three years when I read H. D.'s work, I could still engage in an intense project that would then pass out of my consciousness so completely as to seem foreign six years later.

As I continued reading the poem and my work with it, I felt moved by the critical and creative interpretation that was building as steadily as H. D.'s story. The next day, I shared my experience with the seminar, naming those annotations as a sign of my ambivalence toward my creative voice and as evidence of my slow recovery from years of destructive drinking.

The same day I gave up liquor, I began telling people I was a lesbian. Originally that decision was political and therapeutic, but one long-term effect has been on my writer's voice. Gradually I have found and claimed my truest audience: lesbians and feminists interested in women's culture. Once I conveyed this shift in my focus to my department chairman, my writing became surer, livelier, more engaged. My first public speech from this position was on Valentine's Day, 1977, in the guild hall of a local church. Part of a series sponsored by an alternative women's learning institute I helped operate, my lecture was on the poetry of Olga Broumas, Audre Lorde, and Adrienne Rich as it contributes to a lesbian aesthetic. My typescript was more than twenty pages long, and it was good. The overwhelmingly lesbian audience was alert and supportive; for the first time in my life, I felt that my literary training might be put to some use.

As my journal writing developed, I became open enough to include poems and bored enough with my erratic love life to include entries about work, books, and other people who came into my life at a less intense level. Surveying the thirty-six notebooks I have made since 1975, I discover that sometimes I hardly talk of external conditions at all—my journal is a confidential source for self-exploration. At other times, I seem deeply caught up in the world around me.

In April 1978, I went to New York City to read the correspondence between Louise Bogan and May Sarton housed in the Berg Collection of the public library. I wanted to write an article about ways in which letters served as underground support networks for women hungry for other women's ideas. Amidst their discussions of aesthetics I was surprised to find an unmistakably intimate note. Sarton writes asking to extend their developing friendship into a sensual and sexual relationship. Bogan refuses, pleading her disastrous relationship with her first husband. Sarton values her friendship enough to struggle to readjust her feelings. All this is spoken of tentatively and painfully in the letters; my lesbian perspective and my awareness of my own partial alliances lent me a sympathy I might otherwise have lacked. As I read through their often tortured exchanges, I felt respectful and clear about not wanting or needing to distort what was on the pages. Empowered through my own experience, I was able to articulate what the webs of their caring and fighting looked like.

My journal from that month is full of long, introspective entries about everything from the drunks who stopped me as I walked to the library from the subway to the art, ballet, and drama that were integral to my stay. One of my last days in the city was spent at the Cloisters. I gave myself a whole day at that museum I had wanted to visit for years. Journal entries written there contain my responses to the unicorn tapestries. A segment from that visit indicates my growing desire to direct my critical faculty toward my environment:

> #7 is the famous scene of unicorn in captivity in round white fence. Unicorn looks rather dead in #6, then is set up in stasis in #7 as some ideal to be looked at and controlled even if not

understood. It's so clear—these men could never fathom the complexity of the creature they find, hunt, kill, capture—they are so worldly and decadent, the unicorn so magical and pure—there's just no way for them to connect at all. I need to know what I feel, looking at #7. It's sadness at the small space left for the magic beast—she can sit as she does, or stand—no walking—no movement at all. Not only is she inside a fence but tied to an orange tree as well. And in the center of a huge field of flowers, all free in nature. This series is about hunt—war—blood—violence—sex—*men*. The Cluny ones are about the relationship of the unicorn and the lady—look at Robin Morgan's poem once home; go to Paris some day and see the originals.

When I look at my stack of gray-bound books, I remember Evi. She was an editor of *So's Your Old Lady*, whose staff I had finally joined under my own name. Being part of that enterprise was immensely important to me as a writer, since I learned the mechanics of editing a magazine and found the first outlet for my own words.

Before Evi left the group to enter a martial arts collective, she called me out of the office to make me a present of a handmade leather folder in which she kept her own writing. Once I had admired it, asking where she had bought it. Its San Francisco origin seemed to place it beyond my grasp. Now Evi's own beautiful object sat on my lap with a card that read, "So you can unlock your word-horde." Tears sprang to my eyes at her remembering my telling her about my favorite Old English poem in which a man had kept his story silent until his old master told him to unlock his word-horde, to speak the truth within him.

The most important step toward speaking my truth about literature involved my coming out at the university. My career at Minnesota spans twenty-six years, twelve of which were spent in the closet because I felt residual shame about being a lesbian and because I remained in an alcoholic haze that prevented me from seeing clearly. During those years, I survived but at great cost to myself. Not knowing how to express disagreements without antagonizing my colleagues, I either ranted or sat in stony destructive silence. In a journal entry following a 1978 department meeting, I wrote:

I am home from a four-hour-long meeting—headache, exhausted, drained, mute, nauseated, all stuffed in. I "made nice" all through, not saying how misplaced I find their values, not asking why there are no women writers on one man's list of canonical humanities texts, not saying that they're slanting the fiction writer search so as not to have to pay the woman candidate any heed. And we are going to promote to full professor a dullard, primarily because of his "time in rank" (five years to my thirteen). *Faces:* ashen, cud-chewing, carved in sneers, upturned lip, droopy eye, duck-tailed hard on devil's face leering, white roach grog dead, sunglassed mole, pearly-curly dandy, soft falling waves and deep hurt eyes, impish pucker covering steely-eyed true sight, balding round faced joker in forever pain, dicktracy chinned gentle, baggy-pants baggy-eyed vapid, short-haired thin, insipid loner, barefoot lad with deep set teddy bear eyes—English department rogues' gallery. I feel much quieter now.

Clearly I had no idea how to handle my workplace or its inhabitants. Equally clearly, there is no description of me, who at that stage in life was greatly overweight and stressed out in the face, had wildly curled hair à la Janis Joplin, owned ten picked fingers from agitation without an object, and pretended to like triple-knit suits, heels, and hose when I only felt at home in corduroys and flannel.

At the end of the seventies I took a year's leave without pay. I had to decide if I wanted ever to return to an institution that invested in research of which I did not approve and in companies that fed the defense machine, and to a department that refused to promote me to full professor no matter how hard I tried to be their version of me. I discovered the obvious: a teacher cannot make enough freelancing to keep body and soul together. I also learned that I disliked intensely having to advertise myself or arrange classes under my own aegis. The surprise of the year came during a visit by Florence Howe to our campus. She came to evaluate the women's studies program, from which I had just retired after three years as its first chair. We met for a long dinner away from campus followed by a visit to my house where we kept talking about the current state of women's studies work in the country and at Minnesota.

When I took Florence back to her motel, her hand on the car door handle impelled me to speak about what was really on my mind. I blurted out my dilemma about where to work, saying at one point, "I want to do something radical and going back to school seems so easy and safe."

Florence turned to me and said as distinctly as anyone has ever said anything to me: "No, Toni, you have it wrong. Going back to the university is much more radical than staying away. Don't you know you are one of the handful of lesbians with tenure in America and that teaching and working with students from an open position is far harder than offering courses in a church basement or park building. Take the power of the podium and use it—go back and endure the derision that will come your way."

I drove home with her words burning in my ears, feeling simultaneous shock and relief. Within weeks, I had made my sabbatical decision: I would return to the English department, but not until I had met with my chairman to tell him my plan to return as an out lesbian–feminist critic and teacher. I scheduled that meeting and announced to a man who had worked his way through an English college on a pugilist scholarship: "I want you to know that I will be giving you articles and syllabi that assume a lesbian–feminist perspective on literature. I want you to evaluate them the same way you do anyone else's work. Only on this condition can I return to this place." He blanched momentarily before assuring me, "My theory of administration is to find out what makes my staff happy and then help them do it."

When I told my best male friend about my conversation, he fairly beamed with some pleasure I could not at first fathom. He told me that my declaring myself had destroyed an ancient plan on the part of some old timers in the department. It seems that he had heard them at poker games when everyone was a little drunk boasting that should I ever have the nerve to complain about their refusal to promote me, they had the perfect rejoinder. They were maintaining a secret dossier of incriminating tidbits about my private life and would happily bring it out to challenge my claims of mistreatment.

Since that momentous and rather breathless interview with my chair in 1979, I have consistently offered courses in lesbian literature, culture, and critical theory. I have visited other classes to discuss such matters when the regular faculty either did not know enough to do so or held too precarious a position to risk it. My colleagues gradually have either accepted my perspective or decided to leave me alone and be civil.

Occasionally homophobia surfaces, as on an afternoon a few years ago. I was standing in the hall talking with a friend. Because my back had recently gone out of alignment, I was wearing a spandex girdle to help me sit during our long preschool meetings. In an attempt to hide as much of it as possible, I was wearing a blousy knit top that hid the pristine whiteness entirely in the front. In the back, a band about three inches stuck out below the bottom of my sweater.

As my friend and I were speaking animatedly, we were interrupted by one of the chronically homophobic members of our department. His opener to me was, "Well, Toni, in training for the Vikings (Minnesota's professional football team)?" Determined to show my disapproval, I rejoined, "Actually, Fred, my back is out, and I'm in constant pain, thank you." Covered with embarrassment, since he views himself as a liberal humanist, he stumbled through belated expressions of his concern and empathy, saying, "I know about backs; mine goes out on me, too." I am quite sure that, had he seen one of my heterosexual women colleagues in such attire, his imagination would not have conjured linebackers.

Florence Howe turned out to be exactly right that night over a decade ago. Occupying space as a lesbian at the university has changed virtually everything about working there. No longer do I come home with terrible headaches or a churning stomach; no longer do I deny what I see in the literature I teach or the theory I espouse; no longer am I useless to students interested in talking with someone who has lived and thought as a lesbian for more years than many of them have been alive. My classroom manner has become more relaxed because I no longer fear a question that will force me to lie quickly in order to avoid some devastating revelation that will cost me my job or at the least a reprimand from someone in authority for "corrupting the young." But the single most lasting benefit has been to me—being open in my work has been a tremendous boon to my finding and using my voice. Since 1980, I have published three books and several substantial articles and poems; I write reviews for *Hurricane Alice,* a feminist journal that I help edit, and for *The Women's Review of Books;* I have worked on this memoir for some six years. I no longer become terrified when I cannot write on demand or every day, trusting now that I am a person who writes and who will always do that. My greatest conflict these days is between paid employment and my desire for more time at home to write.

# Everyday Magic

*I*f Freud is correct when he says resolving love and work is essential for psychic health and happiness, then I have finally arrived. The last piece to fall into place, however, has been love, because trust and vulnerability both frighten and draw me. I also am a confirmed introvert, preferring my own company to almost anyone else's, having to force myself to make dates for lunch or walks when I would rather stay home with my animals and read or write or putter around the house and yard. But I also yearn to be known and cared for, to have a special someone to whom I can tell everything without fear of censure or ridicule, to give myself over entirely if briefly to another's wishes.

Thirteen years ago, I made a series of decisions that moved me closer to being able to hold this basic contradiction in solution, like letting oil float on water without demanding emulsion. I remained celibate long enough to review my sexual history and formulate some clear sense of what I wanted in a partner. Simultaneously I entered and completed several therapeutic programs intended to facilitate self-understanding. In 1978, at the end of this period of intense introspection, I began seeing a woman of whom I had known for years.

It began in 1972, when I attended a conference for counseling and guidance workers. My lover at the time, who owned the English sheepdog and nursed her boredom with me, was working toward a Ph.D. in that field and wanted to attend. Having no money, she let her wishes be known, and, as usual, I jumped at one more chance to secure her dwindling attention.

When I expressed a wish to tag along, she could hardly object. At the conference, a panel was held on special counseling needs of gay people. Still closeted at the university but hungry for information and contact with lesbians, I went. In a stuffy room, filled with anxious members of the helping professions, I witnessed a quiet, slight woman speak about the interrelationship between chemical dependency and being a lesbian in a hostile culture. Her words found my heart; when the program was over, I went to the front of the room to thank her. Shaking hands, I felt courageous and asked for her phone number and whether she would like to have tea sometime. Though she agreed, I was never able to complete the requisite telephone call. Twice I tried, once getting so far as actually dialing all seven digits. To my utter relief, the line was busy.

Because the lesbian community in Minneapolis was relatively small, I ran into Susan several times between our initial meeting and our beginning to court. She was at that time driving a city bus after more than a decade of public-school teaching. Every so often I found myself boarding her vehicle, sitting in the seat across from the driver's chair, talking nervously. After about four years of these chance encounters, I joined a group of lesbians that met weekly for dinner and discussion. Susan and her lover were members and I remember paying particular attention when she talked about their life together. I also was especially aware of her the night we abandoned personal consciousness-raising for an old-fashioned swimming party.

In the summer of 1978, two years after our Friday night group experience, we were asked to organize an older lesbians support group. I was determined to set the admission age at thirty-five, since Susan's lover was only thirty-four at the time. After each month's meeting, we found ourselves talking near our cars or arriving before anyone else "by accident." At the same time that her relationship was coming apart, we had lunch—two lunches actually. I suggested a little vegetarian place called the Mud Pie where we sat under a wooden trellis and had enchiladas and fruit juice. Susan took me to her club dining room for an elegant Sunday brunch followed by a spin around the nearby lake in her Fiat sports car. We confessed to wanting to be friends and that attachment grew until by late fall we acknowledged that we were in love. We took long walks along the Mississippi River, scuffing fall leaves, or drove out into the country in her little car with its top down and radio playing classical music, or spoke last thing at night over the telephone. Sensing this connection might be unique, I vowed with Adrienne Rich to "love with all my intelligence."

During the winter of 1979, Susan and I became lovers and after twelve years are still deepening our relationship. Occasionally I recollect with a wry smile the graduate student complaining about there being nothing left to do after six months. Occasionally I also still want to cut and run, finding intimacy just too hard, but I stay put and talk about my fears. Currently, we live in a large three-story house with a singular cat named Slate and a sweet English cocker spaniel called Blue. The past decade has brought enough happiness into my private life that I no longer entertain an old fantasy about living alone, isolated in a tiny apartment where I could die and no one would know it for days.

Household projects have become especially satisfying for us to undertake, and there have been some rare moments along the way. One of these happened during the first few months of our relationship. That winter was harsh even by Minnesota standards. Susan's house had a gently sloping roof on which snow accumulated in vast amounts as we lay snug and passionate in her bed. Having a steeply pitched roof myself, I was unfamiliar with the effects of snow build-up. After a January thaw, her roof began to leak around the insulation vents. To correct the situation, someone had to climb out onto the roof, shimmy over to the vents, and hammer the ice into disposable chunks. While I did this, Susan insisted on holding onto a rope tied around my waist. Remembering my earlier rope episode, I tried to persuade her of the final ineffectiveness of this plan, but she was sure she could save me should I slip. I firmly believed that I would suffocate from its being pulled too tightly around my middle or else pull Susan out the window so that we both would plummet down to the cold ground.

Before the ordeal was over, Susan ventured out onto the roof, admitting to a certain acrophobia. We reversed the rope trick and hoped for the best. Her fear flared up when she found herself further away from the entry window and me than she had intended, and she froze midway between safety and the ice line. Inch by inch, I talked her toward me until she could take my hand and scramble into her house, shaken both by the experience and by her willingness to gamble on my dependability.

From this early fiasco, we have progressed to semiannual hangings of forty-five storm windows or screens, depending on the season; a fall putting in of over a hundred bulbs on a day when finger tips turned blue; laying of bathroom carpet complete with precision cutting around toilet, lavatory, tub, and radiator; a yearly ritual Memorial Day planting of two flats of impatiens in our front garden;

a summer's labor of sanding, priming, and painting all the house screens in light lavendar to match one of the colors in Judy Chicago's Sappho plate. When we fall into old competitive ruts, we have to scream and yell. But mostly we mesh talents, patience, and taste so that we get amazing things done while having a good time.

We first understood how important an element travel would become in our life the spring after our roof adventure. I had planned for some time to take that quarter off from teaching and spend six weeks in England. Three of them were to be spent in London, doing what I liked most to do in that magical city: strolling in Bloomsbury, taking meat pies to the park for lunch, visiting the Tate or British Museum, eating mutton at an old chop house off Bond Street, riding the tube to place names that charmed me and then walking in that district until I felt tired. The other three would find me in Cornwall, at St. Ives where Virginia Woolf spent many childhood summers and of which her earliest memories are composed. I would search out her old family home and lie idly on the beach, listening to the same waves she had so loved. Between this plan and its execution, Susan and I happened. To my amazement, one autumn Sunday as we ambled along the river, talking about my April hegira, Susan said she would join me if I liked. She would spend two weeks in London with me; I would go a week early and find a place to stay. Once we had "done" the city, I would go on to Cornwall for my hermit period.

When we broke out of our parting embrace the day I left Minneapolis, I felt like someone was peeling the top layer of my body off. During my solo week in London, two firsts happened: I felt homesick, and I saw London sober. Each midmorning I lingered over tea, crackers, and cheese at a little shop near the German YMCA where I had taken a room. When it became embarrassing to sit in the same booth any longer, I looked for lodgings, a process that resulted in my renting a two-bedroom flat for ten days. Though it cost more than a hotel room, we could cook and be private in a living room of our own. Several evenings I called Susan and cried into the transcontinental phone for tens of dollars. By the time she flew into Heathrow, I had made a strange decision: I was going to return home when she did, dropping St. Ives from my itinerary. For an entire afternoon before coming to this, I roamed Virginia's streets, sat in her favorite squares, listening for voices warning me about giving up my time alone. Hearing none, I wrote her a poem in which I said, "Your waves will lack my echoes for the present/ I'll not go west to see your childhood shore/ I need to hear my own concentrics." I was choosing to live my own moments of being rather than trying to retrace some of hers.

The day before Susan's plane was to arrive, I cleaned the flat and laid in special provisions: malt wheat bread and sugarless jam from a health food store I located after much searching; fresh scones from the elegant little bakery a few blocks down Queensway; delicately wrapped fruit for our first breakfast; blue and purple flowers for the coffee table. Though her flight was not due until noon, I took an early morning airport bus so I could get a good place at the barrier for incoming passengers. With four hours to while away at Heathrow, I had a second round of tea and toast, paced the waiting area, tried to read but ended up just working at breathing evenly.

An interminable period lapsed between a voice announcing the arrival of Susan's plane at some invisible and unreachable gate and the appearance of a passenger. Since I was pressed against the yellow plastic-covered wire separating arrivals from greeters, I could not miss anyone's walking up the ramp. I watched as well-dressed business men filed off with attaché cases and black umbrellas, couples strolled up arm and arm and bleary-eyed, young families were met by grandparents and older people were welcomed by children and their children. I was sure hundreds had deplaned and still no Susan. As I began to panic, thinking she had fallen ill at the last minute or some other dire circumstance had occurred, I saw a stunning woman striding up the gangway in a broad-brimmed felt hat with a pink band around the brim and a rain garment that was half coat, half cape, all magic. For a split second I thought, "what a terribly handsome creature," feeling instant disloyalty to Susan. Looking again, I discovered the terribly handsome creature *was* Susan. We waved ardently and rushed up either side of the dividing rope until we reached its end and could touch.

Eventually we found ourselves in a traditional Hansom cab on our way into downtown London. In my navy pea coat and short hair, I had been several times mistaken for a man. When we pulled up at our flat, the cabbie said, as I gave him a generous tip, "Thanks, guv'nor."

Since that halcyon trip, we have returned several times to London, cabined in the Tetons, driven through the South to visit my sister and Susan's undergraduate college, lounged at a glacial lake in the Canadian Rockies, trekked around Paris and Florence, eaten lobster off a weathered wharf on the Maine coast, hiked across an island off the tip of eastern Quebec to gaze in wonder at a huge gannet colony, and driven often to the north shore of Lake Superior to watch ice break up in March. A few miles out of the city, things seem to loosen, drop away, leaving us together and close without need for scheduling.

Because our bond is so deep, I am vulnerable to hurt, anger, and disappointment when our moods do not coincide or our needs are not complementary. Occasionally our expectations about some event differ radically. The first Halloween we lived together showed us the disastrous effects of not knowing the other's history. I have never put out candy or popcorn for children, probably because when I was a child, my family did not let me go trick-or-treating. Fearful that something terrible would happen to me, they staged an elaborate substitute in which I dressed in my costume and then rang my own doorbell repeatedly, each time getting some new treat. Their fear was not unfounded, since in the forties in the South, mischievous neighborhood children soaped all our car windows or dragged all the furniture off our front porch and onto our lawn. Halloween did not seem benign or fun to me. Susan's history was much more participatory and pleasant, both as a child who went out in her trusty sheet and an adult who left bags of goodies on her lighted porch if she had to be away during the evening. Contrarily, I either went to a movie or retired to some room at the back of my house, turning out all the lights as I went.

Because we had not shared these Halloween stories, I thought we would go to a picture show, while Susan assumed we would carve pumpkins and hand out goodies. When it became clear that we did not agree, each of us felt devastated. After an exhausting fight that took several days to heal, and in which we shouted and cried such words as "betrayed" and "adrift," we agreed to share our past experiences of all major holidays. The fierceness of our scene had sprung from the intensity of our connection and from a dangerous assumption that because we shared basic values and politics, we would of course agree on how to observe some relatively inconsequential holiday.

Being with Susan has contributed to my finding my voice as a writer as well as my happiness as a woman. During our early courtship days, on a walk around one of Minneapolis's many lakes, I found myself talking about my writing block. Susan tightened her arm around my waist while instant tears welled up in me. As I tried to pull away, Susan pinned me to her side and asked particular questions about what prevented me from writing. I answered with sentences previously imprisoned in my own head: "I'm afraid to write because I may be good at it and then I'll have to be responsible for that gift." "If I write, it takes time alone and when I'm alone too long, I revert to compulsive behavior." "How can I have a life with someone else and still find energy for intense writing?" "No one ever asks me about my writing, so I stay stuck where I am." Having blurted out these taboo words amid still-falling tears, I felt terrified.

Susan said little to cheer me up or change my mind, but what she did say seared into me: "I'll support your writing and ask you about it if you want. I'll listen to you read or read your stuff myself if that will help. I understand because I too want to write." In our twelve years together, she has remembered and kept her promise made in the rush of courtship. Of all my critics, Susan remains the one who will challenge me the hardest and drive me the longest to make my work less wordy, and truer.

In 1979, we decided to make a home together and began looking for a suitable house. We knew that we had to have a space in which to write. One of the most attractive features of the place we bought was a finished third floor, complete with the original 1911 skylight and a bathtub with clawed feet. As we discussed use of space, we returned often to an idea of using the third floor as a common writing area. My decision to risk such closeness brought me up against classic messages about the writer's postures, full of secrecy, self-protection, and isolation. It was fine to have an attic—there was a lot of romantic precedent for that—but letting someone else share it as an equal rather than for purposes of serving the artist's domestic needs was unheard of in my imagination.

The effect of our decision has been quite the opposite of what I feared. With Susan working at her desk while I write, I stay put when all my impulses are to turn off the typewriter or computer and do safe household chores. When both of us are trying to write, I feel an aura of love and creativity sustaining me when the blank page stares back unyielding. Toni at work in her fifties is different from the little girl of four hiding between her bed and the wall, hurriedly shaping animal forms or the older child inventing another girl to accompany her on her most precious adventures.

At the same time that Susan was offering tangible encouragement for my writing, Shirley and Mimi, two friends at work, were struggling toward their own best voices. We decided to support each other by devoting one lunch meeting every week either to reading aloud our latest efforts or to talking about our difficulties. Over the past ten years, we have shared specific pieces of writing, long-range dreams, and deep-seated problems. I have given them drafts, trusting that they will read carefully and critically. Such mutuality is precious and rarely available in an academic world devoted to national visibility and educational upward mobility.

Once a chairman tried to exploit our connection. As usual, he had failed to award us our deserved merit points for the year and we had written letters of protest. One day, I received a note asking me to stop by his office. He was prepared to grant me additional points, but when I asked about Shirley and Mimi, he said that his original calculations stood. Without missing a beat, I looked him squarely in the eye and said, "Well, then, don't give me any more, since it would be unfair; they had even better years than I." His expression was of someone hearing a language totally foreign to his ear. Unable to believe me, he offered again, only to hear me refuse again. I walked out feeling like the winner; I had spoken from a position of unity and love in response to his meager ground of money and competition.

The most dramatic support we give each other turns around what and how we write. All three trained in the English Renaissance, we each began careers assuming that we would write standard essays about works from that illustrious period. While we have written on such matters, the essays have hardly been "standard," and in recent years we have steadily inclined toward quite different fare. Each of us has encouraged the others to write poetry and essays about women writers or feminist topics. Most importantly, we have been unflinching in our support of each other's autobiographical writing.

As three articulate full professors in a department like most others, we are feared by some and listened to by all. In our lighter moods, we joke about being the Three Furies to some of our colleagues. At all times, we are sure we are the Three Graces to one another.

One other woman has contributed in ways she probably does not realize to my recovery of confidence as a writer. While working on *So's Your Old Lady* in the seventies, I met Yarrow Morgan and liked her immediately. Being shy and reluctant to let myself have friends, I kept my distance, preferring to talk shop rather than share anything personal. Over the years, we went for the occasional walk or breakfast, until we wound up in the same writing group. There we heard our first poem about father–daughter incest. Within the next few months, two other group members brought pieces dealing with incest or child abuse. One night Yarrow called and said: "I think we ought to edit an incest book so poems like the ones we are hearing have a place to be published—want to?" I answered yes impulsively, and we never backed away from that moment.

Putting together an anthology of women's creative writings about incest (*Voices in the Night: Women Speaking about Incest,* Cleis Press) took three years of steady and unpaid work. For much of that time, we met weekly to read copy and decide whether to accept a piece. Once that process was completed, we began the terrifying task of writing an introduction. Deciding to do it as a joint venture, we floundered for a few meetings before agreeing on a method: we would go outside unless it was raining, sit apart for ten minutes writing independently about whatever the topic was. Then we would read our words aloud before stopping until the next week. After writing on all our chosen topics, we typed our pages and began arranging them, a process that reminded me of shuffling the Tarot deck until the cards are as you intend them. I was amazed at how unrepetitive we were and at how smoothly sections flowed into one another. Our printed introduction includes virtually everything either of us scribbled in backyards or on porches; from a reading of the prose, it is impossible to identify who authored which sections. At first, I kept our typescript so we could check whose sections were whose, but along the way that has vanished and I am no longer certain which are mine and which are Yarrow's unless we are speaking by name about personal experience.

Given my long history of not finishing things, I am immensely grateful. When I felt discouraged, Yarrow kept us at it. When I saw a title page carrying my name, I cried for a long time. I had thought that could never happen, but with Yarrow's parallel vision and labor, one of my oldest fantasies was realized.

A miracle occurred during the first few years of Susan's and my partnership: I wrote poetry easily for the only time in my life. In one of many love poems, I caught something I firmly believe in—the ineluctable connection between sexuality and spirituality. On our second visit to England, we drove from London to Cornwall, through the heart of ancient Celtic country. In addition to stopping often to visit roadside stone circles, we went purposefully to a little town called Avebury to see the wondrous stones erected there centuries ago. This is the resulting poem:

through mists I watch you   priestess
touch the goddess stones
mammoth and friendly
so thick I cannot hear you through them
so tall I crane to find their tops
slate gray like this rainy autumn morning
except for threadings of pink or mauve
or muted sea-green lichens

your fingers trace the ancient markings
searching recesses of rock and memory
for special meaning in the tiny holes
that house bug-like creatures sleeping upside down
with caterpillar feet and armadillo backs;
eons ago we women walked these circles
touching each stone   touching each other
pilgrims at our sacred stations
carving witches' crosses on the rock face:
cuts with equal arms in four directions
cuts you find today and show me   questioning

slowly yet with knowing steps
you weave your way from outer bounds
through inner ovals to the core of worship
where you stop and let your weight
sink down into the mystic dirt

outside the circle, at the entrance stone,
I wait, transfixed before the scene:
your back resembles all the other stones
mute and misted over
you add yourself to this place
alive with echoes from women
come from barrows near and far
to claim the goddess in these stones
to offer smaller gifts of gentle hands
caressing every surface
healing wind and snow scars,
crystal voices singing in moonlight
lulling this female heart of Avebury
season after season   century after century

finished with your solitary rite
you move away
brushing past me   luminescent
as if you'd caught a whisper from another plane
saying things you've always known

so we came, lovers of each other,
lovers of these mythic stones
standing rooted in their meadows
filled with sheep who munch the grass
beneath the monoliths   unperturbed
they watch us as we find the magic
among their leavings
through the Wiltshire drizzle.

A paradox surrounding me and poetry persists: I know how to criticize a poem far more deeply than I do prose; I go to poetry for my lessons rather than reading the additional words required in prose. Yet I feel more secure writing prose than poetry, at least when I want to speak about my own life and perceptions. When I read drafts of poems nestled into journal pages, I feel a warm affection for the Toni of that time, struggling to like herself enough to risk letting anything out of her storehouse. My first attempts at love poetry sound like most beginners' efforts: lots of passionate clichés and prosaic declarations of fidelity or longing or pain, depending on when the poem was written.

My first nonlove poem centered on a woman who had lived with a member of the Symbionese Liberation Army during the sixties. She was convicted of a crime of passion when she killed him, and my poem is full of anger and protofeminist awareness. Reading it now, I understand that I felt some inner connection but was unwilling or unable to invest emotional energy in the writing.

The third volume of my journal includes a torn-out sheet on which I have scribbled some lines with a green felt-tipped pen about brown-skinned women reclining somewhere. Though very poor, this early effort shows a glimmer of promise in lines like, "a breeze that comes from nowhere," and "as small thin rainfall / caressing backs and fields at once."

Though undated, this poem marks a turning point. Touches of eroticism, a woman-identified point of view, and a sharp eye for

what's in front of me: these qualities mark the best things I have
written and are what I always strive for. Significantly, this poem is not
"to" anyone; in fact, I can no longer recall the occasion for writing it.
The lines may be a response to some painting I had recently seen,
strong enough to evoke not only emotion but a willingness to shape it.
While any artist can say this is the force behind inclusion of details or
events, regaining sharp responses and the ability to record them is
particularly precious to me as I continue moving steadily from fog into
sunlight.

That was 1976 and I clearly was in touch with how art could help
me in my process of assembling the pieces of me and my life back into
a whole picture. In the next three or four years, almost a score of poems
poured out of me about leaving my psychiatrist, teaching my first
course in lesbian literature, loving Susan, coming upon some natural
phenomenon that will not let me go. Here are two examples:


*Love Song for Susan*

when wind blows your face
your forehead veins show blue
like impressionist paintings
or antique lanterns,
your light source is within

I see dark shadows move behind your skin,
I want to part the curtain    enter the scene
act with you in a hundred stories

I sense you through my pores

I want to put my fingers on your veins
and feel you
coursing beneath my whorls
I want to touch your forehead
as the wind does,
as the wind

*A Fall*

driving the New York Thruway
later than I mean to
I feel the sky quite near
with little force, my left hand
could reach the dipper
just outside my moving window,
could tip that dipper,
drink water before it makes itself rain

a giant moon perches on a treetop,
still orange from her rising,
lopsided    on her wane to newness,
playful as she floats up the sky
   "twinkle, twinkle, little star . . .
   like a diamond . . . "
        you fall
before my eyes a long, two-second descent,
burning out in slowed motion

watching you and not the highway
I know an answer to the nursery riddle
       "how I wonder. . ."
   you are splendid
   in your final journey
   then lost to blackness
   without violence
   without alarm,
   you leave a space
   without successor

they used to say the stars
were held in place
by hidden pins, behind the ceiling
of the sky,
like sets of dress shirt studs
or a vast array of jeweled rings
piercing all the ears of heaven

did someone pull your pin,
release you from your constellation?
        in any case,
you've gone to where all fallen stars
sleep away the ages,
while I wonder how I hang and shine
and if I ever fall so slowly
with so much ease and so much grace.

One of my happy anticipations turns around a sense I have that I will write more poems as I get older, as I give myself permission to be fully eccentric. This vision of myself also includes a sterling-silver-headed walking cane and outrageous hats for all seasons. When I consider why I connect eccentricity and poetry, I meet my deep conviction that prose is the respectable, grown-up form of written communication. Poetry is reserved for children and others brave or foolish enough to refuse the mainstream's ability to stipulate what color cows must be, which notes girls may sing, who can make love with whom.